We were not slaves but less than slaves. True, we were
deprived of freedom and became a piece of property which
our masters drove to work. But here all similarity with any
known form of slavery ends . . . The machinery had to be
operated with care, oiled, greased and allowed to rest; its
life span was protected. We, on the other hand, were like
a bit of sandpaper, which, rubbed a few times, becomes
useless and is thrown away to be burned with the garbage.

—Affidavit of a former Jewish concentration camp inmate,
Theodore Lehman, describing forced labor in a German
armaments factory

# LESS THAN SLAVES

Jewish Forced Labor
and the Quest for Compensation

Benjamin B. Ferencz

Published in Association with the
United States Holocaust Memorial Museum
Washington, D.C.

INDIANA
University Press
Bloomington and Indianapolis

This book is a publication of

Indiana University Press
601 North Morton Street
Bloomington, Indiana 47404-3797 USA

http://iupress.indiana.edu

*Telephone orders*   800-842-6796
*Fax orders*   812-855-7931
*Orders by email*   iuporder@indiana.edu

Originally published by Harvard University Press 1979
© 1979 by Benjamin B. Ferencz, assigned in 2001 to the
United States Holocaust Memorial Museum
"A Retrospective Evaluation" by Benjamin B. Ferencz
© 2002 by Benjamin B. Ferencz, assigned to the United
States Holocaust Memorial Museum
First Indiana University Press edition 2002
All rights reserved

The paper used in this publication meets the minimum requirements of American National Standard for Information Sciences—Permanence of Paper for Printed Library Materials, ANSI Z39.48-1984.

Manufactured in the United States of America

Cataloguing-in-Publication data is available from the Library of Congress.

ISBN 0-253-34105-1
ISBN 0-253-21530-7 (pbk.)

1  2  3  4  5  07  06  05  04  03  02

*To the concentration camp inmates of all nationalities and religions and their unsung champions, Saul Kagan and Ernst Katzenstein*

# Contents

# A Retrospective Evaluation

## A Glance Back

The Universal Declaration of Human Rights makes plain that if there is to be freedom and justice and peace in the world, there must be "recognition of the inherent dignity and inalienable rights of all members of the human family." The story told in this book asks the moral question: What does one human being owe to another who is in his power? It records the arguments made when victims confront their oppressors and demand justice. In his foreword to the 1979 edition, Telford Taylor, my former chief at the war crimes trials at Nuremberg and later my law partner, made the following prediction: "I believe that in time, Germans will regret that their industrial leaders did not write a postwar record of generosity, instead of the cold and niggardly one revealed in this book."

All of us who became engaged in seeking compensation for victims of Nazi persecution more than half a century ago were well aware of the inadequacy of the results achieved. The restitution of heirless and unclaimed Jewish property began in 1948 when the defeated Third Reich lay in ruins. "Displaced Persons" camps in Germany were swarming with destitute concentration camp survivors who needed help immediately. Germany's primary focus was on feeding and housing its own citizens. The communist regime imposed on East Germany by its Soviet occupiers was not interested in restitution.

In 1951, the restoration of German sovereignty was being considered by the occupying powers. The dismembered country was virtually bankrupt and dependent on foreign aid. United States High Commissioner John J. McCloy impressed on West German Chancellor Konrad Adenauer that compensating Hitler's victims would encourage reacceptance of Germany into the family of nations. When the new State of Israel formed a coalition with leading Jewish organizations—the Conference on Jewish Material Claims Against Germany, a body known as the "Claims Conference"—to negotiate the terms of reparation, militant Jewish extremists threatened those who, in their view, would betray Jewish honor by accepting "blood money" from the nation that had planned to exterminate all Jews.

After long, difficult, and dangerous negotiations in The Hague, an agreement was finally reached in 1952 for payments to Israel, to the Claims Conference, and to survivors of Nazi atrocities who could qualify under the strict terms of the indemnification law. West German representatives constantly stressed their government's limited capacity to pay. The German indemnification program was unprecedented. Never before had any people subjected to such persecution been compensated for their suffering. That many justified claims would fall between the cracks was unavoidable and inevitable. What was most important was that significant payments would be made, and that a legal foundation would be laid for the redress of injury to innocent victims of persecution.

The West German indemnification law was expanded in 1956, 1957, 1964, and 1965 to cover recognized shortcomings in earlier laws. Modest reparation grants also went to Western European governments to compensate some of their nationals. To cope with some of the most needy cases, the Claims Conference persisted in obtaining limited hardship funds for distributions subject to German audit. Refusal of West Germany to consider claims coming from any communist country meant that many survivors who had suffered most under German occupation in conquered territories received nothing.

The earliest compensation legislation provided just over a dollar a day for detention in concentration camps, but no payment was considered for unpaid wages or for companies' unjust enrichment when inmates were assigned to work for private firms. Government negotiators brushed aside such claims as relatively minor obligations that could be dealt with by the companies themselves. The failure to pay "slave laborers" soon gave rise to lawsuits against a few of the big industrial firms whose abuses had been revealed in the Nuremberg trials. Details of those negotiations between 1954 and 1969, and the paltry settlements, are recorded herein. The choice was to "take it or leave it." Despite intensive litigation on many test cases, Germany's highest court held that all such claims, being in the nature of reparations, could be considered only as part of a peace treaty with a united Germany. The German legal door on forced labor claims was thus closed and has remained closed ever since. The moral issues of industrial culpability and accountability were left unresolved by the courts.

## Litigating in the United States on Behalf of Slave Laborers

From 1948 to 1992, I was deeply involved on behalf of reparation to victims of persecution. Before my employment by the major Jewish organizations to direct the programs for restitution and compensation, I had been a war crimes investigator during World War II and had collected evidence of the atrocities in many Nazi concentration camps. I returned to Germany after the war and became chief prosecutor at the Nuremberg trial against the SS *Einsatzgruppen* who had murdered more than a million innocent men, women, and children. I recognized that both bringing criminals to justice and rehabilitating their victims were vital objectives that had to be vigorously pursued. But I also came to realize that it was even more important to prevent the repetition of such barbarities. When Germany was unified at the end of 1990, and announced plans to extend its restitution laws to include former East German states, I felt I could be more productive if I resigned my various posts and redirected my energies toward the creation of an international criminal court that might deter future crimes against humanity. I have therefore not been involved in any way in recent activities or lawsuits related to claims on behalf of slave laborers.

Beginning around 1995, a flood of litigation was unleashed in United States courts on behalf of victims of persecution. Little consideration seemed to be given to the prior Claims Conference efforts and achievements. Well-known German corporations were accused of abusing slave laborers and profiting at the expense of the now-American plaintiffs. Swiss banks and European insurance companies were accused of misappropriating Jewish assets. Art galleries were accused of acquiring stolen treasures. American corporations that had plants in Germany were sued for allegedly deriving profits during the Nazi era. Asian women, who had been victims of organized rapes by Japanese soldiers, and whose justified claims had never been recognized by Japan, demanded compensation. American heirs of slaves of African descent called for belated compensation. What generated the sudden torrent of new demands for redress is speculative, but some possible influences may be noted.

Following the horrors of World War II, the world community, led by the United Nations and nongovernmental organizations, cried out for the universal protection of human rights. There gradually emerged a body of international humanitarian law that American courts began to recognize. The sovereign immunity of foreign states could no longer be relied on to protect those who kidnapped, tortured, plundered, or violated basic human rights. Furthermore, the West German "economic miracle" had enabled large German firms to expand into the United States, thereby making them vulnerable to that nation's legal process and pressures. The popularity of "class actions," the unpredictability of American jurors, and their generosity in levying punitive damages against those with "deep pockets" may also have encouraged renewed demands. A new generation, unencumbered by past atrocities for which they were not guilty, might be more amenable to humanitarian payments that did not imply a personal legal or moral culpability. Alert American lawyers, attracted by the drama of morally uplifting causes, were not slow in discovering susceptible targets of opportunity.

In the fall of 1996, a class-action lawsuit was filed in New York against three of Switzerland's largest and most respected banks. The World Jewish Congress led the public outcry, accusing the banks of having unjustly enriched themselves in trades with German companies, and of refusing to disgorge dormant accounts worth many billions of dollars that belonged to murdered Jews. The denunciations were hailed by survivors of the Nazis, backed by American politicians and a public eager to demonstrate continued sympathy for the oppressed. The Swiss government was castigated for collusion with the banks and inhumane treatment of refugees. In 1997, it was announced that a Swiss Humanitarian Fund of some $200 million would promptly be distributed worldwide to an assortment of needy survivors of Nazi persecution; each of these individuals was sent between $500 and $1,400 as a gesture of Swiss goodwill.

In courts of law it must normally be shown that there is a direct causal connection between wrongful acts of the defendant and the injury suffered by the plaintiff. The alleged damages must be measurable and proved. To meet these challenges fifty-some years after the injury is nearly impossible. In the court of public opinion, however, different standards apply. The Swiss banks and government were overwhelmed by the barrage of unfavorable publicity. It was made clear that licenses to do business in the United States could be revoked, thereby inducing losses far greater than the cost of any settlement. The threat of devastating sanctions was a hazard that every businessman could understand. The Swiss banks, fiercely denying any culpability, reached for an out-of-court settlement. In August 1998, the banks agreed to pay $1.25 billion for the benefit of claimants still unknown in amounts not yet determined on condition that all sanctions would be lifted and there would be complete releases from all Holocaust-related demands against Switzerland, its nationals, and its companies.

Creative lawyering and imagination, coupled with a desire by all parties to resolve the disputes, made the accord possible. Details were hammered out in later negotiations. It was recognized that the procedures for auditing dormant accounts of all Swiss banks, locating potential claimants, and adjudicating hundreds of thousands of claims would be complex, costly, and time-consuming. It was anticipated, however, that even after lawyers' fees, administrative costs, and all account owners were paid, a sizable residue might still remain and be available for slave laborers and other Nazi victims. Existing charities were named to distribute the anticipated residue to Jews and non-Jews alike, who would not have to prove any specific connection with Switzerland. The residual payments, including up to $1,000 for former concentration camp laborers, could be seen as voluntary humanitarian contributions to victims of the Nazis. On July 26, 2000, the plan was approved by the chief judge of the United States District Court as "fair, reasonable and adequate."

The Swiss settlement animated additional lawsuits against German corporations, who appealed to their government to rescue them from the thundering threat to their American business interests. The defendants, echoing denials similar to those of an earlier generation, rejected the accusations against them, insisting that what they did during the war years was normal and legal; hence they owed nothing. Besides, the German government already had paid significant sums. Bitter debates hinged on issues such as the amounts to be allocated, the classes of beneficiaries, who was to make the distribution, and what airtight guarantees could be given that all future Holocaust-related claims would be forever barred. As in the Swiss case, condemnation by plaintiffs that the defendants were unrepentant Nazi collaborators whose offers were totally inadequate were matched by defendants' retorts that they were being subjected to blackmail and extortion. Despite bitter recriminations, another deal was struck.

On July 17, 2000, it was finally agreed that a German "Foundation for Remembrance, Responsibility, and the Future," endowed with approximately $5 billion (DM 10 billion), half of which would be contributed by German industry, would dispose of all lawsuits and claims once and for all. The Foundation began to make grants to several Eastern European governments in 2001 to compensate previously excluded victims of the Nazis. The Claims Conference received sums for distribution to Jewish survivors worldwide. The combined amount that each surviving concentration camp laborer might get from the Swiss and German funds could reach $8,500. The non–concentration camp laborers could not get more than about $3,500. It will take several more years before all of the hundreds of thousands of pending claims can be processed. In July 2001, the Claims Conference was able to report proudly in its fifty-year commemorative booklet that since its founding it had negotiated German government compensation payments totaling well over $50 billion, which had benefited more than 500,000 survivors of persecution, Jews and non-Jews alike, in sixty-seven countries. It was an unprecedented accomplishment.

## Lessons for the Future

Camp inmates seldom knew or cared which particular company or agency was the beneficiary of their toil, sweat, and tears. Every concentration camp inmate was a slave laborer. Jews in particular were less than slaves, since all of them were marked for extermination; for those unable to work, the next stop was the gas chamber or the crematorium. Non-Jewish forced laborers who were not inmates of concentration camps were also victims of inhumane treatment and persecution. The German term for the varied restitution programs, *Wiedergutmachung,* literally means "making good again." But it was a "mission impossible," since the harms sought to be remedied can never be made good again. No one can possibly gauge or pay for the pain of seeing loved ones murdered, for the constant fear of being beaten or killed, or for the hunger and misery that was the daily bread of all camp inmates. The attempt to heal such injuries, and their resultant hidden traumas, within rigid and precise parameters was doomed to failure. The crimes against humanity committed by the Nazi regime and its accomplices were so enormous that they can never be redressed in a manner that will be seen as fair by either the perpetrators or their victims.

Deep-seated hatreds and animosities cannot be banished by decree, and compassion cannot be coerced. Imposing liability on those who are not responsible for the harm provokes resentment. Yet, for the sake of our own humanity and to help assuage some of the rage and hatred that may linger like a festering wound, an effort must be made to seek public recognition that wrongs have been done. Lawful means must be found to offer psychological and economic relief to persons of all nationalities or persuasions who have been innocent victims of massive human abuse.

Since *Less Than Slaves* was first published, thousands of women have been raped in war-torn Yugoslavia, and hundreds of thousands of innocent humans have been butchered in civil strife in Rwanda and elsewhere. These crimes were foreseeable and might have been prevented if the general public cared enough about the suffering of others, or if political leaders of powerful nations had the courage to intervene. Outrageous crimes against humanity continue to be committed in the name of religion, self-determination, and social justice, without the recognition that just goals can be sought only by just means, and that justice requires punishment of the guilty and not the innocent. Surely there is need for clearer laws, for courts, and for effective enforcement to protect a universal right of all human beings to live in peace and dignity.

Tolerance, respect, and consideration for others cannot be taught easily or quickly. It is to the gradual development of the rule of law that one must look for the future protection of humankind. The temporary criminal courts set up by the Security Council of the United Nations to try some of those responsible for the atrocities in Yugoslavia and Rwanda in 1991 and 1994 point the way to further progress. Another step forward will be the permanent international criminal court now being formed at the United Nations. In addition to holding perpetrators of genocide and of crimes against humanity criminally responsible, the statute for the court took another step forward by stipulating that victims of such atrocities are entitled to "restitution, compensation, and rehabilitation"—as a matter of legal right under international law.

Unfortunately, the United States, seeking a free hand to engage in what it regards as humanitarian military interventions, has not yet ratified the treaty creating the court. Conservative leaders still cling to outmoded notions of national sovereignty and fail to remember the lessons of Nuremberg that war-making itself is "the supreme international crime," and law must apply equally to everyone. Despite such obstacles and hesitations, an evolutionary process that recognizes the individual as the true sovereign is gradually taking place. Patience and determination are essential for further progress.

Only by creating effective global institutions founded on principles of equity and universally accepted legal norms can we curb the violence and inhumanity that still scar the global landscape. Here we have recorded cases of indifference and denial of responsibility for human suffering. But we have also noted a new willingness to compromise and to find imaginative solutions in the elusive search for justice. This book ends with Cain's question "Am I my brother's keeper?" In our shrinking and interdependent world, is it not time to ask: "Are we not all our brothers', and sisters', keepers?" As Sir Martin Gilbert concluded in his 1979 *New York Times* review, "This is a book to ponder."

Benjamin B. Ferencz
New Rochelle, New York
November 14, 2001

## Recommended Readings

Bazyler, Michael J. "Nuremberg in America: Litigating the Holocaust in United States Courts." *University of Richmond Law Review,* vol. 35, no. 1, Mar. 2000.

Conference on Jewish Material Claims Against Germany. "Fifty Years of Service to Holocaust Survivors, 1951– 2001." Also Annual Reports. 15 E. 26th St., New York, N.Y. 10010.

Gribetz, Judah. Special Masters Proposed Plan of Allocation and Distribution of Settlement Proceeds. 2 vols., Sept. 11, 2000, United States District Court, Eastern District of New York.

Murphy, Sean D., ed. "Nazi-era Claims Against German Companies." *American Journal of International Law,* vol. 94, Oct. 2000, pp. 682ff.

For other books and writings by Benjamin B. Ferencz, see **www.benferencz.org**.

# Foreword

Someday soon an enterprising graduate student in history or sociology should write a doctoral thesis entitled, "What Happened to the Participants in the Nuremberg Trials after the Proceedings Were Finished?" The "participants" included not only those actually present in the courtrooms—the two hundred or so individuals who were on trial, the several hundred lawyers who prosecuted or defended them, the judges and administrative staff, the prison guards, interpreters, researchers, and court reporters, and the many witnesses who testified. Physically absent but deeply involved in every other sense were the millions of victims of the crimes charged against the defendants, comprising not just those who had survived but also the families and friends of those who had not.

Benjamin Ferencz's moving, melancholy, and altogether unique book has lifted the veil of time from a small segment of Nuremberg's aftermath by telling us the story of the unflagging efforts, in which he was a leading participant, to obtain a measure of financial atonement from the German industrialists in whose mines and mills legions of workers, forcibly deported from their homelands during the Second World War, labored, suffered, and often died. These wealthy, powerful employers were the immediate beneficiaries of the forced labor programs. Yet with few exceptions, their reaction to requests that they make amends, even if modest, for their share of the responsibility for these nefarious actions can only be described as appalling. Despite the ingenuity and tenacity of the campaign that Mr. Ferencz and his colleagues waged, its fruits were a miserable pittance—barely a token.

What explains this flinty denial of obligations to make amends? It can hardly have been lack of available proof of participation in the process, for that was both abundant and repellent. Did these tycoons, in the absence of compulsion to pay, simply succumb to the love of money? No doubt greed played its part. But deeper reflection on these events suggests that this stony-heartedness was due not so much to the industrialists' personal failings as to far broader causes, and that the responsibility was widely shared.

Consider, for example, what the German industrialists heard from the lawyers representing those few accused of war crimes at Nuremberg. Their defense was not a denial of the facts on which the charges were based, nor primarily a claim that they had done their best to ease the lot of the workers. Although some of the industrialist defendants relied heavily on the contention that they acted under governmental coercion, this argument (generally known as "superior orders") was not the core of the defense: their defense was, in brief, that the forced labor program was not unlawful.

This was the position taken by Otto Kranzbühler, a defense counsel in the first Nuremberg trial of industrialists, the Flick case. In essence, his thesis was that the Hague Conventions (from which the laws of land warfare, including the prohibition of labor deportations, are largely derived) was the product of a liberal, bourgeois ideology that had become obsolete, and that "total war" (which Kranzbühler described as an Anglo-Saxon concept) had relieved Germany of any obligation to abide by the Hague rules for the protection of civilians in German-occupied countries, if military (including economic) necessity dictated their violation.

Kranzbühler, one of the ablest of the defense lawyers, had effectively represented Admiral Karl Dönitz at the first trial before the International Military Tribunal without making any such sweeping arguments as he subsequently put forward in behalf of the Flick defendants. But his new thesis, acceptance of which would exonerate not only the industrialists but the Nazi government itself of any criminal responsibility for the forced labor program, was adopted and presented in the I.G. Farben case by Professor Eduard Wahl, special counsel for the defense on points of law, and was repeated by Kranzbühler himself as counsel for Alfried Krupp von Bohlen in the Krupp case.

The Nuremberg courts did not accept Kranzbühler's thesis, and it may be doubted that he expected it to prevail, or even that he put it forward primarily to persuade the judges. In retrospect, it is clear that he was addressing himself to his clients, to the hundreds of German businessmen similarly situated whose guilt would inferentially follow from the guilt of his clients, and to the German public. Kranzbühler was seeking to establish before the court of public opinion that German industry's participation in the forced labor program was neither criminal nor blameworthy.

He certainly succeeded in ridding the Flick, Farben, and Krupp defendants of any guilt feeling. Addressing their respective tribunals at the conclusion of their trials, Flick, Krupp, and most of the Farben defendants not once acknowledged the slightest responsibility for the terrible consequences of the forced labor program. Flick himself asserted, "Nobody of the large circle of persons who know my fellow defendants and myself will be willing to believe that we committed crimes against humanity, and nothing will convince us that we are war criminals."

When the convicted industrialists who had served their sentences or benefited by commutation emerged from the Landsberg prison, there was nothing to shake their belief in their own innocence. William Manchester, in *The Arms of Krupp* (1964), has graphically described the celebration surrounding Alfried Krupp's release. Soon Krupp was encountering the American high commissioner for Germany at cocktail parties, and within a few years Krupp and Flick were commonly referred to in the press as the richest men in Germany. Imprisonment had been unpleasant, but gave the convicted industrialists the medal of martyrdom, and few were any the worse (or better) for the experience.

The American government's attitude, as manifested by John J. McCloy, United States High Commissioner for Germany, must also have given the German industrialists much comfort. On January 31, 1951, as part of his sweeping act of clemency to the imprisoned Nuremberg convicts, McCloy ordered that all the industrialists still at Landsberg be released. Whatever the pros and cons of McCloy's action (all of the industrialists' sentences had been reviewed and confirmed by McCloy's predecessor in authority, General Lucius Clay), the blanket release of all the businessmen, while a number of generals, ministers, and others remained in prison, must have appeared to the Germans as a signal that industrialists were not to be seriously blamed for their involvement in matters for which Fritz Sauckel had been hanged and Albert Speer and others had been given long prison terms.

Thus, within a few years after the end of the Second World War, German industry was able to present a solid front in support of the proposition that it was in no way to blame for the conduct and consequences of the forced labor program. That is why Benjamin Ferencz's appeals on humanitarian grounds were so often met with the response, "Much as we would like to do something, it would appear as an admission of guilt, and constitute a precedent for demands to other companies." In short, anyone who broke the united front would be endangering the image of innocence upon which all of them relied. The image, in turn, was the product of many hands and was a welcome vision for the German industrial community, as its plants and office buildings rose, phoenix-like, from the rubble of war.

Given this climate of opinion, the remarkable thing about Benjamin Ferencz's story is not that he and his colleagues reaped a meager harvest, but that they achieved anything at all. In saying this, of course I do not mean to condone the attitudes which they confronted. To understand is not necessarily to forgive. And I believe that in time, Germans will regret that their industrial leaders did not write a postwar record of generosity, instead of the cold and niggardly one revealed in this book.

# Preface

In writing this book I have tried to follow the dictum "Do not judge your fellow man until you have stood in his place." It has not been easy. I have tried to present the facts in an unbiased and unemotional way. If there has been any distortion, it was unintentional. In fairness, however, it is necessary to disclose something of my own prior experience which may have impaired my objectivity.

No one in my own immediate family was murdered by the Nazis. We had left Transylvania when I was an infant and, although the Hungarians and Romanians who divided the region were noted for their anti-Semitism, I was too young to have had any personal awareness of persecution. When Hitler came to power, I was thirteen. To a carefree adolescent living in New York City, the newspaper reports coming out of Germany went almost unnoticed. I did not know any Germans, and Berlin seemed very far away. Later, as a student at City College, I joined in protest marches against Fascism, but my first real awareness of the Nazi atrocities came while I was at law school.

What interested me most at that time was crime prevention. I managed to obtain a parttime job as a student research assistant to one of the outstanding criminologists in the country, Professor Sheldon Glueck at Harvard. He was then associated with a group in London that was assembling evidence of German war crimes, and some of the documentation showing the massacres of Jews in Poland passed through my hands. When Professor Glueck prepared to write a book calling for the punishment of war criminals, I was assigned to research the precedents and the law, and thereby acquired a thorough background in a subject about which little was generally known.

The United States Army had no need for my specialized skills in 1943. Upon receiving my law degree from Harvard, I became a typist in the supply room of an antiaircraft artillery battalion being trained for the invasion of France. I reentered Europe by plunging into the sea at "Omaha Beach" in Normandy, and joined in the pursuit of the retreating German army. When we reached the German border, I was transferred to the Third Army headquarters of General Patton. The judge advocate general had been directed to set up a war crimes branch in the United States Army, and much to my surprise, I found myself with a new assignment.

As a war crimes investigator, I gathered evidence of German atrocities that had been committed in areas which were being liberated by the advancing American army. The retreating Germans frequently murdered French and Belgian civilians; for the first time, my knowledge of French and my training in the laws of war were put to use as I reported on the crimes and tried to apprehend the criminals. As we entered Germany, the army began to receive reports about the wholesale murder of Allied flyers who had been shot down over German territory. My duties required that I disinter and try to identify the bodies of young aviators who had been beaten to death by enraged German mobs; yet the depth of Nazi criminality did not strike me full force until I joined the troops advancing into some of the German concentration camps.

What I recall most vividly—in Buchenwald, Mauthausen, Dachau, and the surrounding camps—are the carts loaded with skeletons and the mounds of emaciated bodies covered with lye, piled up like cordwood before the crematoria. It was difficult for me to tell whether the hundreds of inmates who were lying in the dust were dead or alive. Those who had been able to walk had been whipped out of the camps by the retreating SS. As we pursued the fleeing camp guards through the woods, the path was marked by a trail of corpses. The bedraggled prisoners who could not keep up with the retreat had been shot by the SS and left dead or dying along the way. Occasionally we would come upon a ditch filled with ragged bodies or a mass grave that had been covered with a light layer of dirt. The American soldiers rounded up the townspeople, male and female, and ordered them to dig up and carry the cadavers to the nearest cemetery for proper burial.

As I went about my grim duties, I became like a surgeon on the battlefield with no time for feelings. I recall neither fury nor tears, only an emotional numbness and incredulity. There was no cry for vengeance—merely a state of silent shock. The experience left an indelible impression.

For several months after the war, as an infantry sergeant, I continued to investigate war crimes and interrogate arrested criminals. In the Dachau camp itself, as a form of poetic justice, the United States Army established military commissions to try those who had participated in the killing of American flyers and to bring to trial those SS officers and guards who had committed atrocities in the camps liberated by the American armed forces. The judges were United States Army officers.

I found the proceedings uninspiring. All I wanted was to leave Germany as quickly as possible and never to return.

On the day after Christmas, 1945, I was discharged from the army and looked forward to practicing law in New York. Only a few months had gone by when I received a telegram asking me to come to Washington where the army was trying to recruit lawyers with war crimes experience. I met Colonel David "Mickey" Marcus, a flamboyant West Pointer of Jewish origin who had been with the district attorney's office in New York. Marcus, who was later to die as a volunteer general in the Israeli army, urged me to go back to Germany as a civilian war crimes prosecutor with the simulated rank of colonel. It was a tempting offer.

The trial before the International Military Tribunal against Göring and others was already in progress. Many other high-ranking Nazis were in detention. Arrangements were being made for a limited number of subsequent trials to be conducted by the United States, acting pursuant to a quadripartite law of the Allied Control Council. I was interviewed by Justice Robert Jackson's deputy, Brig. Gen. Telford Taylor, who was to be the chief of counsel for the "Subsequent Proceedings." With a distinguished legal background, he was a far cry from the typical army officer I had met during the war. We agreed that I would join his staff.

For my first assignment, Taylor sent me to Berlin with about fifty researchers, most of whom had been refugees from Hitler Germany. Their task was to scour the captured Nazi archives for evidence of crime. No German could be indicted until sufficient proof was assembled to establish individual guilt beyond a reasonable doubt and in accordance with recognized principles of international penal law. Since the Nazi ideology had penetrated all segments of German society, the scan was to go beyond the SS and the army and was to encompass German doctors, lawyers, judges, diplomats, and industrialists.

During the searching, one of the investigators was stunned when he uncovered some very revealing files in the cellar of the burned-out Gestapo headquarters. They were the top-secret daily reports from the eastern front describing and itemizing the number of Jews and others who had been slaughtered by the SS *Einsatzgruppen*—a word for which no adequate translation exists. I counted over a million people deliberately murdered by these special action groups, whose mission it was to secure the areas behind the German lines. Most of the *Einsatzgruppen* commanders were clearly identified and the enormity of their crimes was unmistakable. I flew to Nuremberg with the evidence and presented it to General Taylor. The general recognized the importance of the evidence but his relatively small and overburdened staff was already busily engrossed in preparing other trials. We agreed that the *Einsatzgruppen* prosecution could be squeezed into the division handling trials against the SS and that I would be responsible for preparing the case. Thus, I became the chief prosecutor in what was called by the Associated Press "the biggest murder trial in history."

Back in Nuremberg I was appointed Taylor's executive counsel, with added management functions related to all of the subsequent trials. This overview further enhanced my knowledge of what had happened during the dozen-year reign of "the thousand-year Reich." When the *Einsatzgruppen* trial was ended and all of the twenty-two defendants were convicted, my wife and I prepared to return home. Before we could leave, however, I was approached by an emissary from some of the large Jewish organizations in the United States on a matter of great importance to the survivors of Nazi persecution. The direction of my life was to turn from the prosecution of war criminals to the rehabilitation of those who had been their victims.

Military Government had enacted a restitution law in 1947 requiring the return of all property that had been confiscated or transferred under Nazi duress. The claims were decided by German courts, but the final decisions were left to an American court of restitution appeals. Heirless property taken from those who had been killed, and unclaimed Jewish assets, could be recovered by a charitable "successor organization" which was bound to use the proceeds for the relief of survivors of persecution. The Jewish organizations asked me to set up the agency to recover the heirless Jewish property for the benefit of the Jewish survivors. It was an offer I did not have the heart to refuse.

I designated myself the "director general" of the Jewish Restitution Successor Organization (JRSO), knowing that nothing would impress the German officials and courts more than a title which combined "director" and "general." A sizable staff was assembled to locate, claim, recover, and dispose of hundreds of thousands of confiscated homes, businesses, orphanages, hospitals, and other tangible properties that had been taken from the Jews. General Lucius D. Clay, the military governor, was persuaded to advance the necessary operating capital by a substantial loan from occupation funds.

In 1952 the newly established Federal Republic of Germany indicated a willingness to try to make amends, in the name of the German people, for what had been done to the Jews. By that time I was considered an expert and I joined the Jewish delegation in negotiating a reparations agreement. The final settlement provided for the shipment of goods to Israel in an amount of DM 3 billion (then over $700 million) over a ten-year term, and a payment to the Conference on Jewish Material Claims against Germany, a consolidation of twenty-three major Jewish organizations, of DM 450 million. For the next ten years the

Claims Conference was to distribute about $10 million each year to help reconstruct the Jewish communities of Europe that Hitler had decimated. Even more important than the global sums payable to Israel and the Jewish organizations was the West German government's promise to enact special legislation to provide compensation for a large variety of losses sustained by each of the surviving victims of persecution. The Claims Conference gave me an additional designation as its director for Germany and the added task of protecting Jewish interests in connection with the promulgation and implementation of the anticipated new indemnification laws.

The German government enacted laws providing for individual compensation, but many Jewish claimants were reluctant to turn to German lawyers for assistance in presenting the complicated restitution and indemnification claims. There was need for a Jewish organization to help the individual petitioners. In addition to my responsibilities for the Jewish Restitution Successor Organization and the Claims Conference, I acquired a third title, that of director of operations of the United Restitution Organization (URO), which soon became the biggest legal aid society in the world.

The story of the elaborate *Wiedergutmachung* (reparations) programs enacted and carried out under the Military Government and West German laws, seeking to "make good again" what could never be made good again, goes far beyond the scope of this book. The basic indemnification law enacted by the Federal Republic of Germany in 1956 was expanded in 1967 and covered millions of claims from Nazi victims, Jews and non-Jews alike. The German government estimated that it would be beyond the year 2000 before the final bill was paid and that the cost by then would approach DM 100 billion—over $40 billion at the 1977 rate of exchange. Yet none of the German laws provided any indemnity for the labor of the concentration camp inmates. Those who had been incarcerated or who could show that they had been forced into hiding under inhuman conditions received a small grant of about a dollar a day for "false imprisonment." The German government refused to make any payment for the work performed for private German companies, or for the pain and suffering connected with such labor. There was thus a gap in the legislative program. No special recognition was accorded the fact that large numbers of human beings had been subjected to conditions of slavery.

The Jewish concentration camp workers were less than slaves. Slavemasters care for their human property and try to preserve it; it was the Nazi plan and intention that the Jews would be used up and then burned. The term "slave" is used in this narrative only because our vocabulary has no precise word to describe the lowly status of unpaid workers who are earmarked for destruction.

This book is the historical record of how, long after Hitler had passed from the scene and the threat of Nazi coercion had disappeared, the private German firms responded to a Jewish appeal for modest compensation. The narrative reaches back for a brief review of what it was like for the Jews under the Hitler regime. It focuses on the employment practices rather than on other atrocities and cruelties that took place in, or outside, the camps. The record is drawn from German documents and other unquestionable evidence. There can be no doubt that millions of prisoners were coerced into working for the German war machine, under conditions which the Nuremberg judges said made "labor and death almost synonymous." The most abused among the forced laborers were the Jews. For them the only alternatives were to be killed outright or to be worked to death before being consigned to the flames.

It has been estimated that approximately half a million persons were found more or less alive in the camps that were liberated by the Allied armies. Over one hundred thousand survivors of those camps turned to the Conference on Jewish Material Claims against Germany and asked for assistance in obtaining a measure of redress from the private German companies that had employed them. In the chapters which follow, only half a dozen of the hundreds of German enterprises that used the labor of concentration camp inmates are scrutinized. The choice of these companies and the omission of others was not the result of any prior rational plan, but arose as a consequence of circumstances which were unpredictable and largely fortuitous. Many of the major users of slave labor, such as the Herman Göring Works, Organization Todt, and other official entities of the SS or the government, disappeared with the Third Reich. Others, like the private aircraft companies Messerschmidt, Heinkel, and Junkers, had been reduced to rubble. The identity of hundreds of lesser firms was too obscure to be recalled by inmates, whose only concern at the time was to stay alive.

The United States war crimes trials could deal with only a small sampling of German crimes and criminals. During the Subsequent Proceedings at Nuremberg, indictments were brought against only three industrial firms, which were accused of abusing concentration camp inmates. The Interessengemeinschaft Farbenindustrie Aktiengesellschaft (A.G; the "cartel of dyestuffs industries"), a stock corporation more commonly known as I.G. Farben, was one of those firms. The other two were the privately owned Krupp company and some corporations owned by the industrial baron Friedrich Flick. The corporate directors were surprised and indignant to find themselves in the criminal dock. As far as they were concerned, the use of slaves was a patriotic duty which was both normal and proper under the circumstances.

The drama in the Nuremberg courtroom concentrated on the guilt or innocence of the accused. Very little thought was given to any rights of the former victims. The survivors themselves were grateful to be among the living. Their main concern was to start a new life as quickly as possible in a land of freedom. As the turmoil of the early postwar years began to abate, however, it was only natural that some of those who had received nothing but abuse for their grueling labor should begin to wonder about their legal rights against their erstwhile oppressors.

During the war I.G. Farben had set out to produce a synthetic rubber, "Buna," and had found a convenient production site adjacent to the concentration camp near the town the Germans called Auschwitz (Oswiecim) in Poland. The new Farben plant could draw upon a plentiful supply of labor, and those inmates who became too weak to work could easily be disposed of in the nearby extermination center at Birkenau. The Nuremberg court found that "Auschwitz was financed and owned by Farben" and that what took place there in the utilization of labor was "a crime against humanity." It was not surprising, therefore, that one of the early initiatives taken against a German user of concentration camp labor should come from a *Häftling* — an inmate who had survived the rigors of Farben's Buna plant at Auschwitz.

Within sight of the three big chimneys of the Auschwitz crematoria another one of Germany's most prominent firms planned to augment its contribution to the Führer's arsenal by using the cheap labor from the camp. For over a century, the name Krupp had been identified with armaments for Germany. The distinction of being "armorer of the Reich" was not achieved without Krupp's employing large numbers of forced laborers. The Jews who were compelled to work for him were arming a country which had pledged to destroy them. We shall see how Krupp reacted when hundreds of Jewish girls who were presumed to have been killed reappeared to demand compensation.

The Allgemeine Elektricitäts-Gesellschaft (AEG), Telefunken, and Siemens were three well-known and highly regarded electrical concerns long before Hitler's rise to power. Although none of the directors of these companies faced a Nuremberg court, they too formed a partnership with the SS when they reached into Auschwitz, Ravensbrück, Dachau, Mauthausen, and other charnel houses for some of their wartime labor. Once the passions of war had cooled and Germany was returning to peace and prosperity, would the electrical companies be ready to acknowledge that they had been connected with deeds which called for some measure of redress or would they attempt to deny, cover up, minimize, excuse, or justify what had happened? Would the German companies' response to the Jewish claims be a legal one or a moral one; or would it be strictly an economic response, in which it would be considered "bad business" to allow the skeletons in the corporate closets to be uncovered? Here, without the coercion of Allied laws or a mass of incriminating evidence assembled by war crimes prosecutors, would come an early test of German conscience.

Some of the former inmates who had survived German cruelties were not prepared to rely on German good will to secure their rights. A number of lawsuits were initiated after the war against firms that had employed camp labor. It was hoped that the German courts could clarify the principles of justice which would govern the rights of the parties. Would loss of evidence, expiration of statutory time limits, or intervening political and economic considerations influence the courts or the parties, and would it prove to be too late to win a judgment against a German company?

One German firm, Rheinmetall A.G., which had produced arms for Hitler, resumed the production of cannons shortly after the war, and the American Army decided to purchase guns from it. Some American congressmen questioned the appropriateness of buying weapons from a company which had not only had former Nazis on its board but which was being sued by camp survivors, many of whom had acquired American citizenship. The Pentagon's embarrassment was accentuated by the fact that the Germany company would displace an old American gun manufacturer whose plant would have to be closed down. The issue of compensating the former slaves became enmeshed in military, political, and economic considerations. The outcome was far removed from what any of the parties might have anticipated at the outset.

Neither legal, moral, political, nor economic arguments proved adequate to persuade Friedrich Flick to make any payment. Flick, who had been convicted as a major war criminal, was an expert in corporate manipulation. During the Hitler period he had acquired a company founded by Alfred Nobel, whose fame as a purveyor of munitions for war was later surpassed by the attachment of his name to an annual prize for peace. The company, Dynamit Nobel, was, through a number of cloaked subsidiaries, a major abuser of concentration camp labor. The working conditions of Dynamit Nobel slaves from Auschwitz, Dachau, Buchenwald, and Gross Rosen must have been well-known to the corporate baron, who was also a principal contributor to the personal fund of the SS chief, Heinrich Himmler. In fact, Flick had personally been escorted through Auschwitz by Himmler himself. After release from a war crimes prison, Flick displayed his corporate talents by acquiring control of Daimler-Benz, the prosperous manufacturer of the luxurious Mercedes cars. He showed an even greater talent for leaving Jewish claimants and Jewish organizations suspended in mid-air. When he died at the age of eighty-nine, the convicted criminal was called "the richest man in Germany," but Friedrich Flick went to his grave without ever having paid any of his former slaves one single German pfennig.

The efforts to convince lesser companies and lesser luminaries that they owed a debt to the slave laborers also met with defeat. At one time it appeared that the Federal Association of German Industries, a private chamber of commerce, might play a role in moving some of the leading German firms toward an accommodation. That was before the association was told by the major companies to keep hands off.

When German courts made it clear that this was one problem they would rather avoid than resolve, all further efforts to obtain compensation for the camp survivors seemed hopeless. There was nothing more that the Jewish organizations could do but to distribute whatever money had been obtained from a few companies to those particular classes of inmates for whom the payments were specifically earmarked. There remained the added burden of trying to explain to all the other survivors why they would have to settle for nothing.

There was no doubt that the working conditions for all Jewish inmates were unbearable, but who was employed where, and when, and by whom was by no means obvious. Hundreds of companies put thousands of forced laborers to work in the same geographic region. The workers themselves were often uncertain about the identity of their employer. Documentary evidence and reliable witnesses had to be assembled to clarify the facts. The possibility that some claims might be fabricated by embittered survivors determined to extract whatever they could from the murderers of their kin could not be ignored.

The payments that were finally made by a few German companies were not large enough to have any decisive impact on the lives of the recipients. Because the sums were so limited, claimants who were employed for a longer period than others argued that they were entitled to a larger slice of the meager pie. Some of the disabled, or the most needy, also clamored for a greater allocation for themselves. To play Solomon in such manner that the beneficiaries would recognize that everything possible had been done to reach an equitable apportionment was neither an easy task nor one which could be completed quickly.

In the process of trying to obtain some measure of compensation for the former camp laborers, many new facts were discovered. As the claimants substantiated their claims, a more precise picture of their persecution emerged than had been obtained during the Nuremberg trials, and one could see how the surviving Jewish remnant had been dispersed. The attitude of the German industrialists toward the events of the past and toward the Jewish demands also became transparent.

In assembling this record, I have hoped to provide more than just a footnote to recent Jewish history. The subject has more profound implications, for we deal here with a striking and contemporary illustration of man's inhumanity to man. My focus is not on the magnitude of the wrongs committed during wartime, but on the confrontation, after the war, between victims and victimizers, when they faced each other as free men and women. They see the past from different perspectives. There are many with memories so scarred that the vision of truth is blinded by hate. Some oppressors see themselves as the oppressed; for others the truth is so shameful that it leads to denial, so that self-respect may be preserved. For a few, the acknowledgment of their participation in evil is the beginning of redemption.

Cruelty is not restricted to any one people, or to any one time, or to a single location. And each of us must find his own way to understand the worst in human behavior—and understand what feeds and sustains it. It is my hope that this book will contribute to that understanding and, by making the bleak record plain, will strengthen our determination that the evils recorded here shall not disfigure human history again.

B. B. F.

# Acknowledgments

Appreciation is expressed to Professor Yehuda Bauer of the Hebrew University, who first suggested that this book be written. Dr. Joseph Kermisz, Dr. H. Rosenkranz, Dr. Shmuel Krakowski, and Mr. Emmanuel Brand of Yad Vashem made helpful comments regarding chapter 1. Dr. Bruno Fischer of the United Restitution Organization sent many useful documents, and Professor Lucy S. Dawidowicz gave invaluable support. Former German Armaments Minister Albert Speer kindly agreed that he could be quoted, as did Theodore Lehman. My thanks also go to my wife, Gertrude, for her constant encouragement and aid, and to my son, Donald, and my daughters, Carol and Nina, for a wide variety of assistance. William B. Goodman and Susan Wallace of Harvard University Press made many suggestions, for which I am most grateful.

In order to respect the privacy of camp survivors who may not have wanted to be identified, only the initial of the surname and a fictitious first name have been used.

Map showing seven principal Nazi extermination camps (Belzec, Birkenau, Chelmno, Jungfernhof, Maidanek, Sobibor, Treblinka), fifteen major concentration camps (Auschwitz, Bergen-Belsen, Buchenwald, Cracow/Plaszow, Dachau, Flossenberg, Gross Rosen, Lublin, Mauthausen, Natzweiler, Neuengamme, Ravensbrück, Riga, Sachsenhausen, Stutthof), and some of the subcamps mentioned in this book. The Federal Republic of Germany has listed over 1,600 camps for forced laborers.

SWEDEN

Kaiserwald ■RIGA
▼ JUNGFERNHOF

North Sea

DENMARK

Baltic
Sea

U.S.S.R.

■ NEUENGAMME

STUTTHOF

● Malchow

Bialystok ●

■ RAVENSBRÜCK   Bromberg
● Thorn
TREBLINKA
▼

WEST   Unterlüss
BERGEN-BELSEN ■   Hennigsdorf  ■ SACHSENHAUSEN   Vistula R.
Braunschweig ●   EAST  ● ○ Berlin   Warsaw ○
Brandenburg
GERMANY   Magdeburg   GERMANY   CHELMNO ▼
● Gelsenkirchen   ● Christianstadt   POLAND   LUBLIN
Schwarzheide ●
Essen  Arolsen   Sömmerda  Gröditz  GROSS ROSEN  Freiburg   SOBIBOR ▼ ▼
Hessich-Lichtenau  ● ● ● ● ● Breslau-Hundsfeld   MAIDANEK
BUCHENWALD  Wüstegiersdorf  Waldenburg   BELZEC ▼
Allendorf   Freiberg  Ober Altstadt  Markstädt / Fünfteichen
Geisenheim   Prague ○  Ludwigsdorf  Bobrek   ● Monowitz
Neustadt   Zwodau  Weisswasser  AUSCHWITZ  ■ CRACOW/PLASZOW
LUXEMBOURG   FLOSSENBERG ■   Trautenau   Langenbielau   BIRKENAU
Nuremberg
FRANCE   CZECHOSLOVAKIA
Strasbourg ○   ○ Stuttgart
Kaufering  DACHAU   MAUTHAUSEN
NATZWEILER  ● Landsberg  Gusen ●   Danube R.
● Ebensee

AUSTRIA   HUNGARY

SWITZERLAND

EUROPE

■ MAIN CONCENTRATION CAMPS
▼ EXTERMINATION CAMPS
● Subcamps

0    60    120
|____|____| miles
0    100    200
|____|____| km

Forget

# The Final Solution—A Brief Reminder

Part of the "final solution" was the gathering of Jews from all German-occupied Europe in concentration camps. Their physical condition was the test of life or death. All who were fit to work were used as slave laborers in the concentration camps; all who were not fit to work were destroyed in gas chambers and their bodies burnt.

Judgment of the International Military Tribunal, Nuremberg, Germany, October 1, 1946[1]

# CHAPTER 1

## The Diabolical Design (1933–May 1939)

Next to the Bible, and perhaps in spite of it, *Mein Kampf* was the best seller in all of Nazi Germany. "All who are not of good race in this world are chaff," wrote the National Socialist leader from his prison cell in the fortress of Landsberg am Lech. According to Hitler, "In a bastardized and niggerized world all concepts of the humanly beautiful and sublime . . . would be lost forever."[2] The Aryan German people were considered the highest species of humanity on earth.

Anyone who could read must have been aware of Hitler's attitude toward the Jews: "a typical parasite," "a noxious bacillus," "a contaminator of German blood" were terms that appeared throughout Hitler's book. "The Bolshevistic shock troops of international Jewish world finance" were castigated as agitators "for the complete destruction of Germany."[3] In the eyes of Adolf Hitler and his devout followers, the racially inferior Jew was the main cause of Germany's ills and the main threat to Germany's future.

The man who was to become chancellor of the German Reich proclaimed "eternal wrath upon the head of the foul enemy of mankind." "No nation can remove this hand from its throat," wrote Hitler, "except by the sword . . . Such a process is and remains a bloody one."[4] No one should have been surprised when, upon coming to power in 1933, the Nazis began to carry out the program so clearly and loudly heralded by their Führer. If the German public did not know what the Nazis had in store for the Jews, it was because they did not want to know.

Jews were registered and sorted according to the purity of their racial origins. They were immediately excluded from all public office, the civil service, and the professions. By 1935 German Jews were divested of their citizenship and the protection of the courts. Sexual relations between a Jew and one of "Aryan blood" were made punishable by death. Everywhere, Jews were insulted, taunted, bullied, and beaten without provocation. German Jews who understood what was happening and who had the means to do so began to flee in panic. Those who remained were to be deprived not only of their civil rights and their property but also of their hope. Finally, some six million Jews of Europe would lose their lives in ways which few if any˚could even imagine.

In the Bavarian town of Dachau, near Munich, a concentration camp was erected in March 1933. The post of police president of Munich had been given to a local party stalwart, Heinrich Himmler, who was one of Hitler's earliest disciples and who had been named head of the *Schutzstaffel* or guard unit—the SS—in 1929. His deputy, Reinhard Heydrich, joined the staff in 1931. Their power was soon to be extended to cover all of Germany.

Within a few months another concentration camp was opened at Oranienburg, near Berlin. As the persecution of Jews, Catholics, Seventh Day Adventists, communists, gypsies, and others who were conceived to be enemies or potential enemies of the Reich continued to grow, so did the number of concentration camps to contain them. Buchenwald, near Weimar, was built in 1937; Ravensbrück for women was opened in 1938. All of the camps were to subdivide continuously into branches or *Aussen Kommandos* and *Unter Kommandos*, subcamps administered from the main camp under centralized direction from Oranienburg. The Secret State Police—the *Geheime Staatspolizei* or Gestapo—and the Security Service—the *Sicherheitsdienst* or SD—began to strike terror into the hearts of all who might be labeled opponents of the new regime.

Under the impetus of a militant Nazi policy, German industry was getting ready for war. The first of a long series of German aggressions erupted in March 1938. Austria, confronted with threats of attack and overwhelming German power, capitulated and merged with the Reich. The Nazis of Vienna pounced upon the Austrian Jews, beat them, despoiled them, and, under the direction of a then unknown SS man named Karl Adolf Eichmann, who was in charge of emigration, drove as many as they could from their homeland. In August, on the outskirts of Linz on the Danube, where both Hitler and Eichmann had gone to school, the new concentration camp at Mauthausen was established. Czechoslovakia, abandoned by her British and French allies after being occupied by German troops, was absorbed by the Reich. Hitler informed the Czech foreign minister that the Jews of Czechoslovakia would be destroyed.[5]

On November 9, 1938, the SS launched a massive pogrom against the Jews of Germany. Jewish synagogues were burnt, Jewish shops and homes were smashed and looted, and Jews were assaulted and killed in the streets. Thirty-five thousand Jews were arrested on that "night of the broken glass," the *Kristallnacht*.[6] Among them was a

Jewish lawyer, Hans Oettinger, who had been born Hans Ludwig Jakobsohn but who bore the name of his adoptive parents. Oettinger was sent to Dachau where, after five months of hard labor in the cold Bavarian winter, he was ordered to leave the country forever. He fled to Switzerland and then to England, where he later offered his services to the British Armed Forces. His frozen and mangled fingers would remain as a constant reminder of his days in Dachau, and one day Hans Oettinger would discard his German identity and return as Henry Ormond to the city of Frankfurt, where he had been seized by the Gestapo, and call some of the former Nazi leaders to account.

Three days after the *Kristallnacht,* Field Marshal Herman Göring began to act on Hitler's order that the Jewish question be "solved one way or another."[7] The SS would soon demonstrate that the "solution" was *Vernichtung* or the annihilation of the Jews.[8] Acting in his capacity as plenipotentiary for the Four Year Plan for German Rearmament, Göring levied a fine on the Jews of one billion marks. If war broke out, said Göring, there would be a "big reckoning with the Jews."[9] On January 24, 1939, Göring ordered that "the emigration from Germany of Jews is to be advanced by all means." A central office was established to expedite action throughout Germany, and Reinhard Heydrich, who had been elevated to chief of the Security Service, was named as the man in charge.[10] A week later Hitler addressed the German parliament *(Reichstag)* and warned, in a widely hailed address, that if war broke out it would be the fault of the Jews and it would result in "the annihilation of the Jewish race in Europe."[11]

The reference to the outbreak of war in connection with the destruction of Jewry was an attempt by Hitler and Göring to suggest to the world that the Jews would be responsible for bringing their fate upon themselves. The implication was another Nazi deceit. Both Hitler and Göring knew very well that war was, if not inevitable, at least most likely to erupt as a direct consequence of the planned German march of conquest.[12] The official documents produced before the International Military Tribunal showed that as early as November 1937, in a meeting with all the military commanders, there was a premeditated and carefully prepared plan of aggression to seize the neighboring states of Austria and Czechoslovakia as a prelude to further attacks on Poland and the Soviet Union.[13]

It was not the Jews who were bringing on the war but Hitler himself. He had proclaimed in *Mein Kampf* the need to conquer territory in the east "to secure for the German people the land and soil to which they are entitled on this earth."[14] Hitler's adjutant recorded the minutes of a meeting in May 1939 wherein Hitler made it clear that it was his plan "to attack Poland at the first suitable opportunity . . . There will be war."[15] The attempt to put the blame on the Jews was a transparent attempt at a cover-up. The Hitlerian goal, declared in 1924, was a united Germany of pure-blooded Aryans dominating all of Europe. In war or in peace, the elimination of the Jews was an integral part of the diabolical design.

## Conquest as a Prelude to Annihilation (August 1939–July 1940)

The Nazi–Soviet "nonaggression pact" of August 23, 1939, gave assurance of Russian neutrality and thereby opened the way for the German attack on Poland a week later. Within forty-eight hours England and France, whose self-deluded leaders had desperately hoped for peace, were at war in a vain attempt to defend their Polish ally. The carefully prepared Nazi *Blitzkrieg* successfully swept across Poland. Russia moved in from the east to seize its prearranged share, and in less than three weeks' time, what had formerly been the independent state of Poland was reduced to a carcass divided between two jackals.

Two million Polish Jews came under Nazi control. Those portions of Poland which had been taken away from Germany following World War I (Danzig, West Prussia, Posen, and the eastern part of Upper Silesia) were reincorporated into the Reich. The remaining portion of German-occupied Poland, which was not incorporated into the territory of the Reich, was known as the General Government *(General-gouvernement)*. It was to become the dumping ground for Jews, gypsies, and other undesirables cleaned out of the Reich. It was also to become their graveyard.[16]

The General Government was put under the administration of Hans Frank, a National Socialist legal expert who had joined the party in 1927 and who had earned a reputation for ruthlessness before being appointed the minister of justice in the province of Bavaria in 1933.[17] Like almost all Germans with university degrees, he proudly bore the title of "Dr." before his name. His diary of thirty-six volumes was to become one of the most damning chronicles of mass murder ever to be recorded by man.[18] Faced with his own record, Dr. Frank was later to confess his participation in the murder of Jews, saying, "A thousand years will pass and still this guilt of Germany will not have been erased."[19]

The Reich Security Main Office, *Reichssicherheitshauptamt* (RSHA), was reorganized by Himmler in his capacity as the highest ranking officer, the *Reichsführer* SS, in September 1939. Heydrich, who held the rank of major general *(Gruppenführer)* of the SS, was chief of the Security Police (Sipo) and the SD. SS Brig. Gen. *(Brigadeführer)* Heinrich Muller, also drawn from the Munich police, was put in charge of Department IV, which was the Gestapo, responsible for combatting the "enemies of the Reich." Under him was SS Major

*(Sturmbannführer)* Eichmann to handle the evacuation of the Jews.[20] Eichman would set the pattern to be applied in dealing with the Jews in Poland, then in Russia, and later in Germany and the occupied or German-allied countries. Otto Ohlendorf, who was later to admit to the killing of ninety thousand Jews by his *Einsatzgruppe,* was put in charge of intelligence. Himmler directed that the supervision of all concentration camps would be handled by SS Col. *(Oberführer)* Richard Glücks, but economic matters affecting the camps would be the responsibility of SS Maj. Gen. Oswald Pohl.[21]

On September 12, 1939, as a further manifestation of German intent and the implementation of the plan, a meeting of army generals took place in the special train of the Führer. According to the testimony of one of them, agreement was reached that the groups to be shot were "mainly the Polish intellectuals, the nobility, the clergy and, of course, the Jews."[22]

On September 21, 1939, Heydrich held a conference in Berlin confirmed by a long teletype to all of the *Einsatzgruppen* commanders, with copies to related ministries, including the Army High Command (OKH, *Oberkommando des Heeres*), in which the plan for the extermination of the Jews was clearly laid out. There were to be two stages. The first was a short-range one: The Jews were to be assembled, registered, and evacuated. They would be moved to a few concentration points at railroad junctions or at least along a railroad, "so that future measures may be accomplished more easily." Councils of Jewish elders would be established in each Jewish community and the elders would be charged with the responsibility for carrying out SS orders. They would see to it that all the Jews were listed according to categories of age and vocation, and would be forced to perform their duties under threat of the severest penalties. The second stage was the long-range "final goal" *(Endziel),* which would take longer. It was underlined that *"die geplanten Gesamtmassnahmen streng geheim zu halten sind"* — "the *planned total measures* (that is, the final goal) is to be kept strictly secret."[23]

Since not all the Jews could be killed at once, it was only logical that, insofar as it could conveniently be arranged, the aged, the infirm, and the incapacitated, as well as the children, should be killed first. Those who were able to work could be used as slaves until their turn was reached. Jews working for the German army could continue to do so "for the time being."[24] Every recipient of that teletype of September 21, 1939, must have known beyond any doubt that it was planned to murder all the Jews as quickly as the technical and economic circumstances would allow.

Frank's diary recorded the minutes of meetings held during October and November 1939 in which the planned movement of Jews eastward was spelled out. SS Brig. Gen. Bruno Streckenbach, who was later to transmit to the *Einsatzgruppen* Hitler's order to murder all the Jews,[25] came to Lodz to instruct Frank in his duties as the new administrator of the General Government. It was, he said, Himmler's wish that all the Jews be removed from the territories newly incorporated into the Reich and that approximately one million persons be deported into the General Government area within the next three months.[26]

Although the fate of the Jews was of no consequence—*völlig gleichgültig sei*—it was recognized that the organization of forced labor by the Jews was a matter of particular urgency. Göring authorized Frank to see to it that the area served the economic needs of the Reich. "The question of forced labor by the Jews cannot be solved in a satisfactory way from one day to the next," said SS Lieutenant General Krüger, who was in charge of transportation. First, all the males between the age of 14 and 50 would have to be listed according to location and occupation.[27] Until the plan could be worked out, the Jews could be put to work in labor companies as needed by the district chiefs. Hundreds of *Zwangsarbeitsläger für Juden*—forced labor camps for Jews—sprang up all over the territory, and wherever a dirty job needed to be done—digging a tank trap, a ditch, heavy construction work, or anything else—the slaves were available.[28] In hundreds of small towns throughout Poland, the process of preparing the Jews for slaughter began. Under conditions of indescribable brutality, Jews were seized and shipped to the ghettos, which would serve as the concentration points until the "final goal" could be carried out.

In the territory that had been incorporated into the Reich, the so-called Wartheland, the city of Lodz, which the Germans renamed Litzmannstadt, became the assembly center. The Lodz ghetto would also receive transports from Vienna, Prague, Berlin, and other German cities. Inside the ghetto, Jews tried to stay alive by working for the *Wehrmacht*—the German army—or some other German master. The German press reported that 400,000 Jews were working for Germany in the ghettos of Poland in 1941.[29] Eventually there were over 160,000 Jews working in over a hundred workshops in Lodz producing all kinds of clothing and other war supplies for the Germans.[30] Some with special skills which could not be used in the ghetto but which were needed elsewhere were reshipped to another forced labor camp or to a concentration camp for direct use by the SS. Occupied Poland became the prototype for the procedures to be followed elsewhere as the German army advanced.

The German invasion of Denmark and Norway in April 1940 and the attack on Holland, Belgium, Luxembourg, and France in May brought millions of new victims into the Nazi net. By the end of June, military resistance to the German tanks and dive bombers was over. In accordance with the Nazi plans, the Jews of occupied Western Europe were assembled under the pretext of being "resettled" and were transported eastward to Poland as fast as Eichmann could make the necessary arrangements.

For awhile, there was some discussion that after the war the Jews would be shipped to a distant and deserted place such as Madagascar, which would be taken from the French for that purpose, or to some American or African territory.[31] Göring had attributed such a plan to Hitler during a conference following the *Kristallnacht* of November 1938. The German Foreign Office, concerned with public reactions abroad, continued to talk about the plan in 1940 and 1942.[32] Even Governor General Frank continued to refer to the emigration of Jews long after he clearly knew that the real plan was to murder them. In the light of the previous secret orders for the annihilation of all Jews and the subsequent actions carrying out the planned program of extermination, as well as the explicit prediction in January 1939 that the Jews would be annihilated, the suspicion cannot be avoided that any talk after September 1939 of creating an autonomous Jewish colony was merely diversionary propaganda designed to camouflage the mass murders which were already underway and which were in fact the initial steps toward the "final solution."[33]

In May 1940 SS Brigadier General Streckenbach again discussed the annihilation program with Governor General Frank and other SS leaders. The SS was now in charge of the General Government and they boasted of their achievements in carrying out the extermination plan. There was no need, said Frank, to transport opponents of the Nazis to concentration camps, since they could be liquidated on the spot.[34] More efficient facilities would be needed, however, before the extermination plan could be put into high gear.

In July Frank titillated an audience of German officials in Lublin by his facetious reference to the shipment out of all Jews—men, women, and children—"as soon as the overseas traffic would allow."[35] In the swelling ghettos of Lublin, Lodz, and Warsaw, the Jewish leadership tried to diminish the Nazi terror by helping to organize Jewish workers in the hope that by becoming indispensible to the Germans, the Jews might be spared. They did not know and could not imagine that their destruction was only a matter of time. Before the year was out, Frank would amuse an armed forces battalion in Cracow by apologizing that, "naturally within one year, I could not get rid of all the lice or all the Jews." It was not necessary to do everything at the same time and within a year, he said. He promised, however, that with their help it could be done in due course.[36] Not far from Cracow, the inspector-general of concentration camps, SS Colonel Glücks, had been shopping around for a means to make Frank's job easier.

## Auschwitz and *Einsatzgruppen* (July 1940 – February 1942)

The SS command for Silesia had drawn Glücks' attention to an old Austrian cavalry barracks of some twenty wooden buildings on a marshy plain 35 kilometers southeast of Katowice on the Vistula River. Glücks had promptly seen its possibilities.[37] With some effort, he could expand this small nucleus into a concentration camp capable of accommodating thousands of prisoners. It did not take him long to conclude that Rudolf Franz Ferdinand Höss would be the perfect man for the job. Höss had confessed to murder for the Nazi party in 1923.[38] He had spent years in prison as a Nazi martyr until amnestied by the German authorities in 1928. This condemned murderer had been rewarded for his early party loyalty by a position of responsibility in the administration of the Dachau concentration camp and was now the commandant. at Sachsenhausen. He was tough and cold-blooded and would make a fine commander of a more important new camp.

On receipt of his reassignment, Höss arranged to have transferred with him thirty of the most notorious criminals from Sachsenhausen, accompanied by a contingent of SS guards clad in their black tunics and black boots. Two hundred Jews, seized and turned over to him by the local mayor, were forced to complete his construction crew. By mid-1940 the camp was ready for its first occupants. June 14 saw the arrival of seven hundred prisoners from Cracow. That was the inauguration of the concentration camp to be known as Auschwitz.

To the Poles the township was known as Oswiecim. It was a cold January in 1941 when the representatives of I.G. Farbenindustrie arrived to consider whether the terrain would be suitable for the erection of a new plant to manufacture the synthetic "Buna" rubber needed by the German air force and army. They reported that the scenery was not particularly attractive and the inhabitants, especially the children, made a miserable impression, but there was coal, lime, and water nearby, the communications were good, and a road could be laid on the flat landscape to run from Auschwitz to the nearby town of Monowitz along the railroad track. The seven thousand Jews and the few thousand Poles would, of course, have to be evicted from their ramshackle wooden homes, but the new concentration camp was being expanded and could accommodate them. Yes, concluded the I. G. Farben scouts, it should be a most favorable site. Labor might be a problem but that could be left to the SS Reichsführer, Henrich Himmler.[39]

On February 18, 1941, Göring, acting in response to a request from Farben director Krauch to SS chief Himmler, ordered that concentration camp inmates be made available for the construction of the Buna plant at Auschwitz.[40] On the first of March, Himmler arrived in Auschwitz to check it out for himself. He was surrounded by a coterie of SS functionaries and leading personalities from I.G. Farben. SS Colonel Glücks, who had recognized the potential of the place within his concentration camp scheme, arrived earlier to brief the commandant, SS Major Höss, and to make sure that a rosy picture would be painted when the big shots from Berlin arrived.[41]

Höss properly considered Auschwitz to be "his baby." He had been given the tough assignment to convert the old barracks into a concentration camp capable of absorbing ten thousand inmates. In his postwar autobiography, Höss bragged that with the help of his connections to German industry, he had managed to get the needed building materials and, despite the fact that there was no drainage and the water was not fit for consumption by man or beast, he had done the job. He had looked forward to being able to point with pride to his achievement; it was therefore a bitter pill for him when Himmler took scant notice of his accomplishments and, in addition, ordered that the entire surrounding area be cleared of all inhabitants and reserved for German armaments production. The camp was to be expanded to accommodate thirty thousand inmates, and ten thousand were to be made available immediately to I.G. Farben for the construction of its new plant. A large prisoner-of-war camp was also to be built for one hundred thousand persons, said Himmler, as he pointed in the direction of the neighboring Brzezinka, which the Germans called Birkenau.[42]

Eventually Auschwitz would have its own POW camp, and a women's camp, and a lot more. According to Höss, who noted in his autobiography that he was determined to carry out his orders without sparing anyone, it was only in Berlin a few months later, in the summer of 1941, that Himmler told him that Auschwitz was to be used for the mass destruction of the Jews of Europe, thus making it the greatest *Vernichtungsanstalt,* or destruction institute, in all history.[43]

Höss admitted afterwards, "In the summer of 1941, I was summoned to Berlin to Reichsführer SS Himmler to receive personal orders. He told me something to the effect—I do not remember the exact words— that the Führer had given the order for a final solution of the Jewish question."[44]

By the end of March 1941 Director Duerrfeld of I.G. Farben was able to report to over a dozen officials in the home office that cordial agreement with the SS Commandant had been reached.[45] The Farben directors were invited to dinner by the camp administrators, and all the necessary arrangements were made to put the concentration camp at the disposal of the new Buna works. The newfound friendship between Farben and the SS was working out just fine.[46]

While Farben was getting itself organized at Auschwitz, Hitler issued an order that no Jews from the east should be allowed to enter Germany. The road to death was to be a one-way street. All able bodied Jews in Germany were to be put to forced labor. In May 1941 Heydrich, who had directed the extermination of Jews in Poland, was getting ready to do the same to the Jews of Russia. The *Einsatzgruppen* commanders were assembled in a top-secret meeting and told that it was the Führer's order that they and their special squads, totaling about four thousand men, were to liquidate all those who were even potential enemies of the Reich. "They had the task of clearing the area of Jews, Communist officials and agents . . . by killing all racially and politically undesirable elements seized who were considered dangerous to the security."[47] No one seemed to doubt that Hitler could give such an order, particularly after SS General Streckenbach explained that the Führer was concerned with the permanent security of Germany.[48] It was the very same justification which Streckenbach had heard in Lodz on October 31, 1939, when Governor General Frank had referred to the instructions he had received from Hitler.[49] In its judgment in the *Einsatzgruppen* case, the Nuremberg tribunal found:

At top secret meetings held . . . in May 1941, the *Einsatzgruppen* and *Einsatzkommando* leaders were instructed by Heydrich, Chief of Security Police and SD, and Streckenbach, Chief of Personnel of RSHA, as to their mission . . . the *Einsatzgruppen* were to liquidate ruthlessly all opposition to National Socialism—not only the opposition of the present but that of the past and future as well. Whole categories of people were to be killed without truce, without investigation, without pity, tears or remorse. Women were to be slain with the men, and the children also were to be executed because, otherwise, they would grow up to oppose National Socialism and might even nurture a desire to avenge themselves on the slayers of their parents . . . One of the principal categories was "Jews."[50]

One of the *Einsatzgruppen* defendants admitted, "Streckenbach himself described the activity of the *Einsatzgruppen* in the East to me as MURDER."[51]

Many years later it would be suggested in a popular book that the Führer did not even know about the extermination of the Jews. The author suggests that the most powerful man in Germany was so engrossed in military and political problems that the real fate of the Jews was successfully withheld from him, and he points to the fact that thus far no written extermination order signed by Hitler has yet been produced.[52] However, the author chooses to ignore the fact that murder is usually kept secret and that the circumstantial evidence of Hitler's personal responsibility for the massacre of the Jews is overwhelming.

In fact, after the tides of war had turned, Hitler felt called upon to explain his actions to his generals. In a speech at Platterhof on May 26, 1944, Hitler sought to justify his ruthless *(rücksichtslos)* action against the Jews. He denounced Jews as "a foreign body among the Germans," and according to the führer it was a battle of life or death, since the Bolsheviks, organized by the Jews, could be expected to massacre millions of German intellectuals and German children. He pointed to the warning in his prophecy before the Reichstag in 1939 that if the Jews brought on the war, it was they and not the Germans who would be eradicated *(ausgerottet)*. "I have gotten rid of the Jews," he proclaimed as he denouned the "old morality" as outdated. By the time that speech was made, millions of helpless Jews had been deliberately slaughtered under direct German command, and it was not necessary that Hitler spell out the gory details to the assembled officers and generals who, according to the official top-secret transcript, repeatedly interrupted the speech with outbursts of sustained applause.[53]

The army had provided the logistic support for the extermination squads, and the *Einsatzgruppen* reports from the field, chronicling the massacres of Jews and others, were tabulated in Berlin, mimeographed, and widely distributed to the highest levels of the armed forces and the government. Field marshals and SS generals who had direct access to the Führer repeatedly discussed the objective of the Hitler order among themselves.[54] There is no indication that any of them ever thought or sought to challenge its authenticity.

It is beyond dispute that the SS *Einsatzgruppen* acted in reliance on an order from their Führer. When the German armies attacked the Soviet Union on June 22, 1941, the *Einsatzgruppen* moved in and as each town and village fell to German occupation, the *Einsatzkommandos* promptly massacred in cold blood every Jewish man, woman, and child they could find.[55] The Nazi forces, trailed by the voracious *Einsatz* units, fanned out to the east and north to seize Lithuania with its esteemed Jewish population in Kaunas, which the Jews called Kowno, and Vilna. Latvia, with its capital of Riga, and all of Estonia were overrun. Ancient Jewish communities of Poland and Russia, such as Bialystok, Pinsk, Dubno, and Odessa, soon fell into German hands. A few Jews managed to retreat with the Russian armies or to hide in the woods. Once the initial waves of slaughter passed and Jews were still found, some managed to be spared but only if they were "for essential war work irreplaceable at this time." Those no longer capable of work were "seized and promptly executed."[56] The Reich commissioner *(Reichskommissar)* for the Ostland (the German-occupied area of White Russia, north of the Ukraine) decreed that "as long as further measures are not possible in the direction of the final solution of the Jewish problem . . . Jews capable of working are to be drafted for forced labor.''[57] He would later be called on the carpet by Berlin for being too lenient.

On July 31, 1941, Göring, as a further follow-up on his early instructions of January 24, 1939, directed Heydrich to prepare detailed and coordinated plans for the "final solution of the Jewish problem."[58] "The final solution," admitted Auschwitz commandant Höss, "meant the complete extermination of all Jews in Europe."[59] Secret instructions were prepared for "the handling of the Jewish question." The instructions could hardly have been more specific:

The whole Jewish question will be solved in general for all of Europe after the war at the latest . . . It appears necessary for the purpose of avoiding a later regaining of strength of the Jews to interpret the term "Jews" in its broadest sense . . . Jewish manpower is to be used for heavy manual labor. The standing rule for the employment of Jewish labor is the complete and unyielding use of Jewish manpower regardless of age . . . Care is to be taken that Jewish labor is used only in productions which will suffer no noticeable interruption in case of a rapid withdrawal of these labor forces . . . It is to be avoided in every case that Jewish workers become indispensible in essential production . . . Violations of German regulations and attempts to avoid forced labor are to be punished as a matter of principle by death to the Jews.[60]

Transports of Jews deported from the major German cities began to arrive in the ghettos of Lodz, Minsk, Riga, and other collecting points. The next month, Eichmann stopped the emigration of all Jews from the occupied territories. The trap was closed.[61]

The *Einsatzgruppen* reporting from Cracow described conditions surrounding the Bug River and the swamps in the Pripet marshes. The report, dated August 14, 1941, stated that until the final solution of the Jewish problem could be settled for the whole continent,

The superfluous Jewish masses can be employed excellently to cultivate the large Pripet marshes as well as the marshes on the northern Dnieper as well as the Volga where they can be consumed [*verbraucht*].[62]

The English language has no word to describe precisely how a human being is *verbraucht*, or used up. Forty-eight copies of the report were distributed to the major offices of the SS. *Einsatzgruppe* A reported how difficult it was to organize local pogroms in order to camouflage the German actions.

The Security Police was determined to solve the Jewish question with all possible means and most decisively. But it was desireable that the Security Police should not put in an immediate appearance, at least in the beginning, since the extraordinarily harsh measures were apt to stir even German circles . . . The cleansing action of the Security Police had to aim at a complete annihilation of the Jews . . . It became soon apparent that an annihilation of the Jews without leaving any traces could not be carried out, at least not at the present moment . . . It is not yet possible to displace all employed Jews . . . All Jews who are no longer fit for work are being arrested and shall be executed in small batches.[63]

A detailed chart showed how many persons had been executed by *Einsatzgruppe* A between June 23 and October 25, 1941. The tabulation showed over 135,000 souls dispatched, almost all of whom were Jews.[64]

Beginning on the eve of the Jewish Holy Day, Yom Kippur, one *Einsatzkommando* slaughtered 33,771 Jews in Kiev in the two days of September 29 and 30, 1941. The ravine in which the massacre took place was known to the local inhabitants as "Babi Yar."[65] Over a million helpless and defenseless people would fall prey to the *Einsatzgruppen* murder squads.[66] In October 1941 the incredulous and hesitant Reichkommissar of the Ostland in Riga asked the Reich Security Main Office for clarification and confirmation that his instructions were to kill all the Jews. "I have forbidden the wild execution of Jews," he wrote,

because they were not justifiable in the manner in which they were carried out . . . Of course, the cleansing of the East of Jews is a necessary task; its solution, however, must be harmonized with the necessities of war production. [67]

He was called on the phone from Berlin and then received written top-secret confirmation: "Clarification of the Jewish question has most likely been achieved by now through verbal discussions. Economic considerations should fundamentally remain unconsidered in the settlement of the problem."[68]

When Himmler visited Ohlendorf's headquarters at Nikolayev on October 4, 1941, he reprimanded Ohlendorf for having allowed the Jewish farmers to be excluded from the executions. According to Ohlendorf's testimony, "I was reproached for this measure . . . Nevertheless, after supper, I spoke to the *Reichsführer* and I pointed out the inhuman burden which was being imposed on the men in killing all these civilians. I didn't even get an answer."[69]

The open shooting of Jews in public view created certain problems. A secret letter dated October 25, 1941, proposed a solution which had been approved by Eichmann. "There is no objection to doing away with those Jews who are not able to work . . . Those able to work on the other hand will be transported to the East for labor services." As for those who could not work, the improved technique for getting rid of them quietly was through "the manufacture of the necessary shelters and the gassing apparatus."[70] What was planned, and what was done, at Belzec, Sobibor, Treblinka, and Chelmno, was to build special factories whose only function would be to kill the Jews of Europe as quickly and as cheaply as possible. The technology for getting rid of the Jews was to be a source of continuous discussion within the Nazi hierarchy. There seemed to be a general consensus, however, that all of the Jews would be liquidated one way or the other.[71] *Arbeitsjuden*—"work Jews"—could wait their turn.

In a very candid speech on December 16, 1941, Hans Frank asked the rhetorical question, "What shall happen to the Jews?" "Do you really think they will be resettled in the East," he asked, and then gave the answer he had received from Berlin: "Kill them yourself. [*Liquidiert sie selbst*] Gentlemen, I must ask you to arm yourselves against every feeling of sympathy. We must annihilate the Jews wherever we find them and wherever it is possible."[72] He also informed his SS audience that there would be a forthcoming conference in Berlin in January where Heydrich would arrange for the mass movement of the Jews. He promised to send his deputy, State Secretary Dr. Josef Bühler, to the meeting. What Bühler had to suggest at the conference at the Wannsee in Berlin was most revealing about the Nazi plans and intentions regarding the Jews.

In Auschwitz itself, with Göring's stamp of approval, the construction of I.G. Farben's new plant, Auschwitz III, at Monowitz was in full swing. The original assignment of 700 Jews had been increased to 1,000. Seventy freight cars arrived daily for the construction site and one hundred twenty for the concentration camp, which was being expanded for an anticipated 120,000 Russian POWs.[73]

Höss was convinced that only beatings would make the inmates work.[74] The Farben directors complained that the severe beatings on the Farben camp grounds—"and this always applies to the weakest inmates who really cannot work harder"—were having a demoralizing effect on the German and Polish workers; they urged therefore that the beatings be restricted to "the *Stammlager,*" the main Auschwitz camp itself.[75]

By the end of the year the Farben officials proudly stated in their weekly report to the main office that they had been invited to join the SS guards in a Christmas party, "which was very festive and which ended up alcoholically gay." The three hundred Farben employees had in return invited members of the SS to celebrate with them at their own staff party, where a good goose dinner was enjoyed by all.[76]

The winter of 1941 was quite different for the inmates of the Auschwitz camp. Shorn of their hair, their names replaced by numbers tattooed on their arms, clad in what looked like striped pajamas, their naked and blistered feet covered by wooden clogs, they plodded through the rain and snow to the Farben construction site, a distance of some 7 kilometers. Those who were unable to keep pace were beaten or killed on the spot.[77] At the end of the long day and after the most arduous of labors, many had to be carried back to the main camp on the arms of their comrades. Those who were too exhausted to continue would be sent to the nearby Auschwitz II camp at Birkenau (Brzezinka), to be put to death by gas. Conditions grew increasingly worse as time went by. The 250 watch dogs and even the pigs at Auschwitz lived better than the human inmates, according to reliable testimony.[78] In the words of the judgment of the Nuremberg court, the inmates "lived and labored under the shadow of extermination."[79]

Back in Berlin, Heydrich invited fifteen high German officials, representing various government departments, to meet for lunch in a pleasant lakeside suburb of Berlin. The meeting had been in preparation for many months but had been postponed since some of the participants, like SS Major Dr. Fritz Lange, were already busy killing Jews.[80] What was to become known as the Wannsee Conference took place on January 20, 1942, and its purpose was to coordinate various problems related to "the final solution of the Jewish question." Göring had requested such action on July 31 of the previous year, and Frank had anticipated the outcome of the meeting in his speech of December 16. The basic plan was, after all, a fairly simple one. The eleven million Jews of Europe, as shown on a detailed chart listing the numbers and localities, were to be combed from the west to "reception centers" in the east where they would be either murdered outright or worked to death. Eichmann would take care of the shipments and once delivery was made, his boss, "Gestapo Müller," would finish off the job. The Foreign Office representatives would be responsible for handling public relations abroad.

Bühler, who had been sent along to represent Hans Frank, urged that the *Aktion*—by which was ment the elimination of the Jews—begin in the General Government "since most of the two and one-half million Jews there are unable to work anyway" and there would be no transportation problems. He urged that it be done quickly and agreed that unrest among the population was to be avoided.[81] One of the details which consumed much of the discussion in January was whether Jews of mixed blood or living in mixed marriage with Aryans should be "evacuated," which meant killed, or merely sterilized.

Those who required transportation could also be accommodated. Jews captured in the occupied lands of the west would have to be moved eastward, and the nearest stop could be Auschwitz. Eichmann went to Auschwitz and discussed the timetable of the transports with Höss, as well as the place of execution and the methods to be used. An isolated section of Birkenau was chosen for a new building, not too far from the railway, and the merits of Zyklon B prussic acid versus carbon monoxide poisoning were considered.[82] At the close of discussions, it was concluded that Zyklon B would prove to be the more efficient method of extermination. According to Höss, "It took from three to fifteen minutes to kill the people."[83]

Obviously killing eleven million people would take time. Heydrich acknowledged that while waiting, the Jews could be put to work under conditions which would be consistent with the ultimate goal. Göring's representative, State Secretary (Staatsekretär) Erich Neumann, acknowledged that Jews who were engaged in essential war production could not be "evacuated" until there was a replacement available. "No doubt," said Heydrich in expounding on the Nazi racial doctrines, a great many of the Jews put to work "in a suitable way in the East . . . will drop out through natural reductions. The residue which is finally able to remain, being the most resistant, and representing a natural selection, must be treated appropriately in order to prevent a new Jewish regrowth through a germ-cell which is allowed to go free."[84]

Within a week after the Wannsee Conference, Himmler teletyped Glücks at Oranienburg, from which the fifteen principal concentration camps were directed (see map), to ready the camps for one hundred thousand male Jews and fifty thousand females who would be shipped from Germany within the next four weeks.[85] Since not all of them would be fit for work, the extermination facilities would have to be expanded.[86] Maximum efficiency was essential.

Auschwitz/Birkenau could take care of those from the west. Some Austrian Jews were shipped as far away as Riga, where they were murdered in an extermination facility known as Jungfernhof.[87] In Chelmno, which the Germans called Kulmhof an der Neer, a new extermination camp was being constructed. It was designed to eliminate the "useless" Jews of the ghetto in nearby Lodz.[88] Bigger and better charnel houses were being constructed. Until arrangements could be completed to gas and burn the victims, they could be put to work.

## Extermination by Labor (February 1942–June 1944)

By 1942 the drain on German manpower became so acute and the need for armaments so great that second thoughts had to be given to the wholesale slaughter of the Jews which was taking place. In February Himmler presented to Hitler and to the newly appointed minister for armaments and munitions, Albert Speer, a proposal which would enable him to build armaments plants inside the concentration camps and put able-bodied inmates to work on armaments production.[89] Propaganda Minister Goebbels recorded in his diary for March 27, 1942: "The Jews in the General Government are now being evacuated eastward. The procedure is a pretty barbaric one . . . not much will remain of the Jews. On the whole it can be said that about 60% of them will have to be liquidated whereas only about 40% can be used for forced labor."[90] Goebbels underestimated the number which would be murdered outright. At least two out of three went straight to the gas chambers.[91] With the growing awareness that available manpower would have to be preserved came the need for a reorganization of the SS Main Office. A new department was created, the *Wirtschafts und Verwaltungshauptamt* (Economic and Administrative Main Office), WVHA, to deal with economic problems. Oswald Pohl, who had joined the party in 1926 and had risen to the rank of *Obergruppenführer*—a lieutenant general of the SS—was to be the man in charge of the new Main Office. Glücks' Department D, which was in charge of all the concentration camps, was made subordinate to Pohl. Department D II handled the commitment of inmates for labor and was headed by Colonel *(Standartenführer)* Gerhard Maurer, who was assisted by Karl Sommer.[92] By the end of April Pohl was able to report to Himmler with pride that he had completely reorganized the existing concentration camps "for the mobilization of all prisoners who are fit for work."[93] At the same time all the camp commanders were told that "this employment must be in the true meaning of the word, exhaustive, in order to obtain the greatest measure of performance."[94]

Thus a compromise was reached between the ideological demands that the inferior race of Jews be eliminated and the economic demands for productive labor. The solution was to spare those who could work, as long as they could work, and kill all the others.

On May 29, 1942, Heydrich, Chief of the Security Police and the Security Service, who scarcely four months before had been directing the "final solution" of the Jews, met his own final solution. He was blown up by a bomb thrown by two Czech patriots who had been parachuted into the area near Prague by Britain's Royal Air Force. In reprisal, the Czech village of Lidice was subjected to a vicious German assault, and thousands of Jews who had nothing to do with the assassination were also executed, supposedly to teach somebody some kind of a lesson.

Despite the increasing British bomber raids on the industrial cities of the Ruhr, things seemed to be going fairly well for the Germans during the summer of 1942. Axis victories were mounting in Europe and Africa and a new German offensive against the Russians was being planned. On July 17 and 18 Himmler made a thorough inspection of Auschwitz, urged that Birkenau be extended, repeated his order that all gypsies and Jews who were unable to work were to be destroyed without consideration—"Ebenso rücksichtslos vernichten Sie arbeits-unfähigen Juden"—and ordered Höss promoted to SS lieutenant colonel *(Obersturmbannführer)*.[95] The Farben directors were reporting some technical difficulties in getting their new Auschwitz plant ready. The ten thousand foreign construction workers recruited from the occupied territories were transforming the entire region into a vast industrial complex but, reported Farben's man on the scene, Belgian, French, Croat, and Polish laborers frequently ran away. Inmates from the concentration camp itself could only be supplied in limited numbers, and they had to be closely guarded. There was also the danger that they would spread typhus, which was raging behind the camp's barbed wires. Unable to supply Farben with all of the inmates desired, SS Lieutenant General Pohl, as a gesture of good will, ordered the concentration camp to deliver the civilian clothes—jackets, coats, and trousers—of the camp inmates to the large numbers of foreign laborers working for Farben outside the Auschwitz camp. Those inmates from whom they were taken would no longer be needing them.[96]

A Farben civilian employee at I.G. Auschwitz, in a personal letter to another employee at Frankfurt on July 30, 1942, wrote: "That the Jewish race is playing a special part here, you can well imagine. The diet and treatment of this sort of people is in accordance with our aim. Evidently, an increase in weight is hardly ever recorded for them. That bullets start whizzing at the slightest attempt of a 'change of air' is also certain as well as the fact that many have already disappeared as a result of a 'sunstroke.'"[97]

Forty thousand Jews from occupied France, forty thousand from Holland, and ten thousand from Belgium were scheduled to be shipped to Auschwitz in special trainloads of one thousand per day. Priority was to be given to those who were capable of work.[98] The word *Vernichtungslager*—extermination camp—was added to the human vocabulary as these centers carried out their deadly program.

In 1942, according to the International Committee of the Red Cross, over 70,000 Jews from the ghetto in Lodz were put to death in the camp at Chelmno. The extermination camps at Maidanek, Sobibor, and Belzec (see map) disposed of the Jews from nearby Lublin and Lvov.[99] In the summer of 1942, seventy miles northeast of Warsaw, the extermination camp at Treblinka commenced its operations. It could turn Jews into ashes at the rate of over 25,000 per day.[100] It was reported that in about seven weeks, between July 22 and September 13, about 300,000 Jews from the Warsaw ghetto were killed in the gas chambers of Treblinka, and German judges found in the course of postwar trials in Germany that a total of about 900,000 Jews had been murdered there.[101] Auschwitz commandant Höss was not to be outdone. He boasted: "Another improvement we made over Treblinka was that we built our gas chamber to accommodate 2,000 people at one time whereas at Treblinka their ten gas chambers only accommodated 200 people each . . . Those who were fit for work were sent into the camp. Others were sent immediately to the extermination plants. Children of tender years were invariably exterminated since by reason of their youth they were unable to work."[102]

Gas chambers stuffed with men, women, and children became the screaming, stinking tomb for millions of European Jews. One of the most vivid descriptions has been given by a German eyewitness, Kurt Gerstein, who had been expelled from the Nazi party but who managed to infiltrate the SS in 1941. Because of some work he had done in helping to control typhus in the camps, Lieutenant Gerstein was called upon to advise the camp commanders how to disinfect the enormous mounds of clothing taken from those who had been killed. Gerstein described his visit to the extermination camps at Belzec and Treblinka in August 1942:

One early morning a trainload of 6,700 Jews arrived from Lvov. Fourteen hundred and fifty were dead on arrival. Two hundred Ukrainians armed with leather whips opened the freight car doors and beat the terrified cargo to the ground. Loudspeakers ordered all to strip naked and to surrender their valuables. The hair was brutally shorn from the heads of all females, and the entire shipment, consisting of stark naked men, women, and children, were driven toward the gas chambers. The SS leader assured the Jews that it was only a necessary disinfectant bath. Hesitant and petrified with fear, the victims were jammed tight into the gas chamber. "Many people prayed," wrote Gerstein, "I pray with them. I press myself in a corner and cry out to my God and theirs. How gladly would I have gone into the chamber with them, how gladly would I have shared their death with them."

Gerstein, the SS man, decided that he would try to live to tell the story. When the doors of the gas chamber were opened, the corpses stood, he said, "like pillars of basalt, with family members still grasping hands, their bones covered with sweat, urine and vomit." The bodies were dragged out by the work commandos and the gold crowns were ripped from the mouths of the dead. The cadavers were then dumped into an unmarked ditch to be covered with ten centimeters of sand before another human layer was added to the pile.[103] In the spring of 1942, the *Einsatzgruppen* had been equipped with mobile gas vans which were intended to dispose primarily of women and children. In the words of SS Gen. Otto Ohlendorf: "The victims were told that they would be resettled and had to climb into the vehicle for that purpose. When the doors were closed and the gas streamed in through the starting of the vehicle, the victims died within 10 or 15 minutes."[104] But the gas vans did not always work very well and there were not enough of them to do the job efficiently. A better method would be to organize a pogrom and then drive the Jews into the woods to be killed.

One of the most vivid descriptions of such an action came from a German manager of a construction firm, Herman Friedrich Graebe, who was working in Dubno in the Ukraine in the summer of 1942. When he learned that an "action" was planned against the Jews, he managed to obtain a written exemption for eighty-one Jews who were working for his company. He posted himself in front of the house in which his workers were hidden. Close to midnight,

the Ghetto was encircled by a large SS detachment and about three times as many members of the Ukrainian militia. Then the electric arclights which had been erected in and around the Ghetto were switched on . . . The people were driven out of their houses in such haste that small children in bed had been left behind in several instances. In the street women cried out for their children and children for their parents. That did not prevent the SS from driving the people along the road, at running pace, and hitting them, until they reached a waiting freight train. Car after car was filled, and the screaming of women and children, and the cracking of whips and rifle shots resounded unceasingly.[105]

Graebe managed to get most of his Jewish workers out of town. It merely postponed their death. Shortly after the Jews in Rovno had been killed, the SS expanded their net and called in all of the German managers from the surrounding area to tell them that they were to be prepared for an immediate "resettlement of the Jews."[106] What "resettlement" meant was also described by Graebe. Some weeks later he went to see what was happening to the five thousand Jews of Dubno who were disappearing at a rate of fifteen hundred daily. His words have become a classic description of a typical execution scene.

The people who had got off the trucks—men, women, and children of all ages—had to undress upon the order of an SS-man, who carried a riding or dog whip. They had to put down their clothes in fixed places, sorted according to shoes, top clothing and underclothing . . . Without screaming or weeping these people undressed, stood around in family groups, kissed each other, said farewells and waited for a sign from another SS-man, who stood near the pit . . . I watched a family of about eight persons . . . An old woman with snow-white hair was holding the one-year old child in her arms and singing to it, and tickling it . . . The couple were looking on with tears in their eyes. The father was holding the hand of a boy about 10 years old and speaking to him softly; the boy was fighting his tears. The father pointed toward the sky, stroked his head, and seemed to explain something to him. At that moment the SS-man at the pit shouted something to his comrade. The latter counted off about 20 persons and instructed them to go behind the earth mound . . . I walked around the mound, and found myself confronted by a tremendous grave. People were closely wedged together and lying on top of each other so that only their heads were visible . . . Some were lifting their arms and turning their heads to show that they were still alive . . . I looked for the man who did the shooting. He was an SS-man, who sat at the edge of the narrow end of the pit, his feet dangling into the pit. He had a tommy gun on his knees and was smoking a cigarette . . . The people, completely naked, went down some steps which were cut in the clay wall of the pit and clambered over the heads of the people lying there, to the place to which the SS-man directed them. They lay down in front of the dead or injured people; some caressed those who were still alive and spoke to them in a low voice. Then I heard a series of shots.[107]

Prisoners of the concentration camps could be made available for work under conditions which had to be approved by SS Lieutenant Colonel Maurer of the WVHA. His order to the commanders of all the concentration camps required that all applications for inmate labor be personally signed by the agency applying for the workers; the application had to set forth specifically "the total number of security personnel (leaders, deputy leaders, and men) who would be assigned to guard the prisoners."[108]

On September 14, 1942, the minister of justice, Dr. Georg Thierack, who had just taken office the preceding August and who had been specifically authorized by Hitler "to deviate from existing law,"[109] met with Propaganda Minister Goebbels to consider further action to eliminate so-called "antisocial" elements. Goebbels said that "Jews and gypsies should be exterminated unconditionally." As for Poles and Czechs, and even Germans who had been sentenced to long prison terms, "the idea of exterminating them by labor is the best."[110] Four days later, at Himmler's invitation, Thierack met with him to discuss the same subject. It was agreed that the "asocial elements," which included Jews and gypsies, were to be delivered to Himmler for the purpose of *Vernichtung durch Arbeit*—to be worked to death (literally, "to be destroyed through work").[111] Streckenbach, promoted to SS major general, was also present. Just a year before, Streckenbach had passed on the Hitler order to the *Einsatzgruppen* that all Jews were to be executed.[112] *Einsatzgruppe* A alone reported: "The systematic mopping up of the Eastern Territories embraced, in accordance with the basic orders, the complete removal if possible, of Jewry. This goal had been substantially attained—with the exception of White Russia—as a result of the execution up to the present time of 229,052

Jews. The remainder still left in the Baltic Provinces is urgently required as labor."[113]

By the end of 1942 Himmler received a secret report that about four million Jews had been eliminated from greater Germany and other European countries. Close to 200,000 Jews were in forced labor.[114] On November 26, 1942, Fritz Sauckel, Plenipotentiary for Labor Allocation, in agreement with Himmler and Göring, ordered that even those German Jews who were engaged in essential war production were to be deported and exchanged for Poles, who were to be shipped into the Reich without their families and trained to replace the Jews.[115] "We will strive," said Himmler, "to substitute Poles for these Jewish workers . . . Of course . . . the Jews shall some day disappear in accordance with the Führer's wishes."[116]

There can be little doubt from the quoted official records of such Nazi leaders as Göring, Goebbels, Himmler, Sauckel, Thierack, Streckenbach, and countless others that the Jews were earmarked for outright extermination or for a slower death through exhausting labor for the German war machine. The ultimate goal was racial purity for Germany. The SS sought complete control of Jewish labor as part of the process of eventual annihilation of Jewry in accordance with the Nazi ideology.

Armaments minister Speer's principal responsibility was to increase armaments production. He was skeptical about the effectiveness of Himmler's plan to manufacture munitions and arms inside the concentration camps. The Army High Command was also dubious about the advisability of Himmler's acquiring an independent capacity to produce arms. In discussing the problem with Hitler in September 1942, Speer argued that Himmler's plan was not feasible. The requisite new machinery could not be supplied and there would not be enough space available in the camps for mass production of the wide variety of war-related equipment and supplies. Speer noted that these obstacles did not exist if armaments production continued in the hands of private companies, which were already being scattered outside the cities to avoid the hazards of Allied air attacks. Speer proposed that production could be increased by putting double shifts to work and this would not require any new machines nor any new space. He felt that concentration camp (KZ) inmates could be used on both shifts. Since Speer anticipated that Himmler might take a dim view of allowing "his" prisoners to be used outside the concentration camps, Speer suggested that Hitler offer Himmler a "sweetener" in the form of three to five percent of all of the weapons or munitions which the inmates would produce. Hitler agreed.[117] Under that agreement, 35,000 inmates were made available for use by the Armaments Ministry. Over 250,000 concentration camp inmates were requisitioned directly from the Main Office of the SS by private German firms which by-passed Speer's ministry.[118]

From around the beginning of 1942 until the summer of 1944, when Allied bombing was effectively destroying German productive capacity, the demand for manpower from any source was overwhelming. No German company had to be coerced into taking labor. On the contrary, the firms had to use all their influence and persuasion to get all the help they felt they needed.[119] The private companies were to pour millions of marks into the coffers of the SS for the privilege of using the camp inmates. An elaborate accounting system was set up to be sure that the companies paid the SS for every hour of skilled or unskilled labor and that deductions for the food provided by the companies did not exceed the maximum allowed. The inmates of course received nothing. They remained under the general control of the SS but under the immediate supervision of the companies that used them. The companies were required to see to it that adequate security arrangements, such as auxiliary guards and barbed wire enclosures, eliminated all possibility of escape.

The long and unproductive march of the inmates from the main camp at Auschwitz II soon inspired the Farben directors to have a camp annex built adjacent to the Buna construction site.[120] By October 1942 inmates from the main camp were transported to the new barracks at Monowitz. Four hundred persons were crowded into a "block" intended for 162. Each wooden bunk, padded only with a thin layer of filthy straw, was shared by three inmates. Dysentery and diarrhea added to the misery. Farben also controlled the nearby coal mines known as Fürstengrube and Janina, where Polish workers and later POWs, illegally employed in violation of the Hague Conventions, were replaced by concentration camp inmates in 1943.[121]

The conditions of work for the foreign laborers, the POWs, and the concentration camp inmates were reported by reliable witnesses after the war. It was well-known to all that the inmates were literally being worked to death. They were forced to run while unloading heavy cement bags weighing one hundred pounds. "If a prisoner collapsed at work," reported a British POW to the court at Nuremberg, "he was kicked and beaten in order to determine if he was still alive." Another testified that the inmates "were all starving to death . . . If the German civilians saw us giving the soup (an inedible watery brew) to the inmates, they would kick it over."[122] Inmates were forced to trot like dogs behind the bicycles of their amused German masters. Drinking water was contaminated, clothing was sparse, and the food totally inadequate. Many died of freezing or starvation. The conditions for all the forced laborers were terrible, but by far the worst were the conditions of the Jews. Five times as many Jews were crowded into the barracks as the number of ethnic German workers.[123] Said another British soldier, "Of all the persons working at IG Auschwitz, the Jewish inmates had the worst time of it." "The German civilians often threatened the inmates that they would be gassed and turned into soap." "They looked on killing Jews as killing vermin."[124] The I.G. Farben directors who visited the camp regularly and received all the reports were later to testify in their defense at Nuremberg that they never noticed anything was wrong, and besides, they were only carrying out orders and doing what was "necessary."

In fact the death rate was too high even for Himmler. With more than half the prisoners dying, it was impossible to keep up the inmates' working capacity.[125] Hundreds of new forced labor camps appeared throughout Germany and the occupied territories. Hundreds of thousands of Jews and prisoners of all nationalities were put to work at the mercy of their masters while awaiting deportation or death. As part of the incredible pattern of deception, the entrance gates of Auschwitz and other camps were spanned by the inscription in large metal letters: *"Arbeit Macht Frei"*—"Work Will Make You Free." The words from Dante's Inferno, "All hope abandon, ye who enter here," would have been more appropriate. Nazi arrogance and power repeatedly manifested itself in an unimaginable array of sadistic tortures and bestiality, all of which would later be documented at the Nuremberg trials and other postwar criminal proceedings in the occupied countries and within Germany itself.

Not I.G. Farben alone but almost all of German industry clamored for the cheap concentration camp labor which might help them meet their war production goals. Millions of foreign workers were seized in the occupied territories and sent to work on the farms and in the factories of the Reich. Höss estimated that approximately nine hundred forced labor camps (ZAL), which were hardly distinguishable from concentration camps (KZ), spread throughout the territories controlled by Germany and became the sources of manpower for the German armaments industry. In fact the number was nearly double that amount.[126] Fritz Sauckel, Plenipotentiary General for the Allocation of Labor, who was later tried and hanged at Nuremberg, ordered that the foreign workers were to be exploited "to the highest possible extent at the lowest conceivable degree of expenditure."[127] Competing bureaucracies within the SS and other branches of the German government sought to gain or keep control over the usable human commodity as long as it would last.

Ernst Kaltenbrunner replaced Heydrich as head of the RSHA in January 1943. Before he was to be sentenced to death by the International Military Tribunal in 1946, the court would quote to him his own letter referring to a shipment of Jews and directing that all who could not work would have to be kept in readiness for "special action" which, said the court, "meant murder."[128] Shortly thereafter Hitler was recorded as telling Hungary's Admiral Horthy that if Jews "could not work they had to be treated like tuberculosis bacilli."[129]

By February 1943 SS Colonel Maurer, deputy to General Glücks, promised to deliver forty-five hundred more inmates to I.G. Farben, which was expanding its operations. He also promised that "the departed spirits" of those who were no longer usable *(abgeschoben)* would be moved out promptly, but he insisted that the entire new working area would also have to be fenced in and thereby converted into a concentration camp, Camp IV.[130]

A small group of hand-picked industrial barons met regularly with Himmler and other SS leaders to review the overall economic situation. Formed in 1933, the group was known as the Circle of Friends of Himmler, and the members provided millions of marks for the personal disposition of the SS Reich leader. They met on the second Wednesday of every month to allow "an exchange of ideas between the industrialists and the members of the SS." Himmler attended many of the meetings personally, as did Oswald Pohl. On February 10, 1943, SS Brigadier General Ohlendorf, whose *Einsatzgruppen* annihilated the Jews of southern Russia, showed the group some films of the action in the Crimea.[131] The regular audience included leading representatives of I.G. Farben as well as Friedrich Flick, a prominent armaments manufacturer about whom more will be said later. According to Wilhelm Keppler, one of Hitler's economic advisers, "The relationship between the two groups was always a very friendly one."[132]

The winter of 1942-43 had not been a good one for the Germans. Things at the front were not going well. The Americans and the British had landed in North Africa in November, and close to a quarter of a million German troops were surrounded and about to be wiped out by the Russians at Stalingrad. Krupp's fuse factory in Essen had been destroyed by bombs and had to be relocated to Auschwitz. The tide had turned.

In December 1942 Himmler ordered the Gestapo to seize "at least 35,000 inmates who are able to work" and deliver them to the concentration camps.[133] In Berlin in March 1943, another roundup was taking place as German Jews, many of whom were already employed in armaments production, were whipped and loaded into trucks for deportation.[134] Himmler was determined to fill his camps with a constant stream of slaves. Caught in the net this time was a young Jewish family, Norbert Wollheim and his wife and three-year old son. They became part of one of the last Jewish transports out of Berlin being jammed into freight cars heading for an unknown destination. When the train was unloaded on the platform at Auschwitz, Wollheim's wife and son were "selected" for death. He was never to see them again. The WVHA recorded: "Berlin shipment arrived 5 March 1943. Total 1,128 Jews. Qualified for work 389 men (Buna) and 96 women. Killed [Sonderbehandelt] 151 men and 492 women and children . . . Berlin shipment arrived 7 March 1943. Total 690 . . . Qualified for work 153 men and 25 *"Schützhäftlinge"* [protective custody prisoners] (Buna) and 65 women. Killed [Sonderbehandelt] 30 men and 417 women and children."[135] And so it went . . .

Norbert Wollheim, able to work, was loaded on a truck, together with about two hundred others, and delivered to Monowitz. There he was forced to undress and was stripped of all his possessions. His head was shaved, he was pushed into a collective bath where he was sprayed with disinfectant rather than the poison gas that had showered on the rest of his family. On his arm there was permanently tatooed the number 107984 as his identity disappeared and he became a number in the Nazi extermination machine. Like all newcomers, he was assigned first to "murder detail 4," which earned its title because few could long survive the assignment of unloading the heavy cement bags from the arriving freight cars. Having acquired a skill as a welder he was, after a few months, transferred to welding, without goggles or other protection. Somehow he managed to keep alive and when the war was over, he would appear in the Nuremberg courthouse to offer witness against those who had murdered his family and tried unsuccessfully to work him to death. Wollheim could not and would not forget.[136]

While the few remaining Jews of Europe were being drawn into the deportation net, those who were already trapped began to fight back. In April 1943 the Jews of the Warsaw ghetto, knowing that they were doomed, rose up and attacked the German garrison. It was hopeless from the start but it took the Germans a month, and heavy losses, before the German commander Brig. Gen. Juergen Stroop could issue an elaborate leather-bound report entitled "The Warsaw Ghetto Is No More." The ghetto, with all its inhabitants, had been burned to the ground and the remaining 56,000 of the initial 400,000 Jews were slaughtered.[137] Similar Jewish uprisings took place in such other ghettos as Lvov and Bialystok, but the participants must have known that they were simply chosing to die fighting rather than perish through slavery, starvation, and asphyxiation.[138]

The Farben company seemed quite satisfied with the way things were going for them at Auschwitz. In July 1943 the head of the company, Dr. Carl Krauch, wrote a top-secret letter to Himmler at the Prinz Albrecht Strasse in Berlin urging that another synthetic rubber factory be built, "in a similar way as was done at Auschwitz, by making available inmates of your camps, if necessary. I have also written to Minister Speer to this effect and would be grateful if you would continue sponsoring and aiding us in this matter."[139]

Krauch was proud of "the initiative displayed by my staff in the procurement of labor, a virtue which had proved its worth in the past, must not be repressed in the future."[140] The amiable commandant Höss offered Farben five thousand sets of men's clothing and two thousand sets of women's clothing for Farben's German workers who had been bombed out in Berlin.[141] SS Lieutenant General Pohl, who had honored Farben by visiting the Aushwitz construction site in August, explained apologetically that the company already had more than its fair share of inmates.[142]

Concentration camp prisoners were being traded and transshipped like so many pieces of metal. A Farben factory in Munich selected two hundred fifty Dutch women from Ravensbrück who were to be shipped by freight car to Dachau, where the car was to be refilled with two hundred Polish women to be shipped back from Dachau to Ravensbrück. Any not found suitable would be placed at the disposal of the Dachau commandant.[143] The Krupp company, which had for generations provided arms for the German war machine, planned to expand its production with the help of the Auschwitz inmates. Krupp's plans for Auschwitz did not work out very well, and he was soon obliged to seek his help from other camps such as Buchenwald and Gross Rosen.

Those leading German industrialists, such as Friedrich Flick and representatives of Farben, Siemens, and Rheinmetall, who were heavy contributors to Himmler's personal fund were thereby assured of close cooperation from the SS, the RSHA, and the WVHA. For a Christmas celebration in 1943, Himmler, who had recently been granted the added title of Minister of the Interior, invited the group of his industrialist friends to his headquarters, where he gave them a pep talk about how the war was going. An SS film was shown and the group was entertained by songs sung by a male chorus of SS men.[144]

In addition to Farben and Krupp, the names of other prominent German firms appeared regularly in the SS records. Each company using labor from each camp was given a secret code number which the camp commanders were directed to use on all correspondence relating to that company. These included the aircraft companies like Messerschmidt, Junkers, and Heinkel, automobile companies like BMW (Bavarian Motor Works) and Daimler-Benz, munitions companies like Dynamit Nobel and Rheinmetall, and the electrical companies, Siemens, AEG (Allgemeine Elektricitäts-Gesellschaft), and Telefunken.[145] Many construction companies turned to the nearby camps for labor, and names like Moll, Holzmann, and Hugo Schneider A.G. (HASAG) were frequent customers of the concentration camps. So too were the mining companies like BRABAG (Braunkohle-Benzin A.G.). The Organization Todt, the armed forces, and of course the WVHA itself created its own corporations to employ about 10 percent of the concentration camp inmates for work in the mines and quarries to produce the stone for the highways and edifices of the Reich as well as the equipment and clothing for the SS.[146] In February 1944 Göring offered Himmler a squadron of planes if Himmler would provide the aircraft industry with the maximum possible number of concentration camp inmates.[147] German aircraft production was beginning to have to move underground, and the prisoners were particularly well suited for the work, which was so arduous that even Speer later described it as "barbarous."[148]

From 1942 to 1944 a steady stream of slaves moved into the ghettos and assembly points and then to a forced labor camp. To tighten security, and to give greater control to the SS, many of these camps were made part of the nearest concentration camp in 1944 and became an *Aussen Kommando*. With hundreds of German companies calling for manpower, the emaciated inmates, beaten, bewildered, and terrified, often had no idea which company they were working for or how long it would be before they too would be sent to a gas chamber.

On the 3rd and 4th of April 1944, at Krummhübel (Karpacz), the *Judenreferenten,* the consultants on Jewish questions of the German Missions in Europe, assembled for a conference. A footnote to the file memorandum stated that no minutes were being taken in order to keep the details of the measures of execution secret. The goal remained the total annihilation of the Jews of Europe.[149] In April 1944 Hitler ordered Himmler to deliver 100,000 Jews to help build the new underground aircraft factories.[150] The need for manpower became so desperate that Speer's assistant, Walter Schieber, complained to his boss that the Armaments Ministry was losing an important part of its labor force to the SS by indiscriminate arrests of skilled foreign labor by the Gestapo. Schieber protested that much against the will of the workers, they were being hauled off to work in the dreaded concentration camps.[151]

Despite the shortage of labor, most of those who came down the loading ramp at Auschwitz from the ghettos and cities of occupied Europe went straight to the gas chambers. In only forty-six days, 250,000 to 300,000 Hungarian Jews who were considered unfit for work were put to death in the five gas chambers of Auschwitz by the Zyklon B gas crystals, which could suffocate 60,000 men, women, or children in a twenty-four-hour period.[152] Commander Höss explained: "We executed about 400,000 Hungarian Jews alone at Auschwitz in the summer of 1944."[153] The crematoria could not keep up with the flow of dead bodies.[154] Those who were young and appeared to be healthy, including thousands of Hungarian girls, were spared to be used by German companies. The SS invited the armaments industry to come, look over the stock, and take them away.[155] It was recommended that they be picked up "in batches of 500."[156] Krupp lost no time in putting in a bid.

Auschwitz and its forty-two branch camps held 144,000 slaves available for work.[157] Although no more than 10,000 persons were ever employed at the Buna plant at any one time, it was reported that during the three years of its operations, over 30,000 people perished while working there for I.G. Farben.[158] There was no doubt that everyone was worked "to the extreme limit of his forces."[159] Auschwitz commander Höss, who knew the workings of the system most comprehensively, estimated that in Auschwitz alone "at least 2,500,000 victims were executed and exterminated there by gassing and burning, and at least another half million succumbed to starvation and disease, making a total dead of about 3,000,000 . . . The 'final solution' of the Jewish question meant the complete extermination of all Jews in Europe."[160]

## The German Defeat and Nuremberg

On June 6, 1944, the Allied forces landed on the beaches of Normandy and began their march of liberation. On the same day, what was left of the ghetto in Cracow was designated by the WVHA as a new concentration camp. As the Russian pincers closed in from the east, some of Hitler's generals could see the end in sight, but the belated attempt by some of them to overthrow the Führer on July 20 ended in a debacle.

Just before Christmas 1944 Hitler launched his last desperate attack against the Allies in the Ardennes. He lost his gamble in what came to be known as the Battle of the Bulge. General Eisenhower's armies moved in across the Rhine, and masses of Russian troops resolutely crossed the Vistula and headed for Silesia. In Auschwitz, in an attempt to conceal the evidence of their crimes, the crematoria were blown up by a special SS commando headed by former *Einsatzgruppe* commander Paul Blobel, under whose direction the Babi Yar massacre had taken place. Some of the prisoners themselves had tried to sabotage the crematoria, and a resistance movement inside the camp smuggled out information and maintained contact with representatives of the approaching Soviet army.[161] The uprising of the inmates was suppressed, and as Auschwitz was evacuated on January 18, 1945, "ragged skeletons, milling for scraps of bread or crying for water" were driven westward toward the camps of Germany, leaving an incriminating trail of starved bodies and new mass graves to mark the routes.[162]

Krupp hastily evacuated the camp at Essen and hustled the Hungarian female inmates back toward Buchenwald. There were still some 600,000 inmates, more or less alive, in the camps and about 250,000 of them were employed by private industry.[163] Soviet troops entered Auschwitz on January 27, 1945. One of the last declarations of Nazi defiance was the German News Agency report of March 13, 1945, saying "Above all, when this war comes to an end, there will be no more Jews in Europe."[164] By April American troops had reached Nuremberg and Russian troops were on the outskirts of Berlin. On April 11, 1945, American troops liberated Buchenwald. Four days later, the British marched into Bergen-Belsen. On the 23rd Flossenberg was entered by General Patton's Third Army, and on the 29th Dachau was freed. Mauthausen and all of its surrounding camps were taken by the Americans on May 5. Two days later, the war in Europe was over.

What the Allied armies found in the liberated camps has been amply described in all of its gruesome and grisly detail by the testimony of survivors and witnesses, and will not be repeated here. Many of the camps, like Auschwitz and Dachau, Buchenwald and Oranienburg, have been preserved as permanent museums and memorials.[165] The documentary records produced at war crimes trials in Nuremberg, Poland, and the Soviet Union, and in the courts of Germany itself, have made the facts clear beyond all doubt—even if they are almost beyond belief.

Hitler took his life in his Berlin bunker on April 30, 1945. Himmler, when captured by the British a few weeks later, took cyanide. Göring, sentenced to death at the Nuremberg trials, cheated the hangman by swallowing poison. Kaltenbrunner, whose RSHA was found to have directed the murder of approximately 6 million Jews, Hans Frank, who was found responsible for the brutal extermination of from 2.5 to 3.5 million Jews in the General Government, and Fritz Sauckel, who had overall responsibility for the slave labor program, all felt the Nuremberg hangman's noose on October 16, 1946. Commandant Höss was tried in Warsaw and taken back to the scene of his crimes at Auschwitz and there hanged on April 16, 1947.[166] On September 8, 1951, Juergen Stroop was taken back to the ruins of the Warsaw ghetto, and General Stroop "was no more." Oswald Pohl was sentenced to death by the American Military Tribunal at Nuremberg and, after several appeals for revision or clemency were denied, he was hanged in Landsberg prison on June 7, 1951. Hanged at the same time were SS General Otto Ohlendorf and *Einsatzgruppen* commander Paul Blobel. Adolf Eichmann managed to escape to Argentina, but he was tracked down by Israeli agents, who abducted him, and forced him to stand trial for his crimes against the Jewish people and against humanity. He was convicted by an Israeli court and executed on May 31, 1962.[167]

In contrast with the uniformed SS officers and Nazi leaders, the white-collared German industrialists who had used the concentration camp inmates came off relatively well. Most of the company managers were never even put on trial. The International Military Tribunal (IMT) sentenced Albert Speer to twenty years in Spandau prison for having used concentration camp labor in the industries under his control as Armaments Minister, even though he was not directly responsible for the cruelties in the slave labor program and there was some evidence that he had tried to mitigate the hardships. No corporate director stood before the IMT. It was left to the Subsequent Proceedings under the supervision of Gen. Telford Taylor to call some of the German industrial users of slave labor to account.[168]

In the subsequent trials against the leading directors of I.G. Farben, Krupp, and the Flick combine, several of the defendants were found guilty of having committed crimes against humanity by having deliberately used their influence to obtain forced laborers and by their abuse of the concentration camp inmates. Many of the convicted corporate officers were sentenced to long prison terms, but by January 1951 not a single one was still in jail. As an act of clemency by the United States High Commissioner, John J. McCloy (about which more shall be said later), those corporate leaders who had not already served their terms were given their freedom. The Nuremberg court's decree confiscating the entire fortune of Alfried Krupp, who was convicted of plunder of property as well as abuse of slave laborers, was set aside. Half a dozen years after the war was over, all of the German industrialists were free to resume their normal lives.

Those former slaves who survived the concentration camps with only their tatoos, their memories, and their nightmares began to reflect upon the recent past and to compare their own condition with that of the convicted criminals who had been their masters. As inmates, instead of wages all they had received was maltreatment. They wondered if those who had profited from their labor did not owe them something more.

# Auschwitz Survivors v. I.G. Farben

27 July 1943

To  Reichsfuehrer SS and Chief of
German Police [Heinrich Himmler]
Berlin SW 11, Prinz Albrechtstrasse

Dear Reichsfuehrer,

I was particularly pleased to hear that during this
discussion you hinted that you may possibly aid the
expansion of another synthetic factory . . . in a similar
way as was done at Auschwitz, by making available
inmates of your camps, if necessary. I have also written
to Minister Speer to this effect and would be grateful if
you would continue sponsoring and aiding us in this
matter . . .

    Heil Hitler!

      Yours faithfully,

[Signed] Dr. C. Krauch
[Chairman of the Supervisory Board of I.G. Farben][1]

# CHAPTER 2

## I.G. Farben on Trial

The twenty-three defendants sat glumly in the dock. They had been accustomed to sitting on the boards of directors of some of the most prestigious firms in the world and now, in the same paneled courtroom at Nuremberg where not two years before Field Marshal Göring and other leaders of the Reich had been condemned, they were about to listen to the verdict. More than a year had passed since the indictments had been handed down in 1947 accusing the I.G. Farben directors of plunder, slavery, complicity in aggression, and mass murder. Over six thousand documents had been submitted by the dozen American prosecutors and by some sixty German lawyers selected by the defendants. Nearly two hundred witnesses had been heard. Chief Judge Curtis Grover Shake, who had come from the Supreme Court of the State of Indiana, read the decision. His opinion was shared by Judge James Morris, who had been on the Supreme Court of North Dakota:

Auschwitz was financed and owned by Farben . . . The Auschwitz
construction workers furnished by the concentration camp lived
and labored under the shadow of extermination . . . the defendants
most closely connected with the Auschwitz construction project
bear great responsibility with respect to the workers. They applied
to the Reich Labor Office for labor . . . Responsibility for taking
the initiative in the unlawful employment was theirs and, to some
extent at least, they must share the responsibility for mistreatment
of the workers with the SS and the construction contractors . . .
The use of concentration camp labor and forced foreign workers at
Auschwitz with the initiative displayed by the officials of Farben in
the procurement and utilization of such labor, is a crime against humanity.[2]

Nine of the twenty-three Farben directors were found guilty of corporate plunder in occupied territories. Only five were held to be criminally liable for the abuse of slave labor.[3] Judge Paul M. Hebert, former Dean of the Law School of Louisiana State University, felt that the other two judges had been too lenient: "I conclude from the record that Farben accepted and frequently sought the forced workers . . . The important fact is that Farben's *Vorstand* [executive board of directors] willingly cooperated in utilizing forced labor. They were not forced to do so . . . The conditions at Auschwitz were so horrible that it is utterly incredible to conclude that they were unknown to the defendants, the principle corporate directors, who were responsible for Farben's connection with the project . . . Each defendant who is a member of the *Vorstand* should be held guilty."[4]

As I watched the sad expressions on the faces of the young American prosecutors, it was clear that they shared Judge Hebert's view that the accused had gotten off lightly.[5] They were not alone. Norbert Wollheim had been a Farben slave at Auschwitz and had given testimony at the trial. He was appalled at the mildness of the court's verdict and was determined to make the company pay for what it had done to him and his friends.

Wollheim had been evacuated from Auschwitz in January 1945 as the German army retreated. He was found by the liberating British army in Bergen-Belsen. While waiting to immigrate to the States, Wollheim made the acquaintance of a refugee German lawyer who was with the Intelligence Branch of the British occupation authorities. Hans Oettinger, born Jakobsohn, had not forgotten his arrest by the Gestapo in 1938 and his time in Dachau. He had abandoned his German name and was known as Henry Ormond. But his German legal training was of little value outside of Germany, so in 1950 Ormond decided to open a law office in Frankfurt. Wollheim appeared as a client eager to sue the I.G. Farben Company. All Wollheim could offer was an advance payment of DM 150 (about $30). The paucity of the payment and the uncertainty of the outcome against a powerful economic combine were outweighed by the justice of the cause. Ormond agreed to take the case.

By the beginning of 1951 even the few Farben directors who had been convicted had served their terms. Sales of the old Farben cartel had already risen to billions of marks. In order to break up the monopoly, the Allied High Commission decreed that Farben would be split into a number of successor companies and would be under the control of a liquidating committee.[6] The case of *Wollheim v. I.G. Farben in Liquidation* was filed in the district court in Frankfurt, where the company had its headquarters. One of the Farben attorneys, Alfred Seidl, was an ex-Nazi from Munich whose track record as a defense lawyer was not particularly impressive. He had represented SS Lt. Gen. Oswald Pohl and Governor General Hans Frank, who had been sentenced to death.[7] For the first skirmish Farben was not putting in its strongest team, but in reserve stood the talent and the resources of the entire combine. Wollheim and Ormond stood alone.

Wollheim's complaint set forth that he had been arrested in Berlin with about a thousand others, including his wife and three-year-old son, and that they were all shipped to Auschwitz, where his wife and child were "selected" for the gas chamber. He described his work for Farben during twenty-two months in Auschwitz, and how he lived under constant threat of death. He called a dozen former inmates as witnesses, including a professor of medicine at the Sorbonne, the president of the Bar Association in Nancy, France, other professors from Graz and the Sorbonne, and two British POWs. Wollheim contended that his mistreatment and starvation were well known to the Farben directors, and he demanded DM 10,000 (then less than $2,500) for his labor and his pain and suffering. (The amount claimed was deliberately understated to minimize the court costs, which are set by German statute to vary in proportion to the amount in dispute. German law also, requires the losing party to pay all costs, including attorneys' fees, for both sides.)

In its defense the Farben corporation argued that Wollheim had been neither beaten nor injured, and that whatever happened to him was the responsibility of the SS, the Nazi Party, the State, the subcontractors, or possibly the corrupt inmates themselves. Farben said it tried to improve the conditions of the workers by providing a supplementary soup, and noted how dangerous it was to help Jews, since Auschwitz Commandant Höss was known as the greatest Jew-murderer of all time. Farben was only doing its duty. In fact, said the defendant, if the inmates had not been employed they would have been killed even sooner. The implication was that Wollheim should have been grateful to Farben that he was still alive.

The Farben defense witnesses claimed that they had never been in Farben's special camp at Auschwitz/Monowitz, yet they described life there as not much different from employment by Farben's regular German workers elsewhere. They never heard of "selections" at Auschwitz, they said, until after the war. The supplementary "Buna soup," which the inmates described as "nauseating," was praised by one German defense witness as "delicious." To him, the maccabre skeletons with their zebra-striped pajamas, their wooden shoes, and shaved heads looked "splendid." Former inmates testified that they were forced to carry unbearable loads until they collapsed, and that they were not permitted to use even a piece of newspaper or a scrap of clothing to protect their bleeding shoulders or hands, yet Farben's witness, Engineer Häfele, characterized Monowitz as a "convalescent camp." The Farben business manager, Dr. Heinz Savelsberg, came forward with precise charts to show from his detailed production–cost analysis that Farben had in fact paid the SS more than the inmates were really worth.[8]

The Frankfurt court studied the sixty-four volumes of records from the Nuremberg trial of Farben directors, noting, however, that it did not consider itself bound by the Nuremberg findings but would decide the case solely on the basis of German civil law. After a year of trial and deliberation, the three German judges handed down their forty-three-page decision. The court concluded that what had happened to the Jews in Monowitz exceeded what was considered to be possible or endurable.

The fundamental principles of equality, justice and humanity must
have been known to all civilized persons, and the IG corporation
cannot evade its responsibility any more than can an individual
. . . They *must* have known of the "selections" for it was their
human duty to know the condition of their employees. Their al-
ledged total lack of knowledge merely confirms their lack of interest in the lives of the Jewish prisoners for whom they had a duty of
care, at least during the time the inmates were in their power.
There was a duty to do what they could to protect the life, body
and health of the plaintiff, and not even the SS could free them
from that duty—which they failed to carry out. For that failure,
which was at least negligent, the company is liable.[9]

Before the year was out, I.G. Farben decided to bring up its big guns to knock down the decision of the courageous Frankfurt court.

Newspaper stories of Wollheim's success encouraged other Buna survivors to hope that they too could obtain compensation. Thousands of former forced laborers turned to attorney Ormond, asking that he handle their claims against Farben and other German companies. Ormond was soon overwhelmed. He was realistic enough to know that, although he had won the first round, the going would get tougher and more costly as the case moved up the judicial ladder. He began to look about for help.


## Jewish Organizations Enter the Fray

There were very few places to which the former slaves of German industry could look for assistance. The small Jewish congregations that were reestablished in Germany after the war were impoverished and disorganized. They were hardly in a position to help themselves, let alone take on a legal battle against leading German firms. The Jewish Restitution Successor Organization was designated by United States Military Government Law to recover heirless property, but the JRSO was not authorized to deal with slave labor claims.[10] The Conference on Jewish Material Claims against Germany had only a small staff, and the primary responsibility of the Claims Conference was to work for the enactment of new laws by the German government to provide comprehensive indemnification to those who had suffered a wide variety of losses as a consequence of persecution by the Third Reich. The United Restitution Organization had a few Jewish lawyers on its staff in Germany, but the URO had concentrated on representing indigent clients under the special restitution laws rather than cases before the ordinary German civil courts. If the camp survivors could not find some institution to assist them, it was almost a certainty that their claims against private German firms would be lost by default.

Both the Claims Conference and the URO had to take into account that a large number of lawsuits would cost money, and if the cases were lost it would cost even more. The chances for winning in the German courts were slight, and no one wanted to arouse false hopes among those who had already suffered too much. One could not overlook the possibility that if German industries were provoked, the powerful companies might oppose all indemnification to Nazi victims—which would risk losing infinitely more than the claims related only to forced labor.[11] Whether to come to the aid of the slave laborers or not depended upon the judgment of a few people.

The president of the Claims Conference was Dr. Nahum Goldmann, an old-time Zionist who was chairman of the World Jewish Congress and a senior statesman among world Jewish leaders. It was on his initiative that the conference of major organizations had been convened in New York in 1951 to consider the possibility and advisability of responding to Konrad Adenauer's reconciliation feelers, when the German chancellor publicly declared that Germans had a moral duty to try to make amends for the crimes against the Jews. The senior vice-president was Jacob Blaustein, a wealthy American industrialist and oil magnate, who was also president of the prestigious American Jewish Committee. Moses M. Leavitt, Executive Vice-President of the American Jewish Joint Distribution Committee (AJDC, or "Joint"), which had spent hundreds of millions of relief dollars in aiding and resettling Nazi victims, served as the Claims Conference treasurer. These three were the senior officers, responsible for making the policy decisions, subject to the approval of the entire board of directors representing other important Jewish organizations.

The day-to-day management of Claims Conference activities was in the hands of a small professional staff of highly dedicated and competent individuals. Saul Kagan headed the staff as conference secretary. He shared offices with the AJDC on Madison Avenue and was responsible for keeping the board fully informed and communicating policy decisions to the staff in Germany.[12] In fact, he exercised a considerable degree of independence and was heavily relied upon by the board members, all of whom were fully engaged in other enterprises.

When the Hitler—Stalin pact was signed in 1939, Saul Kagan was a young man of seventeen living with his family in Vilna, the capital of Lithuania. It was an area which had at various times been under Polish and Russian domination as well as German occupation. The approximately 150,000 Lithuanian Jews constituted only 7 percent of the population, and like most Balkan minorities, the Jews were subjected to discrimination and persecution. Despite the prevailing anti-Semitism, Vilna managed to sustain a rich and respected Jewish cultural life.

In 1940 Lithuania was absorbed by the Soviet Union. Kagan's father, who was a hospital administrator, obtained permission for his son to go abroad in order to study medicine. After traveling via the trans-Siberian railroad across the steppes of Russia, Saul boarded a ship for Japan and from there went on to New York, where he found a home with a distant relative. He had escaped in the nick of time.

German troops invaded Russia on June 22, 1941. By mid-October *Einsatzgruppe* A, confirming that it was carrying out orders "aiming at a complete annihilation of the Jews," reported that it had executed over 80,000 Lithuanian Jews, including 7,015 in Vilna.[13] That was just the beginning. Not too long thereafter, the *Einsatzgruppe* reported to Berlin: "The Lithuanian sector was cleansed of Jews of both sexes. Altogether 136,241 were liquidated . . . As the complete liquidation of the Jews was not feasible as they were needed for labor, ghettos were formed, which are occupied as follows: . . . Vilna, approximately 15,000 Jews."[14] Saul's father, mother, and older brother had been in Vilna when Saul left home. He had no way of knowing whether they were dead or alive.

Saul Kagan enlisted in the United States Air Force. He participated in the Normandy invasion and the Battle of the Bulge and was at the Elbe River when the Russian and American troops met to signal the defeat of the Third Reich. Most American soldiers were eager to return home, but Saul was eager to remain in Europe to look for his family. He obtained his honorable discharge and found employment as an investigator with the United States occupation authorities. He soon learned that his mother and his brother had been murdered by the Nazis. Only years later did he discover that his father had survived by pure chance, since, he had been on a trip inside the Soviet Union when the German armies attacked. After the war his father had immigrated to Sweden, where father and son were eventually reunited.

I met Saul Kagan in 1946 when he was with Military Government in Berlin. He was investigating Nazi bankers, and I was collecting evidence of war crimes from the Nazi archives. I was particularly pleased when in 1948 he agreed to help set up the restitution organization to recover heirless Jewish property. Saul had been married in Berlin to one of his co-workers who had earlier fled from Nazi Germany. They moved to Nuremberg, where the JRSO then had its headquarters, but after a few years and the birth of two children they felt they had to return to the United States. By that time Saul had made his mark as a hard working, able man, and the Jewish organizations were pleased when he accepted a new assignment as the JRSO secretary in New York and later as the Claims Conference secretary as well.

The United Restitution Organization had been created by a small group of German Jewish lawyers who had taken refuge in England. When the first restitution laws were passed, they saw an opportunity to resume their profession by assisting needy Nazi victims with claims against Germany. The URO opened offices in a few German cities and received claims through cooperating Jewish social agencies in Israel, the United States, and other countries. The chairman of the URO board was Norman Bentwich, a distinguished British jurist who had been the attorney general in Palestine under the British Mandate and who had played an important role in rescuing Jews from Germany.[15] The board included the principal British Jewish charities, although most of the financial support came from the American Joint Distribution Committee.

When in the Hague negoiations of 1951 the new Federal Republic of Germany agreed to enact special indemnification laws that would open the doors to millions of new claims, the Claims Conference undertook to expand and subsidize the work of the URO to serve as a legal aid office for the Jewish persecutees. In order to centralize and coordinate the various restitution and indemnification activities, I was designated the URO director of operations, in addition to my JRSO and Claims Conference responsibilities. My office, which had been moved to Frankfurt, thus became the operational center for the three agencies. Kagan's office in New York became the focal point for cooordinating the JRSO and Claims Conference policies.

Despite the proliferation of restitution organizations, very little attention had been paid by any of them to the possibility of obtaining compensation from private German companies. After winning his first round in the Frankfurt District Court, Norbert Wollheim, realizing what difficulties still lay before him approached the Claims Conference president, Nahum Goldmann, with a request for assistance. Goldmann passed the problem on to Kagan with a recommendation that it be given sympathetic consideration. Kagan recognized the political and economic hazards should it appear that the conference, which was negotiating the overall indemnification laws, was supporting a collateral assault against the powerful German firms. He felt that it might be more appropriate to have the problem dealt with discreetly by the "nonpolitical" URO.

The head of the Frankfurt office of the URO was Kurt May, who had for many years been a successful practitioner before the appellate court in Jena, in eastern Germany. Like all other Jewish lawyers, he had been expelled from the bar when Hitler came to power. He immigrated to Palestine where, being unfamiliar with the language and the laws, he ran a department store.

May had been following the Wollheim case with great interest and had often discussed it with Henry Ormond. His legal instinct, based on his long practical experience before the appellate court, made him skeptical about the eventual outcome, but he recognized that if Jewish interests were to be protected it would be essential to provide Wollheim with assistance to help offset the Farben advantage. He arranged to have me meet Ormond, and after we all reviewed the situation together it was agreed that, without disclosing the source, a small fund would be created by the Claims Conference to help defray some of the legal costs. In addition, the URO offices were instructed to render all necessary assistance in support of Wollheim's position.

It was clear from the very cautious approach that no one on the Jewish organizational side was very eager to jump into the fray, but I.G. Farben could not be allowed to strike down the Jewish claims without a fight. At the same time there was the hope that perhaps some means could be found to settle the problem in a more amicable way. Whether that would be possible might depend upon a man named Walter Schmidt, whose official title was "liquidator."

## Bargaining about Auschwitz

Schmidt's title had an ominous ring in Jewish ears. The designation merely signified that the liquidator was one of the three German lawyers appointed by Military Government to supervise the dissolution of the I.G. Farben cartel. Although his real bosses were the Farben managers, Schmidt had been accepted by the Allied authorities because of his impeccable anti-Nazi record. The lawyer from Berlin had been married to a Jewish woman whom he had refused to divorce despite pressure from the Gestapo, and he had earned a reputation as a person of strong moral character.

The Frankfurt court's ruling that German companies might have to pay their former slave laborers created potential liabilities of unpredictable magnitude. The fiscal uncertainty could impede the speedy distribution of the assets which Schmidt was supposed to liquidate. When Schmidt discussed the problem in Bonn, he was told that under no circumstances would the German government pick up the Farben bill. It was suggested instead that he try to work out some arrangement with the Claims Conference.

The person in charge of the conference liaison office in Bonn at that time was Dr. Herbert Schoenfeldt, who had been practicing law in Berlin when the Nazis came to power. Although he had been wounded and decorated as an officer in the German army during World War I, he was, as a Jew, forced to flee to France to avoid arrest and deportation. He escaped over the Pyrenees, carrying his aged mother on his back. He became an American citizen and returned to Germany after World War II to join the United States prosecution staff at Nuremberg. When the trials were over, he accepted an appointment as head of the Stuttgart office of the JRSO, and then, after the Hague agreements, was reassigned to Bonn to oversee the promised new indemnification legislation for Nazi victims.

Walter Schmidt and Herbert Schoenfeldt had been colleagues and friends in the pre-Nazi days in Berlin. When Schoenfeldt returned to Germany after the war, he had sought out his old associate. It was a pleasant spring day in 1954 when Schmidt, taking his cue from the Finance Ministry, paid a visit to his friend Herbert Schoenfeldt in Bonn to chat about forced labor claims.

Even though they represented conflicting interests, Schmidt and Schoenfeldt could speak openly as friends who had known each other for almost thirty years. Schmidt was convinced that in the end Wollheim would lose his lawsuit, but he was mindful of the bad impression that the rejection of a small slave-labor claim would have on Farben's reputation abroad and of Farben's moral obligation to do something for the camp survivors. He had succeeded in persuading the other two liquidators that a settlement was essential to expedite the winding up of Farben's affairs, and he was ready to face opposition from other German firms that had also used concentration camp labor.

What Schmidt had in mind was the payment of a fixed sum by Farben to the Claims Conference, which would then divide the money among all the known forced labor claimants, and in exchange the conference would guarantee that there would be no further Jewish claims against Farben. Schmidt said that he could recommend an average payment of about DM 5,000, which was then about $1,200. He guessed that there might be two thousand claimants and the total cost to Farben would therefore not exceed DM 10 million.[16]

A few weeks later Schoenfeldt invited Walter Schmidt to present his plan to the Claims Conference headquarters in Frankfurt. The building on the Friedrichstrasse shared by the conference, JRSO, and URO was a restituted Jewish schoolhouse attached to the synagogue in what had once been the fashionable west-end of Frankfurt. The temple, with its massive Byzantine dome, had hardly been damaged by the bombs that fell all around it. Almost all of the Jews who had prayed there were gone. Although it was available for daily use by the new Frankfurt congregation, the temple stood practically empty except on the High Holy Days. The majestic organ that had been used in the religious services of the assimilated Jews of Frankfurt was saved from decay by a kindly German musician who came to practice on it from time to time; Thus the discussion of Jewish restitution problems frequently took place against a faint musical background unwittingly provided by a visiting German organist from the local church.

Schmidt lost no time in conveying the views of the Farben company. Farben would not recognize any legal liability, he said, and any payments the company might make would have to be accepted as a gesture of good will rather than as the discharge of an obligation. I replied, as had been previously agreed with Ormond, Schoenfeldt, and May, that an agreement might be considered which set forth the amount to be paid by Farben for every month of labor and which formulated the procedures to be followed by the conference in validating the claims. I argued that even if the number of claimants should reach ten thousand and each were to receive DM 10,000, the total cost of DM 100 Million, which would be a tax deductible expense to the company, should not be considered excessive.

Schmidt replied that such an amount was outside the realm of Farben's consideration. He said he would have to consult with his clients, with the Federal Association of German Industry (Bundesverband der Deutschen Industrie), as well as with the Finance Ministry before giving a definite response.[17]

A few weeks later Schmidt sent back his answer. The plan could not be carried out "at this time." The main difficulty, he explained, was the impossibility of knowing in advance how many claimants would have to be satisfied.[18] In a private note sent me the next day, Schoenfelt expressed his view that my mentioning the figure of DM 100 million had scared Schmidt off. We were thrown back to reliance on the court. At the next court hearing the presiding judge of the appellate court was told that Farben was ready to offer DM 10 million to dispose of the Wollheim case and all similar claims. The court suggested that the company try to go to DM 15 million.[19] The proceedings were adjourned to give the parties time to reconsider.

Figures received from Israel indicated that there would be about six thousand survivors of the Farben Auschwitz plant. At the next meeting with Schmidt I argued that each one should receive DM 10,000 and that an additional 10 percent should be added for cases of extreme hardship. The total cost to Farben would therefore be DM 66 million instead of the DM 100 million I had previously mentioned. Schmidt replied that he would recommend that the Farben offer be increased from DM 10 million to DM 20 million.[20]

In the meanwhile the legal proceedings were resumed in the old red stone court house in Frankfurt. The first attorney who stepped forward for Farben was Dr. Alfred Seidl. At his side stood Otto Kranzbühler, the man who had represented Alfried Krupp and other industrialists at Nuremberg. Kranzbühler was a skilled advocate as well as a staunch defender of many of the Nazi actions.[21] This time Ormond did not stand alone as he had stood in the lower court two years before. Among those who joined him was Otto Küster of Stuttgart, who would make the summation on behalf of the former Jewish victims of German persecution.[22]

Küster, a lay leader of the Evangelical Church, was a man of rigid moral principles. He had distinguished himself with the Jewish organizations when, as co-chairman of the German delegation at the Hague negotiations, he had resigned in protest when he felt that the German government, which he represented, was not acting in good faith. His defiant action had brought about a reversal in the German position. A towering man of stern visage, Küster began his summation in a low voice. It was a duty of honor, he said, to defend in its entirety the decision of the lower court. He went on to describe the many grisly abuses to which the inmates had been subjected and the "slavery of those who had been humans." He argued that the Farben company was responsible not merely for what its agents and employees had done but for what they failed to do when they had a legal duty to act. They had a duty, he said, despite their "horrible lack of interest," to show a minimum of humanity to those who were unwillingly in their employ. The victims never could tell who would be the next one to be killed. "Collective fear" was a form of pain and suffering which alone would justify the compensation sought.

On March 2, 1955, under the headline "Slave Laborers Find a Champion," the *New York Times* hailed Küster as one who had the courage to denounce I.G. Farben. He was called "the conscience of Germany" and a man who had sacrificed his public career by his support of the Nazi victims.[23] The *Allgemeine Wochenzeitung* of Düsseldorf, the organ for the Jewish communities of Germany, gave the case the entire first page on March 11. The *Frankfurter Allgemeine* (March 4) called it "Ein Schwieriger Prozess"—a difficult trial—and the *Bremer Nachrichten* (March 3) warned that "billions are at stake."

Instead of handing down a decision, the appellate court in its ruling of March 15 called for further evidence. Half a year later the court issued an order again calling upon the parties to consider a settlement. It stated that Farben, regardless of its legal position, should be aware that certain injustices had occurred before its eyes and should make an offer within its capacity to pay.[24]

There were certain considerations which did not appear on the surface. When Germany declared war on the United States, all German property in the United States had been seized, as was customary under international law. After the war the German government agreed that the properties could be used, in lieu of reparations, to compensate American nationals whose property had been taken or damaged in Germany during the war. Nonetheless, a number of German firms whose property in the United States had been taken into custody began to lobby in Washington, with the help of important law firms and senators, for the return to them of the vested assets which were worth hundreds of millions of dollars. If the Wollheim case was not settled and it became necessary to hear witnesses in the United States describe what had happened to them at Auschwitz, the impact of American public opinion might destroy all German hopes of ever getting the former German properties released.[25]

During the first week of 1956 the settlement negotiations that had been initiated in the early months of 1954 were resumed. Schmidt reported that Farben would be willing to put up a maximum amount to satisfy all claimants equally, Jews and non-Jews alike. Farben estimated that the non-Jews would be no more than 5 percent of the total. The previous Farben offer of DM 20 million was increased to DM 25 million, based upon Farben's new estimate that there would be a combined total of five thousand claimants, each of whom would receive DM 5,000.

The Claims Conference could not accept responsibility for distributing funds to non-Jewish claimants, since it was outside the authorization of the conference by-laws. As a step toward compromise, I indicated that I could recommend acceptance of an amount of DM 42 million to cover six thousand Jewish claimants at an average payment of DM 7,000 each.[26] The original Farben offer had been more than doubled and the original Jewish request had been cut to less than half. The gap was narrowing, but bridging the difference was not going to be easy.

Nahum Goldmann, the conference president, agreed with Kagan's recommendation that the conference had an obligation to settle on the best terms possible. It was the same basic line that Goldmann had taken when he had persuaded some reluctant and suspicious Jewish organizations to sit with the Germans in the Hague. Moses Leavitt, the tough administrator of the charitable funds of the American Joint Distribution Committee, and Jacob Blaustein, the pragmatic industrialist, were concerned about the financial and political consequences that might ensue from an inadequate deal. They were finally persuaded to go along, providing the Claims Conference would not be directly involved. The prior consent of leading Auschwitz inmates would have to be obtained, and a special agency would have to be created to screen the claims and distribute the funds.[27]

There were similar doubts on the Farben side. At one of the subsequent negotiations in the Farben office on the Bockenheimerlandstrasse, we soon detected that the atmosphere had noticeably cooled. Schmidt began by drawing attention to the difficulties claimants would have if every one of them were forced to conduct individual lawsuits. He stated that any settlement would have to make it explicitly clear that Farben had no legal responsibility for what happened. The company owed that much, he said, to German industry's reputation. Furthermore, the agreement would have to contain a new clause that there would be no criminal prosecutions against any Farben employees. The claims of non-Jews suddenly loomed much greater than before, and Schmidt announced that the whole settlement would have to be reconsidered.[28]

Schmidt had dropped a clue from which an explanation for the change in his behavior could be deduced. He mentioned that he had received a letter—from the vacation resort of Arosa in Switzerland—which had been sent by the new chairman of the Farben supervisory board of directors *(Aufsichtsrat),* Dr. Johann August von Knieriem.

During the days of Farben's greatest glory, from 1932 to 1945, von Knieriem had been the company's top lawyer. He had been a member of the executive board and chairman of Farben's legal committee. The former Nazi had also been indicted at Nuremberg but had persuaded the majority of the court that there was insufficient evidence to convict him beyond a reasonable doubt.[29] Now he surfaced as the top man in the firm.

At the time when von Knieriem reappeared I was about to resign from my various restitution posts and return to the United States. My four children had been born in Germany and neither my wife nor I wanted them to start their education there. My position as director general of the JRSO was taken over by Dr. Ernst Katzenstein; Kurt May took over as director of operations of the United Restitution Organization, and Herbert Schoenfeldt moved up to the director for Germany of the Conference on Jewish Material Claims. I was retained as a consultant to the Claims Conference and the URO, as I returned home to practice law in New York.

When Schoenfeldt and May saw the latest Farben draft, they reported that Farben did not really want a settlement.[30] In due course Schmidt let Schoenfeldt know, however, that the new Farben chief had been brought around to supporting an accord. But it was "more with his head than his heart."[31] Von Knieriem, in charge of the negotiations, was prepared to increase the Farben offer from DM 25 million to DM 30 million, but certain other conditions would have to be accepted. Farben would withhold a fixed amount which it would use to satisfy the claims of non-Jews. If the amount proved to be more than was needed, Farben would return the excess to the Jewish claimants. Thus, von Knieriem placed the Jewish and the non-Jewish claimants into a competitive position, which was bound to lead to conflict.

Farben held its 1956 annual stockholders meeting in the Palmengarten in Frankfurt—a lovely botanical park with winding scenic walks amid exotic shrubs and flowers. Signs throughout the park marked the way to the reception hall. Tickets were collected at the door and checked against the list of the thousand expected guests. The floor around the dais was richly bedecked with summer floral arrangements. The table on the first tier of the stage was reserved for the chairman of the managing board, August von Knieriem—who had seen poorer days in the Nuremberg jail.

Microphones were all in place when von Knieriem opened the meeting. He turned the podium over to Schmidt, who reported on the status of the negotiations regarding the forced labor claims. Some shareholders stood up to protest against any settlement with the former camp inmates. Some wanted to know why other companies were not paying *their* former forced laborers; while others argued that the money should be spent on the former *German* employees. No one spoke up in favor of a settlement with the Jews.[32]

The next draft submitted by Farben offered DM 30 million, but DM 3 million was to be withheld for payment to the non-Jewish claimants and an additional DM 3 million had to be held in reserve in case of further litigation. Thus, instead of getting DM 28-1/2 million, as had previously been indicated by Schmidt, the new proposal would enable the Claims Conference to dispose of only DM 24 million. The conference protested, and Schmidt tried to keep the negotiations going by suggesting that the conference submit a counter-draft. He asked for twenty-five copies, which indicated the number of people he would have to convince before further progress could be made.[33]

One of those whom he could no longer consult was Herbert Schoenfeldt. On the eve of the enactment of an expanded indemnification law that provided new benefits to hundreds of thousands of former Nazi victims, Schoenfeldt, who had worked so hard for the legislation, suffered a heart attack which proved fatal. Leading German officials came to pay their respects at his funeral in Bonn. Herbert Schoenfeldt, who was esteemed and beloved by all who knew him, made a notable contribution to the welfare of the survivors of persecution. To help fill the gap caused by Schoenfeldt's demise, Ernst Katzenstein took on the additional duties as the Claims Conference director for Germany.

Katzenstein had been raised in the town of Hameln, whose legendary Pied Piper had taught the world the hazards of not paying one's bills. His career as a lawyer was cut short by Hitler, but he was able to resume his legal studies in England and Jerusalem, where he built up a successful practice. It was quite a sacrifice for him and his wife to leave their newly established home in the Jewish state and to set foot again on the soil of Germany, but it was seen by both of them as an essential duty to be endured for a brief period in order to help right some of the wrongs of the past. His skill as an advocate and his warm personality made him a fitting replacement for Herbert Schoenfeldt, and Katzenstein soon picked up the Claims Conference reins which had dropped from Schoenfeldt's hands.

Several times it appeared that negotiations between Farben and the conference would have to be broken off, as conflicting drafts were considered and rejected. No one on the Jewish side objected to Farben's proposed payment to the non-Jewish claimants, but there was considerable objection to their doing so by subtracting the money from the amount that had been promised to the Jews. Norbert Wollheim, who was particularly bitter, wrote to Henry Ormond on November 24, 1956: "If the IG, whose slave masters in Buna treated us so inhumanely, now uncover their good hearts to the non-Jewish persecutees the Jewish Buna victims will certainly have nothing against it if they are compensated for the injustices which were also done to them. That, however, cannot be done at the expense of the persecutees, but must be at the expense of the IG Farben which was the beneficiary of our slave labor." He instructed Ormond to warn Farben that the former inmates who were now American citizens were prepared to fight. It was too late in the day for threats.

Saul Kagan and I sought the intervention of a prominent German-American Jewish banker, Eric Warburg, to try to persuade Farben to go a bit further. The Warburg Bank in Hamburg had been highly respected in Germany before Hitler. It was "aryanized" during the Nazi period and became Brinckman-Wirtz & Company, but it had been given back to the Warburg family, and Eric Warburg had returned to Hamburg from New York to continue the business. Warburg was on good terms with Schmidt and served as an honest broker in trying to convince both sides to reach an accommodation and put an end to the haggling. Farben was about ready to do so, and so were the Jewish organizations.

## Farben Settles

I.G. Farben made its last offer. It would pay no more than DM 30 million, of which 10 percent would be withheld for non-Jewish claimants. Only a strictly defined group of persons—those who had been employed by Farben at Auschwitz—could share in the fund. The Claims Conference Executive Committee, fed up with the indignity of the continuing hassle about how much should be paid to which Auschwitz survivors, authorized the staff in Germany to close the deal.[34] Comprehensive stories appeared in all the German newspapers and Farben "liquidation" shares jumped 10 percent on the German stock exchange.

The signing of what was in effect only a provisional or conditional agreement took place in the Farben offices in Frankfurt. Norbert Wollheim's written consent was attached, but it would only become valid when, and if, the contract went into effect. It was understood that the Farben board of supervisors as well as the shareholders would have to give their consent. Both sides reserved the right to revoke the deal. Farben would have to be sure that no further claims could be made, and the conference would have to be sure that the amount received would be adequate to satisfy the claimants. These were only some of the conditions which would have to be met before the contract would become binding and irrevocable, but as far as the public was concerned, none of the uncertainties were noticed.

To present its position in the most favorable light, Farben retained the public relations firm of Julius Klein, a retired United States general who at one time had been the commander of the Jewish War Veterans of America. Klein's offices in Chicago, Washington, and Frankfurt also handled public relations for several other German firms and was actively engaged in seeking the return of Farben's assets seized during the war by the United States and other countries. In Farben's press release all legal liability was denied and reference was made instead to the responsibility of the SS and the former Reich. On February 7, 1957, the *New York Times* headlined "Farben Will Pay Slave Laborers: Liquidators of Big German Trust Reach Agreement with Jewish Committee." The *Milwaukee Sentinal* in its Sunday editorial (February 10) said: "One of the most significant, encouraging and important events since the formal cessation of World War II took place, in relative quiet in Frankfurt, Germany last week. It was the signing of an historic agreement between the trustees of the former I.G. Farben chemical combine and the Conference on Jewish Material Claims Against Germany." The *Chicago Sun Times* (February 7) ran an editorial entitled "Cartel with a Conscience" and hailed Farben for wanting to "clear their conscience as well as their books." The settlement was seen as a sign of a new spirit in Germany which "the rest of the world should know about and appreciate." In the House of Representatives Congressman Herbert Zelenko of New York rose to praise the agreement as holding "great moral significance to the free world" as the Farben liquidators "welcomed the opportunity to redress some of the wrongs of the Nazi era." [35] The senator from Wisconsin had the entire editorial of the *Milwaukee Sentinel* read into the Congressional Record, and called it "the sort of action which helps to bring a brighter tomorrow for the world."[36] Julius Klein had earned his fee, but for those of us who knew the facts the picture seemed far less rosy, and we looked to the future with considerable trepidation.

When the stockholders were assembled in the Palmengarten at the next annual meeting, Walter Schmidt rose to present the proposed agreement for ratification. The complete text of the proposed contract was attached to the printed report of the company for the year 1956. Schmidt did not fail to note the moral implications as well as the favorable impression abroad which the proposed agreement had created. These arguments were not persuasive to *Rechtsanwalt* P.H. Gordan, a lawyer from Giessen and leader of the opposition.

Gordan saw neither a moral nor a legal basis for an agreement which benefited only a select group of claimants. He argued that to pay all those who worked for Farben would be impossible. The clear implication was that no one should be paid. Several of the speakers pointed out that the federal government was already paying reparations to the state of Israel, and that there was also a major German indemnification program for the survivors. They argued that the victim should not expect to be indemnified three times for the same suffering.[37] No one noted that for their labor for Farben, the concentration camp inmates had received nothing but beatings and the threat of death.

The big banks held proxies for the overwhelming majority of Farben shares and ratification was assured. The management still retained the right and indeed the obligation to revoke the agreement if it appeared that the contract would not settle the slave labor problem once and for all. One of the preconditions was satisfied when the *Bundestag* approved and the Allies consented to a special law which required all former forced laborers against Farben to assert their claims by Decemeber 31, 1957, or be forever barred.[38] The parties to the contract still had three months after that date to exercise their right of revocation. By that time each side would have to know whether the number of claimants would exceed expectations and thereby render the deal unworkable.

The Claims Conference had to start the preliminary screening of the claims, and a new agency and a new man had to be found to do the job. Dr. Ernst G. Lowenthal was a journalist who in the pre-Hitler days was active in Jewish affairs in Berlin. In 1938 he had fled to Great Britain, where he helped to form an association of Jewish refugees. He came back to Germany after the war with the Jewish Relief Unit attached to the British army and was soon employed by the Jewish Restitution Successor Organization. He agreed to become the managing director of a new organization to be created by the Claims Conference to deal with the Jewish claims against Farben. The name for the new agency was Compensation Treuhand.[39]

Nazi victims throughout the world had to be informed via the media and other channels about the terms of the Farben agreement in order that only those who might qualify could apply for payment. A questionnaire, in German, English, and Yiddish, was sent to each applicant, from which his elegibility for payment under the restricted terms of the contract might be ascertained. Local advisory committees of former Auschwitz inmates were recruited to advise the board of Compensation Treuhand.

No sooner was the screening agency organized than a delegation from Poland arrived in Germany to demand payment for Polish forced laborers who had also worked for Farben at Auschwitz. Farben had refused to pay them on the grounds that Poles were not in Auschwitz because of their "race, religion, or ideology" but because of their "nationality," and therefore they did not qualify as persecutees within the restricted definition of the German indemnification laws. The delegation spokesman was Hermann Langbein, Secretary General of the International Auschwitz Committee, who threatened to block any agreement that failed to include the "national persecutees."[40]

Katzenstein explained that although the conference was sympathetic to the objective of the International Auschwitz Committee, the conference was only competent to deal with Jewish claims, and had done its best to assure basic equality in the contract with Farben.[41] The threat of additional massive lawsuits and the commencement of some new legal actions in the United States, Holland, and Israel served to make more uncertain whether Farben would really stick to its agreement with the Claims Conference. German newspapers carried headlines "Wollheim Settlement Endangered" and "Auschwitz Negotiations Break Down."[42]

If the number of eligible claimants proved much greater than expected, the conference might be forced to revoke the provisional agreement. Lowenthal rushed lists of applicants, together with completed questionnaires, to the screening committees in Israel, New York, Paris, and other locations.[43] The committees, themselves inexperienced and inadequately informed, were asked to make preliminary estimates of how many persons on their lists might finally prove to be entitled to payment under the contract. On the basis of these guesses, the conference had to decide whether to stick to the agreement or not.

After difficult deliberation, Compensation Treuhand recommended that the agreement should not be revoked. Farben had reached the same conclusion. The company announced that it would be possible to make a major distribution to its shareholders of assets that had been held in reserve. Farben shares again advanced briskly on the Frankfurt stock exchange.[44]

After the contract became irrevocable, I wrote to Walter Schmidt and thanked him. He replied that it was for him also "a matter of heart."[45] For the first time in history, a settlement had been concluded between a worldwide Jewish organization and a German company for the company's use of concentration camp inmates as forced laborers.

## Verifying the Claims

Farben paid DM 27 million to the Claims Conference, and the process of determining the validity of the claims was set into motion. The documentary evidence was usually inconclusive, and it was therefore necessary to await the recommendations from the screening committees that personally interviewed the applicants. A small office was rented in an old building on Ann Street in New York to deal with claims from the United States and Canada. A former Auschwitz inmate, Simon Gutter, was hired on a parttime basis. Gutter had fled from Leipzig to Holland in 1938, but he had been caught by the Gestapo when Holland was overrun by Germany. He was sent to Sachsenhausen and then deported to Auschwitz in 1942. He knew all about Monowitz from his personal experience. He and Norbert Wollheim invited some of their former comrades to help with the screening of the claims. At the first meeting seventeen of them showed up.

Max Spira, an old-timer who had managed to be assigned to the Auschwitz kitchen, remembered many of those who had been with him in the early days on the *Aufbaukommando*, the original construction gang; he volunteered to come on Tuesday and Thursday evenings. Emanuel Polkow could come almost any night, and he knew many of the Greek inmates. Hugo Cahnman knew the Dutch group, and Hans Marek, who had come from Theresienstadt (Terezin) knew the Czechs. Herbert Kalter came with a Polish transport and Martin Gurenfeld came out of Lodz. Fred Sarne, who had come to the meeting from Philadelphia, was a goldmine of information; he had been a *Schreiber* or registrar and seemed to remember everybody.

The *Kameraden* (old comrades) would come to the dilapidated New York office late at night to screen applications, interview persons whom no one seemed to remember, and give their opinion whether the claimant had really worked for Farben at Buna. An applicant who did not know when the typhoid epidemic had broken out or where the latrines were located was soon disqualified. Many ineligible claimants conceded that they must have been mistaken and their claims were apologetically withdrawn.

Persons whose documents showed that they had unquestionably been in Monowitz were recruited to help screen claims in Prague, Vienna, Budapest, Melbourne, London, Sao Paulo, and Oslo. Although the committees worked at different tempos, all of the recommendations were factual and objective and could be accepted in Frankfurt almost without exception.

Detailed information was received from surprising sources. Hershel M. of Paris had engraved into his memory the specific tatoo numbers assigned to the various transports that arrived at Buna. He knew by heart that the first transport was composed of German, Austrian, and Polish Jews from Buchenwald and that they all received numbers between 68000 and 69000. The next thousand numbers went to the second transport, which came from Sachsenhausen, and the thousand after that went to the Czech Jews from Theresienstadt. He knew the numbers assigned to Jews from dozens of villages in Poland, and he remembered that the Greek Jews all had numbers between 116000 and 117000. He could provide the tatoo numbers for the three transports from Maidanek, almost all of whose members were later killed. He even knew the numbers of the German criminals who were assigned to Buna. Hershel M. had been seized by the Gestapo in Warsaw, and his whole family had been murdered by the Nazis. In his mind he had been carefully storing the information, which he hoped would one day help to bring the criminals to justice.[46]

It reminded me of the time I had entered the concentration camp at Mauthausen/Gusen as a war crimes investigator for the United States army. Piles of corpses littered the area. Starving *"Musselmänner,"* the inmates' slang for walking skeletons, stared with vacant eyes at the liberating American troops. An inmate registrar embraced me joyfully. One of his jobs had been to type identification cards for the SS guards; when the guards were reassigned, the card was to be destroyed. The inmate, whose name I shall never know, had, at great risk to his life, failed to burn the cards. Instead he had buried them carefully in a field. After he greeted me he left the barrack and, a few minutes later, returned, unwrapped a soiled box, and handed me a complete record and picture of every SS man who had ever been in the camp! It was invaluable evidence for a war crimes prosecutor. I was moved by the blind faith which inspired the unknown prisoner to risk his life in the conviction that there would come a day of reckoning.

Compensation Treuhand managed to obtain a list of all of the Auschwitz inmates who bore tatoo numbers from 150000 to 200000. From it could be seen which ones had been assigned to Buna. Many of them bore the simple notation "Escaped." That meant that the bearer of that particular number was dead.

No one could foresee that the process of deciding the claims would take as long as it did. The questionnaires, which came from all parts of the world, were often illegible or incomplete. Addresses changed and envelopes were returned unopened. The information received had to be compared with records stored at the International Tracing Service of the Red Cross in Arolsen, where millions of concentration camp dosiers were filed. Screening committees, working after normal working hours, could handle only a limited number of cases at a session. They frequently would ask the claimant to come back with additional evidence or witnesses. Their recommendations had to be sent to Frankfurt for final action, and the claimant had to be notified of the decision. Without knowing how much he would finally receive, the applicant was expected to waive all further claims. It was thus necessary to explain the nature of the contract and to offer at least a partial advance payment. Legal forms had to be signed and authenticated.

Those claimants who had been in the camps for less than six months were offered an advance of DM 1,500 ($375) and those who had been there longer received DM 2,500 ($625) as a first installment. The payment of the balance would have to wait until the total number who would have to share the fund could be ascertained.

Although the West German indemnification program precluded any payments to countries with which Germany did not have diplomatic relations—and that meant all of the countries behind the Iron Curtain—the Claims Conference decided as a matter of policy to make remittances to Jews wherever they might be. Very advantageous rates were negotiated with the finance authorities of Poland, Hungary, and Czechoslovakia, which proved to be a great benefit to the recipients in those countries.

Thousands of claims had to be turned down when the applicant was unable to prove that he had been a concentration camp inmate employed in one of four designated Farben plants at Auschwitz. Rejected claimants had a right to appeal to an "arbitration court" headed by Siegfried Ikenberg, a former judge.[47]

It took several years of screening before the initial advance payment could safely be increased. Those who had been at Buna for more than six months were given another DM 2,500, to bring the total up to DM 5,000 ($1,250). Those who had worked for less than six months and who had already received DM 1,500 were given another DM 1,000. It did not look like much to the board of Compensation Treuhand, or to the claimants, but to Farben it looked like too much.

Dr. Benvenuto Samson, Farben's staff lawyer, insisted that not more than DM 2,000 ($500) could be paid to those who had worked for Farben for less than six months, even though the contract specifically stated that DM 2,000 was the *minimum* payment.[48] The Claims Conference refused to alter its decision.

The agreement authorized payments only to those inmates who had been employed "in den Werken," which meant in the Buna factory itself. The construction workers were technically not eligible. Yet Farben had accepted the claims of Polish workers who had helped to build Monowitz before the Farben plant had been put into operation. Compensation Treuhand had honored the strict terms of the contract by initially rejecting claims of Jewish construction workers, although it was known that they had been miserably beaten and abused. Back in August 1941 the Farben managers supervising the construction of the Monowitz campsite had complained to the Farben main office: "The inmates are being severely flogged on the construction site by the Capos in increasing measure, and this always applies to the weakest inmates who really cannot work harder. The exceedingly unpleasant scenes that occur on the construction site because of this are beginning to have a demoralizing effect on the free workers (Poles), as well as on the Germans." The concerned Farben supervisors did not hesitate to tell the SS what to do: "We have therefore requested that they should refrain from carrying out this flogging on the constructon site and transfer it to the inside of the concentration camp."[49]

The official Farben report sent from Auschwitz showed that Poles may have been more observers than victims of the floggings, but if Samson decided that the claims of the Polish construction workers should be paid, the Claims Conference did not protest Farben's liberal interpretation of the contract, for it created a precedent which the Claims Conference was eager to follow. It allowed "the weakest inmates" to share in the fund.

Farben insisted that claims submitted after the legal filing deadline should be rejected.[50] Compensation Treuhand refused to do so, arguing that the contract contained no such requirement and that since the conference had guaranteed that Farben would be free of any further liability it was none of Farben's concern how the Jewish fund was divided. Many Jewish claimants were dissatisfied with the small payments received and, in cases of severe hardship, Compensation Treuhand wished to make a supplementary payment. Farben felt that no such payments could be made without its consent.[51]

In the meanwhile some of the rejected Gentile Polish claimants took their cases to the courts. A complaint filed in the name of *Leon Staucher et al. v. Farben* demanded DM 10,000 each for 2,295 listed persons, or a total of DM 22,950,000. The argument was made that a claim for unpaid wages under the ordinary German Civil Code could not arbitrarily be restricted, as had been done in the special indemnification legislation, to those who had been persecuted for "racial or political" reasons.[52]

The Farben shareholders had been assured by Schmidt that the agreement with the Claims Conference would dispose of the forced labor claims. Farben would have to fight the case through to the end. This jeopardized not merely the demands of the national persecutees but also the claims of all forced laborers who might be contemplating suits against *other* German companies.

The class action which had been brought by the 2,295 Polish claimants soon ran into trouble. Several hundred petitioners were struck off the list when the lawyer failed to produce powers-of-attorney. The district court concluded that all of the claims had been filed too late.[53] The claimants appealed.

By the time the appeal of the Polish claimants came before the appellate court, one important Farben representative was no longer on the scene. Walter Schmidt had died at the age of seventy-one. Without his sympathetic support, the settlement with Farben would not have been possible. There was no doubt where his personal sympathies lay, yet he always had to be looking over his shoulder toward those who seemed determined to pay as little as possible. With Schmidt's departure, the tone and the contents of Farben's argument would drastically change.

The lengthy brief submitted by Farben to the appellate court in opposition to the Polish claims argued that, despite Farben's strong resistance, the Reich had *ordered* Farben to build a Buna factory at Auschwitz. It quoted in full a decree from Field Marshal Hermann Göring on February 18, 1941, in which Göring directed that the Jews be cleared out of the neighborhood around Auschwitz, that their homes be confiscated, and that eight to twelve thousand prisoners be taken from the concentration camp to build the Farben plant. As further proof that they were merely carrying out orders, the Farben lawyers offered the testimony of three former leading Farben directors—Krauch, ter Meer, and Ambros.[54]

The fact was that all three of the designated witnesses were convicted war criminals. Furthermore, what the Farben brief failed to mention was that the order signed by Göring had actually been requested by Krauch, the chairman of the board of Farben. Judge Hebert of the Nuremberg tribunal had stated: "I conclude, from the evidence, that they were bound to know, as a prerequisite to the proper discharge of their duties, of such a major development as the Göring order of 18 February, 1941, issued at the request of the defendant Krauch."[55] Another captured document showed that on April 12, 1941, Ambros was actually bragging to ter Meer about Farben's success in overcoming the organizational difficulties at Auschwitz, and how all the arrangements had been made "to obtain the outstanding management of the concentration camp for the benefit of the Buna works." It was in that very letter, written when neither Ambros nor ter Meer dreamed that they might ever be called to account, that Ambros said, "Furthermore, our new friendship with the SS is working out blessedly."[56] Farben's enthusiasm for being in Auschwitz was again confirmed when, in 1943, Krauch wrote to SS chief Himmler that he was "particularly pleased to hear that during this discussion you hinted that you may possibly aid the expansion of another synthetic factory . . . in a similar way as was done at Auschwitz, by making available inmates of your camps, if necessary. I have also written to Minister Speer to this effect and would be grateful if you would continue sponsoring and aiding us in this matter.''[57]

When the Farben directors were on trial for their lives during the Nuremberg prosecution in 1947 and 1948, they denied having anything to do with the terrible deeds that had occurred; and again in 1960, but this time in a German court, in a civil proceeding, when all the directors were at liberty and immune, Farben made the same discredited excuses, based on the testimony of three top Farben officials whose own words, written among themselves during the Hitler years, proved the contrary. Farben also argued that in the London Debt Settlement Agreement between Germany and the Allied powers the Allies had agreed to postpone claims against the Reich until there was a peace treaty, and therefore the Polish demand was premature. To drive the final nail into the claimants' coffin, it was argued that all Polish claims had been discharged by virtue of the Potsdam Reparations agreement. The Farben contention, in short, was that the claims of the Polish concentration camp inmates had been submitted too late, had been submitted too soon, and had already been paid!

The Polish claimants knew that they were fighting a losing battle. At the end of November 1960 the distinguished Polish judge Jan Sehn of Cracow came to Frankfurt to suggest to Samson that all the Polish claims be settled by a total payment of between DM 4 and DM 5 million, a rather paltry sum in the Farben balance sheet. Samson refused and suggested instead that Sehn go to the Claims Conference and see how much the Jewish organizations would contribute to the national persecutees from Poland.[58]

The appellate court confirmed the lower court's decision by rejecting the Polish claims—but for a completely different reason. According to the appeals court, Farben had been an instrument of the Reich, and the London Debt Settlement Agreement postponed claims against Reich agencies until a formal peace treaty would be signed with Germany. Thus, said the court, the claim was not too late but too early.[59] Some of the claimants decided to fight it out to the end by appealing to the German Supreme Court.

When it appeared that the German courts were not prepared to open the door to those who were in Auschwitz only because they were Polish nationals, many of the claimants decided to try to enter through another door. They could be paid if they proved that they had been sent to Auschwitz not because they were Poles or criminals or ''volunteers'' but for ''ideological reasons.'' Many of them set out to prove that they had been arrested only because they were communists, and therefore they qualified as political opponents of the Nazis. If Polish witnesses swore that the claimant wore a red triangle on his jacket, signifying that he was a communist, it was difficult for Farben to deny the claim.[60]

The contract with the Claims Conference required Farben to reject claims of "non-Jewish inmates who mistreated other inmates." This was a point on which there was great sensitivity on the part of the Jewish survivors, and they raised a hue and cry when it came to their attention that a German *Kapo* (the name given to selected camp inmates who served as camp police or guards and who often were more brutal than the SS) from the Auschwitz Buna plant who had in fact been detained by the Poles as a war criminal for several years had his claim approved by I.G. Farben.[61]

Farben was prepared to be generous to the former *Kapos* but was not prepared to pay those whom Farben regarded as "racial Jews"— that is, persons who had been baptized but who had been persecuted because of Jewish ancestry. Farben sent them to the Jewish fund for payment, but the Claims Conference was not willing to accept Nazi racial concepts and looked to the declaration of the claimant himself to determine whether or not he was a Jew. The point was not strongly pressed, however, since the conference recognized that many Polish nationals had converted in an attempt to save their own lives and were still professing to be Christians because it was politically safer for them to do so. Many of the "nonprofessing Jews" later showed up in Israel, and Compensation Treuhand approved the payments to them without further delay. But dispute about which fund should pay which claimants soon gave rise to a major disagreement.

## Farben Demands a Refund

In October 1961 Farben demanded a refund from the Claims Conference. According to Samson, DM 2 million more would be needed by Farben to dispose of the non-Jewish Polish claims. Katzenstein and I refused to consider a repayment. We argued that if Farben wanted to be generous to persons who did not qualify under the agreement, it should not be done at Jewish expense. There was sharp disagreement about the correct ratio of Jews to non-Jews who had been employed by Farben at the Auschwitz/Monowitz camp, and I offered to try to clarify the picture.[62]

As a gesture of appreciation for having helped to obtain compensation from Germany for Polish women who had been victims of Nazi medical experiments, I had been invited to Poland as a guest of the Polish Red Cross. I had acted as a member of a committee of volunteers, organized by Norman Cousins, editor of the *Saturday Review,* to help rehabilitate the Catholic women from Ravensbrück who had been used as human guinea pigs.[63] Several of the committee members had been invited but, as I had been unable to go with the group, I later went alone. My main interest was to see Auschwitz, and a visit under such favorable sponsorship offered a unique opportunity for me to seek the information needed in connection with the Farben agreement.

It was a moving scene when my plane landed at the Warsaw airport. The weather had been bad and the plane was hours late when it touched down during a pouring rainstorm. A small group of women whom I had never met were waiting eagerly at the gate. They were some of the Ravensbrück *Lapins* or "rabbits" who had been used for Nazi medical experiments. They had stood for hours, clutching small bouquets of drenched flowers, to welcome me to their country. The "guide" sent by the government to escort me whisked me off to attend the ballet in accordance with the prearranged program for entertaining the American guest. I had not come to see the ballet or to be thanked. Within a few days I persuaded my hosts to fly me to Cracow and from there we proceeded by car a short distance over the flat roads leading to Oswiecim.

We drove through the entrance gate and under the massive sign ARBEIT MACHT FREI—"Work Will Make You Free." The Polish government had preserved Auschwitz to serve as a reminder of the German crimes.[64] I could not fail to compare my vivid memories of Mauthausen, Gusen, Ebensee, Flossenberg, Dachau, Buchenwald, and other camps with what I saw as we drove past the long rows of wooden barracks toward the chimneys of the crematoria.

The director of the Auschwitz Museum, Kazimierz Smolén, a former inmate, having been informed that I had been the United States chief prosecutor against the SS *Einsatzgruppen* and that I was a guest of the Polish Red Cross, received me most cordially. He escorted me on a tour of the former SS warehouses in which were retained enormous mounds of prosthetic appliances torn from the arms and legs of cripples, hundreds of thousands of crutches, eyeglasses, and shaving brushes, rooms full of children's shoes, and large bales of human hair. He showed me what was left of the crematoria. They were similar to crematoria I had seen in other camps, while the furnaces were still burning. As he pointed to the adjacent fields, covering many acres, he explained sadly that many of the ashes had been buried there. I kicked over a large clump of wild grass and reached into the soft earth. In my hand, among the ashes, I found a few small bones, which I carried away with me as a reminder.

We surveyed the places set aside for whipping, torture, experiments, and execution of prisoners. Smolén showed me the unused cannisters of Zyklon B, the crystals releasing hydrogen cyanide poison, which had been found near the gas chambers. When he mentioned that Farben had owned the company which produced the poison that could suffocate nearly 60,000 human lives per twenty-four hours, I asked that we adjourn to his office so that I could explain to him an important objective of my visit.

I told him candidly that I was negotiating with the Farben company, and I needed to know more about the number of Poles who had worked for Farben at Buna. He assured me of his full cooperation. We searched through several volumes of documents captioned *Widerstandsbewegung*—"The Resistance Movement." In volume 2 on page 96 we finally found exactly what I had been looking for. It was a small piece of paper that had been rolled up like a cigarette and smuggled out of the camp in August or September 1944. It was to inform the Soviet army what to expect when the Russian troups entered the camp. In very fine script it stated explicitly that there were ten thousand inmates in the Buna Works and that two hundred of these were Poles and 95 percent were Jews. By confirming that 95 percent were Jews, it was proof that 10 percent of the overall settlement sum—the amount Farben wanted to withhold—was double the amount that should have been required to satisfy all the legitimate Polish claims.

Smolén insisted that he could not officially divulge the information to me without clearance from the person who had smuggled out the note. He hesitated to ask for such permission for he was confident that it would have to be refused. The note to prove that Farben was overpaying the Polish claimants had been smuggled out of Auschwitz by the Polish leader of the communist resistance movement inside the camp. That man, Jozep Cyrankiewicz, was then the minister president of Poland![65]

Jan Sehn, who lived in Cracow and was in charge of a large institute of criminology, was the author of several books on Auschwitz. I had known Sehn since he had been a Polish representative at the Nuremberg trials, and I had maintained friendly contact with him. When I visited him and his wife at their home, we spoke about the efforts to obtain compensation from Farben and other German companies. In the evening Sehn took me to his institute. From a large safe he removed several piles of documents and files, which we scoured till past midnight when only the bitter November cold drove us out of the unheated rooms. He revealed new information that was to be of value in connection with the Farben case and others.[66]

Nearly half a year went by before the Farben representatives repeated their demand for a refund. This time they asked for DM 1.5 instead of DM 2 million. I had been convinced by the evidence found in Poland that it was Farben which should have made a further payment to the Jewish fund. After hours of debate, I suggested that both sides be content with what they had received and make no further claims against the other. Farben rejected the compromise. The parties were at a stalemate and Farben threatened to invoke arbitration.[67]

The claimants had no idea of what was going on behind the scenes. As far as they could see, it had taken several years for the Claims Conference to pay out even DM 22 million of the DM 27 million received in 1958. They could not know that Farben had required the Claims Conference to keep DM 3 million in reserve to cover possible lawsuits against Farben. That provision had to be kept secret lest it encourage the type of legal action it was designed to prevent. The claimants began to protest and clamor for "their money."

Not all claimants were dissatisfied. A Czech claimant, Manfred G., expressed his "immeasurable thanks," wishing in one word that Compensation Treuhand be *gebentscht*—the Yiddish word for "blessed." Perhaps his blessing helped, for the path was soon opened toward a new accord with the Farben company.

The conference officers were not eager to provoke other German firms by appearing to be uncompromising. They approved an offer to Farben of DM 750,000 as a final settlement, in return for which the conference was to be given a free hand to dispose of the remaining claims and funds as it saw fit.[68] As far as the conference was concerned, it was a price worth paying for it would buy the freedom to handle the remaining claims in a more equitable way, to alleviate cases of extreme hardship, and to be able to do something to honor the memory of those who had remained forever in the fields of Auschwitz.

I.G. Farben was ready to close the entire account; it had no fear of any new demands. The German Supreme Court had confirmed that claims of forced laborers were in the nature of reparations, which would have to await a final peace treaty with Germany.[69] It was not likely that any slave laborer would live long enough to see that day.

## A Hardship Fund for the Destitute

The hands of the Claims Conference were untied. Borderline cases that had been rejected were reviewed, and the petitioners were given the benefit of every reasonable doubt. Those construction workers whose claims had been dismissed because they had not worked in the Buna factory received an award. Laborers who had come to work for Farben from a place the Germans called Heydebreck (now Kedzierzyn) were paid despite Farben's protest that they were not entitled because Heydebreck was a forced labor camp rather than a concentration camp. Where the claimant could show that through no fault of his own he had been unable to submit a timely claim, his petition was accepted by

Compensation Treuhand. Cases of extreme hardship could now be considered for a supplementary payment.

But how was one to determine hardship among those who only recently had walked out of a camp with nothing more than scarred memories and a tatoo on their naked arms? Norbert Wollheim was asked to canvas other Buna suvivors and come forward with a specific plan. Gradually, a consensus began to emerge. Supplementary payments of either DM 2,000, DM 3,000 or DM 4,000 would be made to widows, minor children, the aged receiving public assistance, and other especially needy persons. The existence of the hardship fund was announced in a final report sent to all of the claimants.[70] It set forth the guidelines and urged all recipients to be in touch with any known widows of fallen Buna comrades or others who might be eligible for a grant.

Contacting the claimants behind the Iron Curtain presented a particularly delicate problem. The non-Jewish Polish claimants resented what they regarded as discrimination by Farben in favor of the Jews, and any indication that the Jews might receive a supplemental hardship grant could make the lot of the Jews in Poland even more difficult. Even in Hungary and Czechoslovakia, prudence seemed to be advisable. Local social agencies were called upon in many countries in order to evaluate the hardship applications in a reliable way.[71] Specific standards of need had to be established for different countries, since an allocation based on deutsche marks would have a different impact depending upon the rate of exchange and the local living standard. After consulting with welfare agencies around the world, Dr. Hans Seidenberg, who took over as the general manager of Compensation Treuhand after Ernst Lowenthal resigned, was able to prepare a comprehensive chart showing how much one deutsche mark would buy and what the minimum living standard for that country was.[72]

Not all former Buna workers were pleased with the idea of a hardship fund. The Association of Jewish Victims of Nazi Persecution in Melbourne expressed strong opposition, demanding a pro rata payout of the residual fund and the right to make the distribution themselves.[73] Seidenberg sent a temperate reply, noting that only the accumulated interest earned on the Farben fund was being used to benefit needy widows and orphans and that he could not understand how the survivors in Australia could withhold those payments merely to obtain some small additional benefit for themselves. Similar replies went to protesting groups in Belgium and France.[74] Protesters in Israel began collecting names to seek an injunction against Compensation Treuhand. Seidenberg met the leader of the group and persuaded him of the inappropriateness and futility of the threatened action.[75]

The Claims Conference had been recognized by the West German government to be the most suitable and representative partner to deal with indemnification and restitution problems of Nazi victims. Its officers were all kept closely informed by Saul Kagan of everything being done by Compensation Treuhand, and they had to approve every important policy decision. At least once a year either Ernst Katzenstein or I reported in detail to the full board of directors, composed of almost fifty Jewish leaders, which had to ratify the actions being taken. Such extensive controls should have provided complete assurance that the interests of the Nazi victims were being fully protected, yet not all of the suspicions could be allayed.

Those who had survived the camps had learned to suspect everyone. They were as a group apart—those who had returned from another world—and it could not escape their attention that among all the distinguished Jewish leaders connected with the Claims Conference there was not one who had personally been imprisoned in Auschwitz or any other concentration camp. It was resentment not so much against the outside world for not having intervened sooner or even for having escaped the tortures that the inmates had endured but against the paternalism of those who were really strangers. Norbert Wollheim shared the opinion of most of the former Buna workers that what the Claims Conference had received from I.G. Farben because of their labor was "their money" and they alone should have the right to determine what was to be done with it. In fact, the feelings and needs of the former Auschwitz laborers were uppermost in the minds of the board of Compensation Treuhand, and the views of responsible Buna spokesmen were eagerly solicited before final decisions were reached.

The processing of thousands of hardship applications was both difficult and painful. The reviewers had to decide who was the poorest among the poor. They were faced with the constant reminder of the permanent scars of persecution. Verification of the facts often required the assistance of an independent Jewish welfare organization in some remote locality where the claimant had found refuge. In Israel, where most of the claimants knew each other and were familiar with their own social circumstances, it was not quite as time consuming.

Over 1,800 individuals from twenty-one countries received supplementary grants totaling close to DM 3.5 million. Almost half of the hardship grants were to persons in Israel. France, which had given refuge to many Nazi victims, was also a major recipient, as was Hungary and Czechoslovakia. The United States, with its higher standard of living and relatively generous welfare system, had less than a hundred approved cases. It had been possible to pay out to the survivors of the Farben plant at Auschwitz not only every penny of the amount received from Farben under the contract but also a substantial additional sum from the accrued interest. The board had also kept a small reserve for a purpose which had never been forgotten.

### Memorializing Those Who Perished

Thirty thousand Jews had died in the Buna camp. To honor their memory, Norbert Wollheim proposed in 1958 that a suitable memorial be created. What he and a dozen of his former comrades had in mind when they met in Tel Aviv was the erection of a convalescent home, a hospital, or a museum which would be financed by each claimant's waiving 2 percent of what he would receive under the Farben settlement. The proposal never got off the ground. The contract with Farben did not allow diversion of funds for such a purpose. Wollheim's next effort was to try to raise the money in 1960 by voluntary donations from former Auschwitz inmates, or anyone else who might want to contribute. An Auschwitz-Buna Scholarship Memorial Fund was incorporated in New York.[76] The big fund-raising event was to be a memorial dinner with New York Senators Herbert H. Lehman and Jacob K. Javits as honorary co-chairman and Nahum Goldmann as a principal speaker. The occasion was also to be used to express the gratitude of concentration camp survivors to "the People, the Congress and the Government of the United States and to the United Jewish Appeal."

It was a Sunday evening in March 1960 when the former concentration camp survivors assembled at the Concourse Plaza Hotel in the Bronx to honor the memory of their dead. Many came formally attired in black tie, a far cry from the tattered pajamas at Auschwitz fifteen years before. There were touching scenes as former Buna inmates slowly and hesitantly approached each other in uncertain recognition and joyful reunion. The meeting was well attended. The speeches were dignified and the expressions of appreciation were sincere. Almost everyone there considered himself lucky and happy to be alive. There was a spirit of comraderie which exists among those who have faced death together and survived; there was sadness, too, as some lost friend or relative was recalled. Lurking behind the laughter and the tears could be sensed the ever present question, tinged with unearned guilt, "Why me?"

The Claims Conference had advanced a small sum to cover some of the expenses of the dinner. Compensation Treuhand had been very careful to make sure that no claimant would feel coerced in any way, and no lists of claimants were made available for solicitation. Despite their festive appearance at the memorial dinner, most of those who had walked out of Auschwitz with only their skin and bones were still poor people. The hope that substantial amounts would be received for the scholarship fund proved illusory. The dinner itself produced a deficit, and pledges from former inmates came to less that $15,000.[77]

In 1963 Nahum Goldmann, visiting Auschwitz, learned that the Polish government planned to erect an international pavilion to commemorate all the nations whose citizens had perished in the camp. Since the Jews had always been segregated as a separate group rather than as citizens of their home country, Goldmann asked how the Jews would be memorialized. He received assurances that the special sacrifices of the Jews would be appropriately indicated and consideration would be given to the erection of a special Jewish pavilion in the memorial.

Wollheim urged that the survivors be allowed to personally participate by contributing up to DM 50 each to pay for the design of a Jewish colonnade. Goldmann recommended that Compensation Treuhand set aside DM 250,000 for that purpose, which was less than 1 percent of the amount received from Farben, and he established a Committee of Friends of the Auschwitz Jewish Museum at the offices of the World Jewish Congress in Geneva. The head of the Auschwitz Museum, Kazimierz Smolén, and his assistant, Adam Rutkowski, were invited to Paris, where they received two thousand documents and six hundred photographs from the Centre de Documentation Juive for possible exhibition in a Jewish pavilion. Marc Chagall and other artists were consulted about the design of the Jewish hall.[78]

In June 1967 the Six-Day War erupted in Israel, and Poland severed all diplomatic relations with the Jewish state. It began to be obvious that anything honoring the memory of Jews was not likely to appear in Poland for some time to come. The Frankfurt committee screening hardship claims urged that all available funds be rushed to Israel, where the needs were greatest. The Israel committee petitioned that the idea of a Jewish memorial in Poland be abandonded: "Let us," said the committee, "erect a monument to the victims in Israel in their holy memory."[79] The plan they put forth was one which had been mentioned many times in the years past, but now its time had come.

It was proposed that, as a memorial to honor those who had died in Auschwitz, a special loan fund be created in Israel. Many Buna inmates had been forced to close their small businesses and leave for the front during the Six-Day War. When they returned, they would need small loans to get started again. The Israel Advisory Committee asked that the funds earmarked for the Auschwitz pavilion be transferred to Israel. The petition closed with the hope "that peace may reign and that Israel will stay secure." It was signed, "In friendship and with blessings from the eternal Jerusalem." It was an appeal that could not be denied.

On April 21, 1968, the Polish government inaugurated a two-story pavilion to honor the dead of Auschwitz. According to the *New York*

*Times,* only one foreign Jew, a Mexican citizen, was present to hear the speeches condemning Zionism, Israel, and American aggression. Only half a dozen Polish Jews were present to lay a wreath.[80] Professor Robert Waitz of Paris resigned from the International Auschwitz Committee in protest.[81]

The DM 250,000 that had been held for a memorial in Auschwitz was transferred instead to Israel to serve as the basis for a new loan fund. Upon dissolution of the fund, any remaining assets would go to Yad Vashem, the permanent memorial in Israel to all victims of the Holocaust.[82] The public accountants designated by the Claim Conference confirmed that hundreds of loans were being granted each year and were being promptly repaid. The former Auschwitz inmates had succeeded in establishing a self-perpetuating revolving fund with which to help themselves. It was a useful and practical memorial, created by survivors in Israel to commemorate in word and deed those who had perished in the Auschwitz-Buna concentration camp and who would never be forgotten.

Compensation Treuhand paid out to the Auschwitz survivors more than it had received from I.G. Farben. The net amount that Farben had made available, after claiming a refund of DM 750,000, was DM 26,250,000. The final audit of Compensation Treuhand showed that it had given the claimants DM 27,841,500. The surplus was interest earned in excess of the administrative expenses.

The 5,855 Jewish claimants who received awards were located in forty-two countries. Those in Israel received about DM 8 million, including the DM 250,000 to start the revolving loan fund. In the United States, 3,713 claimants received over DM 6,600,000. In France, 899 claimants divided DM 3,472,000. Over DM 1 million was sent to the claimants in Canada and the same amount to those in West Germany, Czechoslovakia, and Hungary. Over half a million went to Australia, Belgium, and Holland. About a quarter of a million went to Austria, Argentina, Greece, Poland, and Sweden. Lesser sums were distributed to former Buna workers in such countries as Brazil, Bolivia, Chile, Italy, Great Britain, Yugoslavia, Norway, Uruguay, Venezuela, and even Paraguay and Peru. Over 600 persons who missed the filing deadline were given a payment. Over 1,800 needy persons received special hardship grants.

To most of the former Buna inmates the DM 5,000 ($1,250) or more received, and even the lesser sums, made their lives just a little bit easier. This was particularly true for those living in Israel, the countries of eastern Europe, and South America, where the purchasing power of the strong deutsche mark had a more valuable impact. To some it meant a new start in a new direction.

There were a few who were completely dissatisfied, who criticized, who complained, who were suspicious, and who condemned Wollheim and the organization for not getting more and paying it out faster. When dealing with thousands of people who had come from an environment where fear, hate, suspicion, greed, and abuse of one's fellows was the daily bread, it is almost surprising that there were not more complaints of that kind. They had no idea that dedicated Jewish public servants had poured their hearts and minds into obtaining the maximum benefit possible for the survivors of the camps.

Then there were others from whom nothing was heard because the very idea of accepting a payment from a German was anathema. A poignant letter received from a pious Jew expressed their feelings. He wrote that he was badly in need of compensation to help him recover from the injuries which the Germans had caused, but he would not ask for or accept any payment. He described how he and his wife and seven children were seized and how they, together with his brothers and sisters and their entire families, numbering fifty-six persons, were shipped to Auschwitz. Within twelve hours all of the women and the small children were gassed. The twenty-five who were kept alive were sent to work for I.G. Farben at Buna. He saw his two brothers beaten to death with a shovel by a German foreman and the others were tortured or worked to death. He was ruptured carrying the heavy bags of cement and beaten until his ribs were broken. The gold crowns were torn from his mouth and when he begged to be shot he was told by the foreman that it was not for him to decide when to "croak" but he would give up his mongrel soul when it suited the Germans. Of all of his fifty-six relatives, he alone survived—"a miracle of God." Writing the letter to Compensation Treuhand had obviously been very difficult for the crippled survivor. He expressed appreciation for the efforts made on his behalf but his conclusion was firm. His conscience dictated that he should accept no money from the sadists.[83] He asked not to be identified. How many others there were like him we will never know.

# Accounting with Krupp

SECRET

7 September 1943

To   Lt. Col. Dr. von Wedel
    Army High Command . . .

From you letter of 26 ultimo I gathered that you are of the
opinion that the firm of Krupp did not do its best to start
the production of fuses at Auschwitz as soon as possible. I
think there must be a misunderstanding . . . I can only
say that a very close cooperation exists between this office
and Auschwitz, and is assured also for the future.

   With kind regards and Heil Hitler,

      Yours faithfully,

      A. v. Bohlen[1]
      [Alfried Krupp von Bohlen]

# CHAPTER 3

## Krupp's Rise and Fall and Restoration

It was a rousing speech that Adolf Hitler made on February 20, 1933, to the twenty-five German industrialists who had assembled in the home of Herman Göring. They were so impressed with the Führer's ideas that three million marks were pledged to the coffers of the Nazi party. Herr Dr. Gustav Krupp von Bohlen und Halbach convened the Reich Association of German Industry, and they promised to "do everything in their power to assist the government in its difficult task."[2]

The Krupp concern was one of Germany's oldest, most distinguished and largest industrial combines. It consisted of a vast complex of coal, iron, and steel enterprises which had been accumulated to support its renowned armaments production. For almost a hundred years Krupps had been known as the "cannon kings" of Germany. With Gustav's declaration of loyalty to the Führer, it was inevitable that Krupp would become the armorer for the Third Reich.

Gustav Krupp's oldest son was Alfried Felix Alwyn von Bohlen und Halbach, and he was first in line to become the heir to the Krupp empire. At eighteen, Alfried was serving his apprenticeship in the firm. When he was twenty-four, in 1931, he was a dues-paying member of the SS.[3] He acquired a degree in engineering, and by the time Hitler's illegal rearmament of Germany was in full swing, Alfried was exercising important responsibilities in the departments of war materiel and artillery construction. Alfried's father suffered an apoplectic stroke in the spring of 1942, and the management of the family enterprise was entrusted to the oldest son. By 1943 Alfried Krupp, at age thirty-six, was chairman of the board and *alleiniger Inhaber*—sole owner—of all the Krupp companies.[4] One of Alfried's first directives was to confirm that "the owner of the family enterprise has the full responsibility and direction of the entire enterprise."[5]

On April 11, 1945, troops of the United States Army converged on Krupp's palatial mansion, the Villa Hugel in Essen, and placed Alfried Krupp under arrest.[6] It did not take long to locate his ailing father,

Gustav Krupp von Bohlen, but half a dozen medical experts from Paris, Moscow, England, and the United States soon confirmed that Gustav had for some time been "incontinent of feces and urine" and was speechless except for sporadic expletives such as "Oh, God!" All legal proceedings against the senile seventy-five-year-old Krupp were soon suspended by order of the Tribunal president, Sir Geoffrey Lawrence.[7]

There has grown up a rather widespread misconception that Alfried Krupp was put in the dock at Nuremberg to pay for the sins of his father. Nothing could be further from the truth. Justice Robert H. Jackson, on leave from the United States Supreme Court to serve as chief American prosecutor at Nuremberg, was convinced that Alfried was as guilty as his father of the crimes charged in the indictment. As soon as it became clear that Gustav could not stand trial, all of the prosecutors joined in a motion, first put forth by Jackson with the approval of the secretary of state, to indict Alfried Krupp, the owner of the concern.[8]

By that time it was too late. The new defendant would have to be given adequate time to reply, but the date of the international trial had been publicly announced, and was awaited eagerly all over the world; it would not be postponed. The court refused to let anyone be added to the indictment just three days before the scheduled opening. Alfried Krupp was saved by the bell.[9] But that was only the first round. In the very same courtroom two years later, a dozen responsible officials of the Krupp concern, led by their director Alfried Krupp von Bohlen, were asked to answer to the charges filed against them.

There were four counts to the indictment brought in the Subsequent Proceedings under the direction of General Telford Taylor. Counts one and four charged the accused with committing crimes against peace by helping to wage aggressive war. These two counts were dismissed by the court without waiting for the defendants to present their case. The prosecution, said the court, had failed "to show beyond a reasonable doubt that any of the defendants is guilty . . . there can be no conviction without proof of personal guilt."[10] Count two charged the defendants with plunder and spoliation, and count three accused them of war crimes and crimes against humanity involving prisoners of war and slave labor. On those counts the defendants did not do so well.

Alfried Krupp declined to take the stand in his own defense, and the other defendants followed the lead of their chief. More than 250 witnesses were heard, and over three thousand documents were presented. Thirty-seven lawyers, including one American, appeared for the defense. The judgment of the court covered 122 printed pages. Its findings set forth at least part of the truth about what had really taken place in the Krupp plants during the days of Hitler's glory.

The horrors of the concentration camp are well known. The Krupp firm was the beneficiary of these camps . . . In the early summer of 1944, the SS offered a large group of concentration camp inmates to the armaments industry . . . This labor was merely offered to industry, not allocated to it. It was not a matter of refusing to accept an allocation; it was up to the enterprises to put in requests. Many armament firms refused to request concentration camp labor for employment.[11]

The Nuremberg Tribunal of three American judges from the states of Tennessee, Connecticut, and Washington found Alfried Krupp and ten of the other eleven defendants guilty beyond a reasonable doubt.

On order of the court, the defendant, Alfried Felix Alwyn Krupp von Bohlen und Halbach stood at attention. "On the counts of the indictment on which you have been convicted, the Tribunal sentences you to imprisonment for twelve years and orders forfeiture of all of your property, both real and personal."[12] The convicted prisoners, who had been leaders of German industry, were transported to the town of Landsberg in Bavaria in the spring of 1949, there to join other distinguished colleagues in War Criminal Prison No. 1.

Alfried Krupp's imprisonment coincided with a dramatic change in Allied policy in Germany. The Russians had walked out of the Allied Control Council in 1948. The Soviet blockade of Berlin had been broken by an airlift under the command of General Lucius Clay. About a week after Krupp arrived in Landsberg, the foreign ministers of the Western Allies announced that they had agreed on an economic and political merger of the three western zones. Military Government was to be replaced by a High Commission. No sooner had the new United States high commissioner, John J. McCloy, established himself in his new office in Frankfurt than he began to receive petitions on behalf of the condemned war criminals. The prisoners of Landsberg were, after all, not without friends.

Jack McCloy, as he was known to his intimates, was a lawyer of outstanding reputation who had served as assistant secretary of war. In taking over from General Clay, he was inaugurating a new relationship between Germany and the United States. Petitions poured into his office on behalf of the prisoners of Landsberg. His wife, who was of German ancestry, was also besieged by women's groups pleading for mercy and denouncing the Nuremberg trials as "victor's vengeance."

McCloy was confronted with a difficult human problem. Fifteen of the prisoners convicted at Nuremberg were still awaiting execution. Their cases had all been carefully reviewed by General Clay, who had commuted only one death sentence and confirmed the rest. He had stayed execution, however, in order to allow the defendants to complete legal appeals to federal courts in the United States.[13] As Clay handed the reins over to McCloy, he apologized for not having been able to complete this bit of unpleasant business.[14]

When the rights of the prisoners had all been exhausted, and there was no longer any possibility to challenge the validity of the Nuremberg decisions, the pressure on McCloy became intense. It was then up to him to sign his name to an order directing that each of fifteen human beings be hanged by the neck until dead. It was not something which he was inclined to do lightly.

In July 1950 High Commissioner McCloy established the Advisory Board on Clemency for War Criminals to help him with his difficult decision. The board was directed not to review the jurisdiction or the decisions of the Nuremberg tribunals on questions of law or fact, but to consider disparities among sentences, facts tending to show that a sentence was excessive, and the "physical condition and family situation of the particular defendant and other pertinent facts tending to warrant mitigation of his sentence." The board was only authorized to hear from counsel for the defendants.[15] It was, as its name implied, created only to consider clemency. Because it was humanitarian in nature, McCloy did not restrict the review to those fifteen condemned men still awaiting execution but directed the board to deal with the cases of all of those who were still imprisoned.

David W. Peck, a distinguished judge of the appellate court in New York, was chairman of the panel. He was joined by Brig. Gen. Conrad Snow of the Department of State and Frederick A. Moran of the New York Board of Parole. The Clemency Board spent the summer of 1950 in the pleasant environs of Munich, reviewing part of the record and receiving petitions from scores of lawyers retained by the prisoners or their friends. No member of the Nuremberg prosecution staff was consulted in any way. The board, noting that "murder, pillage and enslavement are against the law everywhere" and that "if we have erred we have erred on the side of leniency," submitted its recommendations to McCloy.[16] The final decision was up to him.

Thirteen of those who faced execution had been defendants in the *Einsatzgruppen* trial. They had been condemned for having led the SS extermination squads that had murdered over a million defenseless people in cold blood.[17] The others in the death cell included Oswald Pohl, who had been responsible for the murder of millions of Jews in the concentration camps. In that company the demure Alfried Krupp and his colleagues from the *Direktorium* (council of directors) must have appeared to McCloy as lambs among the lions.

McCloy agonized for months before he announced his clemency decisions. "Striving to temper justice with mercy," ten of the death sentences were commuted. Four of the remaining five who were to face the gallows were the *Einsatzgruppen* leaders like Otto Ohlendorf, who had admitted killing 90,000 Jews, and Paul Blobel, who had been in charge of the two-day massacre of over 33,000 Jews at Babi Yar. Oswald Pohl, head of the Main Economic Office of the SS and administrator of the concentration camps, was also beyond clemency. In McCloy's words, Pohl was a "slave driver on a scale probably never before equalled in history."[18] The white-collared collaborators who had been the beneficiaries of the slave labor were seen quite differently by the former Wall Street lawyer. Every one of the nine Krupp directors was hardly distinguishable from normal corporate clients. The high commissioner ordered that all of them be released, and thus not a single German industrialist was left in a war crimes prison.[19]

There was an extra bonus in store for Alfried Krupp. In addition to receiving the return of his liberty, he also received back his entire fortune. In its report to McCloy the Clemency Board, referring to the assertions made by none other than Krupp himself, repeated his claim "that Hitler ordered concentration camp inmates assigned to the concern . . . and that concentration camp inmates allocated to the concern were under the strict control of the Gestapo, and their food, billets and discipline beyond the jurisdiction of the firm." The board failed to emphasize or even notice that a contrary conclusion was found in the judgment of the Tribunal. Instead, pointing to the dissenting opinion of one of the Nuremberg judges in the Krupp case, the Clemency Board recommended that the twelve-year sentence be reduced to seven years and that the confiscation of property be lifted. The board noted: "The property of even the most criminal of the defendants, those sentenced to death, was not confiscated." McCloy, relying on the three men he had appointed to advise him, felt that property forfeiture was somehow repugnant to American justice, and he was concerned by the fact that it had not been invoked against anyone except Alfried Krupp. According to McCloy and his advisors, Alfried Krupp had been a victim of discrimination.[20]

As he walked out of prison a free man, the wan but smiling Alfried Krupp was handed an enormous bouquet of flowers. The Associated Press reported: "Steelmaker Alfried Krupp von Bohlen und Halbach, four generals and twenty-four other Germans walked out of the Landsberg war crimes prison yesterday into a festival of freedom . . . Krupp, gray and drawn, motored to Landsberg's best hotel in a gleaming black sedan with his younger brother Berthold. Several of the eight Krupp executives released with Krupp joined them there for a champagne breakfast."[21]

Within a fortnight of Krupp's release, a conference of western powers took place in Paris to consider the establishment of a European army. Germany had been invited to participate on a basis of equality.[22]

A few weeks later, the Schumann Plan was signed for the pooling of western Europe's coal, iron, and steel industries. The occupation statute was revised to further relax Allied controls. Germany, with four billion dollars of Marshall Plan aid, was about to embark on an economic miracle of recovery from the ravages of war.[23]

The return of the steel plant at Rheinhausen was part of McCloy's liberation gift to Krupp. The high commissioner insisted, however, that, as required by the Allied High Commission law, Krupp would have to sell it.[24] Since Alfried could pocket the proceeds, he did not hesitate to accept the high commissioner's condition.

German sovereignty was restored in 1952 and this inaugurated a new period of prosperity for West German industry and for Alfried Krupp.[25] McCloy returned home to become chairman of the board of the Chase Manhattan Bank. Having played an important role in the establishment of an independent and prosperous German state, he continued to enjoy considerable influence in German circles.

McCloy's decision to restore all Krupp assets caused a storm of protest throughout the world. In England's House of Commons, the question was raised: "The restoration of such a vast sum of money to the families whose activities were of such assistance to Hitler has deeply shocked people everywhere . . . Inasmuch as Krupp has been found guilty of using slave labor and taking other people's property, is it not possible to devote some of this wealth to the people who have suffered?"[26]

At the age of forty-five, Alfried was once more the owner of a vast industrial kingdom. The second wife he had acquired shortly after his release from prison revealed during a divorce action a few years later that, apart from his holdings in Germany, Alfried had deposited over a quarter of a billion dollars in Swiss and other foreign accounts.[27] He began to look around for someone who might relieve him of some of the burdens of running the empire of industries, and he found that man in the person of Berthold Beitz.

Beitz, at age thirty-seven was the director general of a large German insurance company. He was a self-made man who was noted for his sharp elbows and American-style drive. In 1953 Alfried decided to give Beitz almost complete authority over the running and rebuilding of the Krupp empire. His title became *Generalbevollmachtigter*—the bearer of the general power-of-attorney to act for Krupp.

Alfried Krupp resumed the life of a German monarch at the Villa Hugel. Kings, emperors, chancellors, and ambassadors were among the guests received in the three-hundred room Krupp mansion.[28] The energy of Krupp and Beitz restored the firm to its position of wealth and power.

## Former Slaves Demand a Payment

Mordechai S. was born in the same year as Alfried Krupp, but beyond that they had nothing in common. They were to be joined together, however, in the caption of a lawsuit. In January 1954 the Essen District Court received the complaint of *Mordechai S.v. Krupp.*[29] The pleadings set forth the plaintiff's story:

Mordechai, who had come from a small town in Poland, was seized in 1941, together with his wife and three children, and transported to Auschwitz, where his wife and all of his children were promptly murdered. He had number 135936 tatooed on his left arm, and so branded, was ready for employment as a slave for the German war machine. In September 1943 a number of high officials and doctors from the Krupp company came to Auschwitz and inspected the inmates. Mordechai was among those who were chosen, loaded on freight cars, and shipped to a camp at Fünfteichen in Silesia. Other Krupp officials gave the prisoners their work assignments in a new Krupp munitions factory at Markstädt, some 4 kilometers away. At four o'clock each morning, the prisoners were forced to stand at attention during an hour long *Appel* or roll call before they were marched off. At the plant they were supervised by Krupp *Meisters* (foremen) and, under threats of beatings or worse, were worked to total exhaustion. Mordechai's thumb and forefinger were sliced off by a Krupp lathe.

As the Soviet armies advanced toward Markstädt, the inmates were marched westward through the woods, from one concentration camp to another. From Gross Rosen they plodded to Flossenberg and then on to Dachau. Those who faltered were shot by the SS guards. I was with the liberating American army and remember the trail of bodies very well.

Mordechai S. initially asked for DM 40,000 ($10,000) but as soon as Krupp demanded that cash be posted to cover court costs, Mordechai was stopped in his tracks. To save expenses he reduced his claim to DM 2,000 ($500).[30] The defendant was in fact stone poor.

Alfried Krupp, on the other hand, had his picture on the cover of *Time* magazine which described him as "the wealthiest man in Europe—and perhaps the world" (August 19, 1957). It was obvious that Mordechai was no match for Krupp. If former forced laborers were to have their claims taken seriously, it would be necessary for the Jewish organizations to roll out some of their own big guns.

Jacob Blaustein, Senior Vice-President of the Claims Conference, was a man of temperate disposition, but he was also a man of determination and power. He had amassed a sizable fortune through the ownership of several oil companies and was on the board of directors of various important American corporations and banks. He also played a leading role in the American Jewish Committee, which was politically active with regard to Jewish problems. He made no secret of the fact that he had frequent access to the White House. Blaustein had known John J. McCloy for many years, and McCloy's law firm had represented the American Oil Company, of which Blaustein was a principal stockholder. It occurred to industrialist Blaustein that his old friend Jack, now bank president McCloy, might try to persuade industrialist Krupp to be more reasonable. After all, had it not been for McCloy, Krupp would still be a pauper sitting in the Landsberg jail. Blaustein lost no time in phoning McCloy, who, true to pattern, promised to help if he could.[31]

To bolster whatever efforts McCloy might make, the Claims Conference authorized the preparation of a new test case that would reinforce the claims of the slave laborers by a carefully documented presentation of the facts. The Nuremberg trial that had resulted in the criminal conviction of a dozen Krupp defendants had ended in 1948. Most of the evidence had been shipped to the National Archives in Washington or otherwise dispersed. The problem years later was one of reassembling and reconstructing the incriminating picture in so compelling a way that even a German judge in Essen would have to rule against Essen's most prominent citizen.

A treasure trove of documents was discovered in a garage in Lexington, Kentucky. The Nuremberg records had been sent home by Rawlings Ragland, who had the main responsibility under General Taylor of preparing the Krupp prosecution. The files, weighing over five hundred pounds, were shipped to New York for screening by a former Nuremberg researcher.[32]

As more and more persons wrote to the New York Committee of Former Jewish Slave Laborers, the gaps in the overall picture began to be filled. One young man, Theodore Lehman, born Tadeusz Goldsztajn, who had found refuge in New York, was particularly well informed. He gave the most vivid description of one of Krupp's major plants:

During the third week of September 1943, a Director of the Krupp installation at Fuenfteichen, Germany, arrived at the Birkenau quarantine Lager of Auschwitz to select able-bodied inmates of the KZ [concentration camp] to work at his plant. The prisoners, completely naked, were paraded before him . . . I was one of those chosen and thus became separated from my father . . . I was 16 years old . . . I remember very distinctly how . . . at a motion from the Krupp representative the SS man, standing nearby, hit my father across the face with force that broke his eye-glasses. This is how I left my father and made my acquaintance with the Krupp enterprises for which I was destined to work for 15 terrible months . . . I was always hungry, sleepy, filthy, tired beyond any normal human comparison, and most of the time by any normal human standards, seriously ill . . . Whenever a prisoner sneaked closer [to the oven] to warm his stiff hands, he was chased away and usually beaten by the Krupp people. Beating and torture administered by the Krupp supervisory personnel was not uncommon. At work we were Krupp's charges . . . Hungry, cold, stiff from hard labor, lack of sleep and beating, and in constant fear of our masters we were forced to exert all of our remaining energies to make guns for our oppressors. We worked until we dropped.[33]

Lehman described how he and other inmates, suffering from dysentery, were forced to run naked in the freezing cold to latrines hundreds of yards away. If a worker tarried too long, he was ordered sprayed with cold water. Although both of Lehman's parents had been murdered in Auschwitz, and the absence of objectivity on his part would have been understandable, his descriptions had the ring of authenticity. He confirmed the usual story of the early morning awakening, the standing roll call, the meager breakfast, the long march to the plant, the inadequate food and shelter, the absence of sanitary facilities, the lice-infested filthy rags that the prisoners were unable to wash or change, the beatings with rubber truncheons and iron bars and the threats of worse if any prisoner should falter. "Yet," said the young Lehman, "there is nothing unusual in my story. It should be quite familiar to Krupp, his Directors, supervisors and employees. They were not blind and saw the fate of the living skeletons tending their machines." Lehman's description was brought to the attention of the former high commissioner who had freed the Krupp directors from the Landsberg jail.

John McCloy hesitated to make a direct appeal to Alfried Krupp lest it be viewed as an attempt to extract some consideration in exchange for the humanitarian grant of liberty to Alfried and his friends. The former high commissioner arranged, however, to get the word back to Essen that Krupp's liberator would look with favor upon a settlement of the Jewish claims.[34]

A few weeks later, in the course of a visit to the United States, Krupp's right-hand man, Berthold Beitz, met McCloy in New York and requested a more detailed proposal. Jacob Blaustein promptly sent a messenger to McCloy at the Chase Manhattan Bank with a plan which suggested an overall agreement with Krupp following the global pattern set in the contract with I.G. Farben.[35] McCloy reported that Krupp was interested in the proposal, but he wanted any payment to come as a result of his own initiative, without outside pressures.[36] The Claims Conference agreed to suspend further action in order to give Krupp a chance to come forward with a "voluntary" act of generosity.

Several months went by and there was not the slightest indication that Krupp intended to do anything about the Jewish claims. The suspicion arose that Krupp was deliberately stalling to await the outcome of lawsuits which had been commenced against other German firms. If the claimants were defeated in the other cases, the precedent could provide Krupp with an impenetrable legal shield. Ernst Katzenstein was instructed to request a meeting with Beitz in Essen to clarify the situation.[37]

Beitz, once described as a man "who ladles out charm in what seem to be carefully prepared dosages,"[38] replied that the West German government was then in the process of negotiating compensation agreements with a number of states. Nonetheless, Beitz said, he would be glad to see Katzenstein if he would call in about six weeks.[39] The clear implication was that compensating forced laborers was not a Krupp problem and surely it could wait. Alfried Krupp had more important things on his mind, as the *New York Times* reported:

Herr Krupp, 51 years old, is the absolute monarch of an empire now bigger, richer and stronger than ever before in its 147 year history. If he is the monarch, then Berthold Beitz as managing director is Krupp's ruling premier . . . But there is one decision which Herr Krupp seems to have reserved for himself. It concerns the Allies post-war order that he sell his coal and steel holdings. Herr Krupp has no intention of complying with the order which he now says was signed under duress . . . Herr Krupp was imprisoned by the Allies as a war criminal. He seems intent on getting at least a measure of vindication by forcing the same Allies to withdraw their deconcentration order.[40]

At the Leipzig Fair in East Germany, Beitz and Soviet Premier Khruschev toasted the good health of Alfried Krupp in anticipation that Krupp would build a network of oil and gas pipelines in the Soviet Union.[41] A Krupp team was reported to be studying a $200 million iron-ore project in Canada. Krupp engineers were building a $168 million steel plant in India and a $75 million plant in Pakistan.[42] In the context of the big deals Beitz was arranging, the slave labor issue was like a flea biting an elephant—a petty annoyance, but it might be best to get it out of the way.

When Katzenstein finally was summoned to Essen, Beitz was accompanied by the company's house counsel, Dr. Hermann Maschke, a former Nazi who had been one of Krupp's defenders at Nuremberg.[43] Maschke noted that Mordechai S. had reduced his claim to only DM 2,000 and then, along with some others, had asked that all court action be suspended. The thrust of Maschke's recitation was that since other claimants had gone away quietly, the Claims Conference should be reasonable and do the same.[44]

According to Maschke, Krupp's connection with forced labor was purely nominal, it was only for a brief period, very few people were involved, they were all well-treated, and the inmates were really employed by the Reich or some other company. He disregarded the fact that all of these spurious contentions had been discredited by the Nuremberg court.

After an appropriate period of skirmishing and debate, Beitz let it be known that he had more important things to do. He was flying off in his private plane with his private interpreter to meet the Soviet foreign minister at the Kremlin, in defiance of the German chancellor's policy against dealing with the Soviet Union.[45] The next day Maschke asked Katzenstein to come back with exact information showing the number of Jewish claimants, their addresses, where they had come from, and when they had worked in which Krupp plant.

Preliminary estimates drawn from the Nuremberg records indicated that, of the Jewish inmates who had worked for Krupp, there might be about two thousand survivors. Assuming a payment of at least DM 5,000 for each one, an amount of DM 10 million would be required from the Krupp company. No one could be sure how many inmates were still alive, let alone how many might submit a claim. If Krupp wanted a guarantee against all further Jewish claims, the payment would as a matter of safety have to be increased. In subsequent discussions with the Krupp lawyers, the Claims Conference indicated that the cost to Krupp would, in any case, not exceed DM 20 million. Maschke confirmed that the final word would rest with Alfried Krupp.[46]

Alfried was combing the world for more trade and was getting quite annoyed with the failure of the Allies to drop the requirement that he dispose of his coal and iron holdings. "I am well aware, " Alfried was quoted as saying before he left Essen, "that this question called for patience so long as the wounds of war were not healed. I think we have shown much patience."[47] Even Beitz did not dare to decide the slave labor question while Krupp was away.

Katzenstein, who had been expecting an offer from Krupp, was surprised to receive a letter from Beitz saying:

Despite the fact that at the last mentioned discussion Mr. Ferencz placed special emphasis on the fact that the Conference did not regard the proposed settlement as primarily a legal matter but much more as a humanitarian gesture, nevertheless the Krupp company, after careful deliberation of all points of view, has come to the conclusion that a positive stand with regard to the proposal of the Claims Conference could also have legally prejudicial significance for other firms, which we believe we cannot justify, at least not until the legal question concerning whether the firms can be held legally liable has been finally clarified.[48]

Krupp's sense of solidarity with other German firms was given as the justification for refusing to proceed. The reasoning was not persuasive. A humanitarian gesture by Krupp, without acknowledging any legal liability, could not be legally prejudicial. Postponing action until there was a final decision by the German Supreme Court would mean a delay of several years. Even if the court then found in favor of the forced laborers, it would by that time be too late for most of the claimants to start new litigation. If the court ruled in favor of the German companies, the claimants would certainly be out. Therefore delay was a no-win proposition as far as the former camp inmates were concerned; it would have placed them completely at the mercy of Alfried Krupp. It was far better to proceed quickly and try to bring a strong test case against Krupp to be pressed with all possible speed through the highest German court. The time had come for the Claims Conference to decide whether it would play the game on Krupp's terms or whether it would move to the offensive and even raise the stakes.

## The Chips Are Down

During the next few months the conference response moved forward in what Germans might have regarded as a *Blitzkrieg* of pincer actions. There was a velvet-glove approach, in which several persons whom Alfried might regard as friends were recruited to try to persuade him to change his mind. There was also an iron-fist approach, which was designed to impress upon Krupp the risks he would run if he did not settle promptly. It was our hope that when Alfried weighed everything in the balance, he would recognize that it was clearly in his own interest to come to an early agreement.

The amiable approach was led by Jacob Blaustein, who obtained the renewed intervention of John McCloy. Nahum Goldmann, who was constantly in and out of Bonn in connection with problems related to Germany's indemnification program for Nazi victims, sought aid from the German government. Eric Warburg, the Jewish banker from Hamburg who had been helpful in connection with the Farben settlement, lent valuable assistance through his personal connections with Beitz and Krupp.

The hard line followed two courses, one directed toward Krupp personally and the other toward his most cherished possessions. Krupp had fostered the idea that he had been forced to employ concentration camp inmates against his will and therefore had been unjustly convicted at Nuremberg. We decided to puncture that myth by taking legal action in Germany and the United States that would disclose the truth. It was our intention that the unfavorable publicity would have an impact not only on Krupp's reputation but also on the expansion of his business throughout the world.

We knew that Krupp resented the Allied law that required him to sell his Rheinhausen steel operations, so we decided to try to persuade the United States government to hold Alfried to his agreement and to enforce the law.[49]

McCloy, who was about to depart for meetings of the Chase Bank in London and Frankfurt, recognized that it would be "good business" for Krupp to settle, and he expressed his disappointment at the negative attitude shown in the Beitz letter.[50] He was still hesitant about talking to Alfried directly, but he promised Blaustein that he would talk to Chancellor Adenauer and others. He requested a detailed memorandum and received assurances that the evidence

> supports the conclusion that Alfried Krupp did in fact exercise effective control of the Krupp company and all its enterprises, that they deliberately sought concentration camp labor for the Krupp industries, that there was absolutely no requirement that such labor be used, that the inmates were employed as slaves without pay under the most inhuman conditions and that Alfried Krupp was personally aware of all of this, and encouraged it. These original documents are still available and served as the basis for the criminal conviction of Alfried Krupp beyond a reasonable doubt. It is felt that they will suffice for the establishment of civil liability under ordinary concepts of German or American law.[51]

Blaustein wrote to his friend Jack at the Chase Bank in London:

> The case against Alfried Krupp is a good one and we feel that if there is no early indication of real willingness to settle amicably, we will have to proceed with full force . . . good conscience does not permit further protracted delays. However, before we proceed legally, we want to be sure that the Krupp people are really aware of the gravity of such action and have had an opportunity to reconsider their present position. As I stated to you in my cable from Berlin, it seems so shortsighted for Krupp, even from a public relations standpoint alone, quite aside from the legal aspect, not to settle this matter, and especially in view of the relatively small sum involved.[52]

David Bruce, the United States Ambassador in Germany, was reportedly on good terms with Alfried. Germany's leading magazine, *Der Spiegel,* had only two months before featured a two-page centerfold photo showing Alfried Krupp, together with a smiling Ambassador Bruce, British Ambassador Steel, and Berthold Beitz, all bearing shotguns, on a pheasant hunt.[53] It was quite a jolly scene, considering that the star was a former convict from Landsberg.

Bruce arranged for Alfried to invite McCloy for lunch at Villa Hugel.[54] The gist of McCloy's report after his luncheon was that although Krupp and Beitz were prepared to recognize the moral aspects of the claims, they could not enter into a settlement, since other companies and the German government had asked them not to do so. They acknowledged that the amount involved was small, and Alfried had implied that he was inclined to settle even if the plaintiffs against other companies were defeated in the courts, since that would then strengthen his own moral position.[55]

Blaustein felt that Krupp should be given time to reconsider, and he therefore wrote to Beitz saying:

The acceptance of a moral committment by Krupp on humanitarian grounds alone could, in our judgment, only enhance the reputation of Krupp and of German industry as a whole . . . We would regard it as unfortunate if you were to leave us no choice but to turn to the courts and to public opinion pursuant to our heavy obligation to assist these needy persons . . . Consequently, we do ask you to reconsider your decision which will permit us to resume discussions designed to bring about an amicable settlement at an early date. If we do not receive any further indication of such an attitude, we shall most reluctantly have to proceed with the assertion of our claims with all of the means at our disposal.[56]

While efforts were being made to induce Krupp to change his mind, the preparations for court action against him were intensified. If a settlement was to be reached, Krupp would have to know that the Claims Conference was not bluffing. Here Eric Warburg could again play a very useful role. He was asked to render a service to both sides by conveying to Beitz and Krupp the fact that the Claims Conference was an organization not to be taken lightly and that if the conference was driven to go public through Congress and the press, Krupp might lose more than the paltry sum in a settlement.[57]

The State Department was asked to report on the status of the order requiring Krupp to sell Rheinhausen, and at the same time inquiry was made about progress on the Jewish claims discussions. The stirring and the linkage did not go unnoticed, and Beitz responded by fixing a date for another meeting in Essen between the Claims Conference and Krupp representatives.

Two days before the scheduled meeting in Essen, I dropped into the United States Embassy and called upon the American member of the Mixed Commission that had been designated to enforce the Allied divestment law.[58] Of course Krupp had not sold his Rheinhausen properties. Each year he had obtained another extension, during which time he had in fact expanded his holdings. I explained that the Claims Conference was trying to negotiate a settlement of slave labor claims and that it would probably be in Krupp's interest to avoid unfavorable publicity. I had no doubts that Krupp would receive a report on my visit.

The Claims Conference was ready for either the hard or the soft approach. Test cases were ready for trial, but a draft of an agreement was also on hand. Saul Kagan was standing by his phone in New York, waiting for a report that he could pass on to the senior officers. We were not quite ready for, and we did not expect what actually happened. The day before the scheduled meeting, Katzenstein received a phone call from Krupp's lawyer in Essen informing him that, on instructions from Beitz, the meeting had been canceled.[59]

The only choices left for the conference were to "put up or shut up." Instead of meeting with Krupp's lawyers as planned, Katzenstein and I met with another German lawyer to brief him on four new test cases that he was instructed to file against Krupp in the court at Essen. He was handed a trial memo supported by about two hundred German documents and the names of about a thousand witnesses.[60] It was left to Kagan to give the final signal to proceed.

Kagan, who was then on one of his regular inspection trips to Europe, contacted Warburg and urged the Hamburg banker to see Beitz immediately. Warburg went to Essen and showed Beitz some of the incriminating documents. Knowing that we were serious and on the verge of turning to the courts and the public, Warburg tried to impress upon Beitz the importance of acting quickly before things got completely out of hand. He urged Beitz to fly to New York and settle the matter at once.[61]

Beitz recognized that he would have to come to grips with the problem without delay. Waiting for the supreme court decision had been Maschke's idea, Beitz acknowledged, and he was inclined to accept Warburg's argument that there were more important considerations than purely legal ones. He did not seem to be overly concerned about the reaction from other German firms, for he said that they had shown little concern for the predicament in which Krupp found himself. Beitz indicated to Warburg that he was ready to go to the United States and meet with McCloy and Blaustein and wind it up quickly, but he would require clearance from his boss. According to Beitz, Krupp realized how much he owed to McCloy, but he had been very annoyed by all of the pressure that had been applied and did not want to seem to be yielding to threats. Beitz promised to discuss the whole subject thoroughly with Alfried and the highest government officials within the next few days.[62]

At just about the same time, Katzenstein received word from the chancellery that, if necessary, Adenauer would be prepared to sign a supportive letter.[63] Goldmann was also planning to talk to the finance minister. The new wind seemed to be blowing fair, and Kagan rushed off instructions for me to hold everything.[64]

Kagan's warning arrived just in time. Krupp International, Inc., was doing business in New York and had assets in the Chase Manhattan Bank. I was considering a class action on behalf of all of the known Krupp forced laborers, each suing in the New York Supreme Court for $100,000. The New York courts, however, would never get a chance to try the issue.

## A Deal Is Made

Beitz obtained clearance from Alfried Krupp. He prepared to go to the States, meet with McCloy and the leaders of the Claims Conference, and settle the Jewish claims. In return, Krupp expected the Jewish organizations to guarantee that there would be no further lawsuits against him.

The gears had to be thrown into reverse. Instead of launching the litigation against Krupp in Germany and in the United States, a settlement contract had to be prepared in a form that Beitz might be able to accept when he arrived in New York.

We did not know it at the time, but Beitz had other and bigger fish to fry during his visit to the United States. It was reported in the press that Krupp was refusing to manufacture arms for NATO until his war crimes conviction was stricken from the record.[65] The Mixed Commission, which was to enforce the divestiture of the Rheinhausen holdings, had recommended that the obligation be canceled. State Department consent was essential, and Beitz planned to make his first stop in Washington.[66]

On Thanksgiving Day 1959, Berthold Beitz flew into New York for a twenty-four-hour visit. First he paid his respects to his boss's benefactor, the former United States high commissioner. Businessman Beitz then set out to settle the Jewish claims. Carrying with him a letter of introduction from the German chancellor to the president of the Jewish Claims Conference, Beitz lost no time in telling Goldmann that Krupp was prepared to put down DM 5 to 6 million in order to provide each claimant with DM 5,000, and Krupp would pay up to a maximum of DM 10 million, or perhaps even a little bit more.

Goldmann was, as usual, very cordial and charming, but he referred Beitz to Blaustein as the senior officer in charge. McCloy had arranged for a midtown office of the Chase Manhattan Bank to be available where the parties might meet. Beitz repeated the offer he had made to Goldmann and stressed that he had to rush off to catch a plane for Germany. Blaustein was not one to quibble, and he made no effort to have the offer increased. It did not take long before a gentlemen's agreement was confirmed in a one-page memorandum of understanding. Everything was to be kept strictly confidential until Katzenstein and Krupp's lawyers could hammer out a final text that could be ratified by the Claims Conference board and accepted by Alfried Krupp.[67]

After six hours of difficult negotiation in Essen, the text of a contract was agreed upon.[68] The opening paragraph declared that Krupp, without recognizing any legal liability and "without prejudice to any other German firm," was making money available to ameliorate the suffering endured by Jewish concentration camp inmates "as a result of National Socialist action" while they were employed in plants of Krupp or its subsidiaries. Six million deutsche marks was to go to those Jewish claimants who could show to the satisfaction of the Claims Conference that they were concentration camp inmates assigned to work for Krupp. If the DM 6 million would not suffice to provide each entitled claimant with DM 5,000, Krupp would pay up to DM 4 million more. Krupp's total obligation was not to exceed DM 10 million. If the DM 10 million proved insufficient, the amount for each claimant would have to be reduced. In exchange, the Claims Conference would have to guarantee that Krupp and its subsidiary companies, as well as persons acting on their behalf, would not be called upon to make any other payments arising out of forced labor claims by Jewish concentration camp inmates or their heirs.

Ratifications were soon forthcoming and letters of appreciation were exchanged.[69] The news of the settlement between Alfried Krupp and the Jews received publicity everywhere. On the day before Christmas 1959, the *New York Times* carried a front-page story under the headline, "Krupp Will Pay Slave Laborers." It announced that the agreement provided for a payment of up to $2,380,000 (the dollar equivalent of DM 10 million) to former Jewish slave laborers, who could expect to receive $1,190 each for having worked in a Krupp enterprise. The story noted that Krupp spokesmen rejected any legal liability and agreed to pay to help "heal the wounds suffered during World War II."[70]

The *London Sunday Dispatch* condemned the agreement as "mean spirited and tawdry" and termed it "the most grasping, clutching, derisory 'gift' in recent memory."[71] It condemned Krupp for having made a fortune on "the blood and misery and starvation of 12,000 Jewish slaves who worked for him during the war."

"Lieber Herr Blaustein," cabled Berthold Beitz from Essen, "I am extraordinarily happy that the agreement concluded between us has been signed." He conveyed his "heart-felt thanks for the friendly and agreeable atmosphere" and expressed his confident hope that the agreement "would lead to a time of more pleasant and understanding association between all the parties."[72]

Although the exchange of compliments was brimming with cordiality, the feelings between Germans and Jews was far from tranquil. By coincidence, in a city not far from Essen there would be a glimpse of the smoldering volcano the very next day.

It was 2:30 in the early morning of Christmas Day that two young German ex-convicts approached the new Jewish synagogue in the city of Cologne. "Juden raus"—"Jews Get Out"—and "Germans Demand: Jews Get Out!" they scrawled in German. The red and white paint defaced the entrance and walls of the synagogue with large Nazi swastikas. The acts of two hoodlums might have passed unnoticed had it not sparked a fire that raced like the wind over all of Germany. Within a month, there would be almost seven hundred reported cases of desecration of Jewish houses of worship and cemetaries in every state of the Federal Republic of Germany. Within a few days the virus of hate was spread to other countries throughout the world. In Vienna, Oslo, Antwerp, Brussels, East Berlin, Paris, Johannesburg, Capetown, Melbourne, London, New York, and Hong Kong swastikas and anti-Semitic slogans appeared as proof that widespread Nazi sympathies were not dead, but only dormant.[73]

Resentment against the settlement with the Jews could also be detected in the house of Krupp and even among the non-Jewish forced laborers. Upon hearing of the Krupp settlement, the International Auschwitz Committee, led by Hermann Langbein, who had been so energetic in trying to obtain compensation for the Polish laborers who had worked for Farben at Auschwitz, placed his demands before Krupp's door at Essen.[74] The first reply which he received was an outright denial. "We had no plants at Auschwitz and therefore no prisoners could have worked for us there. Former prisoners who now make such an assertion are incorrectly informed."[75]

Langbein knew that the Krupp lawyers were either mistaken or lying, and he promptly issued a press release denouncing Krupp for having forgotten about Auschwitz and for rejecting the Gentile claimants. He then proceeded to the Claims Conference office in Frankfurt and demanded to know why, unlike the Farben settlement, no provision had been made in the Krupp agreement for any payment to non-Jews.[76] It was explained to him that when the subject had been broached during the early negotiations, the Krupp representatives had brusquely noted that the Claims Conference had no mandate to speak for non-Jews. Krupp had decided that the non-Jewish claimants would be left out in the cold.

An organization associated with Langbein's group, the Amicale Internationale de Neungamme (International Friends from Neungamme), also called upon the Claims Conference to oppose the discriminatory action by Krupp.[77] Their appeal that all forced laborers should be paid regardless of their religion was certainly justified. Yet their reference to the EINHEIT *aller Verfolgten*—the unity of all persecutees (emphasis theirs)—could not help but remind me of the May Day celebration I witnessed as an American soldier in the liberated concentration camp at Ebensee. The inmates paraded around the camp carrying the flags of Poland, the Soviet Union, Czechoslovakia, and the other lands from which they had come. Only one group, the most emaciated and tattered, marched without a banner. When I asked some of the other inmates, "Who are those who carry no flag and why are they not marching with the national groups?" I was told scornfully, "Oh, they can't march with us. They're the Jews!"

Whenever the Krupp company received a claim from a non-Jewish forced laborer, the applicant was advised to be in touch with Compensation Treuhand. The Krupp attorneys conveniently failed to mention that the settlement contract only authorized the funds to be used for payments to Jewish claimants, and not a penny had been provided to meet the claims of any non-Jews. When Krupp's lawyers came face to face with the discrimination against the non-Jews, they simply gave the claimants a misleading reply and even implied that if Gentiles were not being paid it was all the fault of the Jews. Thus the Central Committee of Nazi Victims Refugees in the Free World, a non-Jewish group in London, received a letter saying; "Gentlemen: With reference to your letter of Jan. 7, 1960, we must inform you that in view of the considerable financial expenditures on behalf of the Jewish concentration camp prisoners, we unfortunately do not see ourselves in a position to make any further voluntary payments. We ask that you have understanding for this."[78]

If Krupp did not want to pay the non-Jewish camp inmates, there was apparently nothing that anyone could do about it. When the question was raised in Parliament, the British under-secretary of state for foreign affairs replied that although the government had a natural sympathetic interest in seeing Krupp pay compensation to the non-Jewish survivors, it was not a matter with which the government was directly concerned. Another Labour Party member, Emanuel Shinwell, commented bitterly: "This rascal got away with murder and is now getting away with the swag."[79]

## The Truth about Krupp's Camps

Krupp was never really successful at Auschwitz, but it was not for lack of trying. On April 14, 1942, a member of Krupp's council of directors showed Hitler a new antitank gun and advised the Führer that "Krupp is also interested in manufacturing automatic weapons in connection with a concentration camp in the Sudetengau."[80] The seed so planted soon bore fruit. Krupp was given an order for artillery spare parts and was informed that the necessary factory would be erected in Auschwitz. The SS would lease the workshops to Krupp, and the company would provide the machines and the management. "The concentration camp at Auschwitz will place the required manpower at our disposal," said the secret staff report to Alfried Krupp, who allocated RM 2 million to set up the facilities. It was anticipated that five to six hundred prisoners would be made available and that fifty to sixty of Krupp's men would have to come down from headquarters in Essen to train and supervise the inmates.[81]

Auschwitz prisoners were put to work constructing the work halls that Krupp would need to produce the gun parts, and production was scheduled to start in March 1943.[82] On March 5, however, the Royal Air Force paid its respects to the Krupp plants in Essen, and Krupp's facilities for the manufacture of artillery detonators went up in flames. Krupp had to alter its plans.

Krupp's man in charge of detonator or fuse production, engineer Weinhold, proceeded to Berlin for a meeting in the "Krupp House" with the army and SS Lieutenant Colonel Maurer, Pohl's deputy in the Main Economic Office of the SS. He proposed that the plan to manufacture spare parts be dropped and that the Auschwitz facilities be made available instead for the mass production of half a million detonators per month. Fifteen hundred workers would be needed.[83]

According to the Krupp representatives, "We could count on the full support of the SS."[84] When Army Ordnance urged Weinhold to try to use German workers, at least in the beginning, Weinhold reported: "I pointed out that the main purpose of evacuating the plant to Auschwitz had been to employ the people there."[85] The SS promised to deliver its human shipments in usable condition. Auschwitz commandant Höss told Weinhold that the construction of washrooms at the worksite was not necessary "since the camp inmates are clean."[86] Weinhold met with Höss and reported:

If anything at all is to come of the mass fuse manufacture at
Auschwitz, very far-reaching measurers are necessary. If we arrive
too late with the planning of the building then the building firms
will have left Auschwitz again; if the production starts too late then
the workers will have been taken meanwhile by other firms . . .
the latter is of decisive importance; because up to now it was always supposed that the supply of workers in Auschwitz is unlim-
ited as regards quality and quantity. It might therefore happen in
case of a belated start of production that the whole reason why we
accepted the unusual difficulties which are present in Auschwitz,
namely the free disposal over workers, will no longer exist.[87]

In the contract with the SS, it was agreed that Krupp would have complete control over production, and "punishment is to be inflicted by the SS at Krupp's request."[88]

The workshops were erected by March, but by mid-July Krupp's detonator machines were not yet in place. SS Lieutenant Colonel Sommer demanded to know when production was going to start. The Krupp teletype whipped back to him in Oranienburg the next day said: "Production in Auschwitz has started, i.e., about 50 men are already engaged in the manufacture of equipment and tools for the fuse production and about 150 additional men on repair work and installment of machinery, etc. Altogether about 200 men are employed."[89] Krupp's reply was a bit of an exaggeration, as the next sentence indicated: "Actual production to start immediately after current is available." The power plant was not working, and there was no electricity, but as far as Krupp was concerned the heat was on.

Army Ordnance and the SS were getting very annoyed with the sight of the near-empty Krupp workshops. Krupp's engineer Weinhold again warned the management in Essen that the SS was considering reassigning the space to another company. Alfried Krupp himself intervened to reassure the Army High Command:

7 Sept. 1943
Secret . . .

We hope to be able to start the delivery of fuses in October and we shall try our best to reach the highest possible output before too long . . . A very close cooperation exists between this office and Auschwitz, and is assured also for the future.

With kind regards and Heil Hitler,

Yours faithfully,

A. v. Bohlen[90]

Army Ordnance was not convinced. At the end of September the army canceled its order. Krupp was told to get out, and the space was given to another company that had been manufacturing fuses in the Ukraine until they were forced to clear out by the advance of the Soviet armies.[91] Krupp's attempt to use Auschwitz inmates to mass produce antiaircraft guns, or even spare parts for the guns, or even detonators, turned out to be a complete fiasco. Little wonder that the company lawyers in Essen would just as soon forget about what Krupp did in Auschwitz. Besides, very few of the Auschwitz inmates who worked for Krupp could have survived.

Hardly had the dust of Auschwitz been cleared from their shoes than the Krupp representatives began to erect a substitute plant nearby. War production was moving eastward out of the range of Allied bombers. Krupp obtained top priority to build a plant in the area of Wüstegiersdorf, near Lublin. Krupp's man in Auschwitz, engineer Weinhold, and his crew of supervisors were reassigned to the new camp. By October they were urging the home office to put the pressure on the SS for more help in order that construction could be completed before the severe winter set in.[92]

By the time Krupp was able to start production, in the spring of 1944, only female inmates were available. The Nuremberg judgment set forth the facts:

After the production of fuses at Auschwitz had been taken away from the Krupp firm, immediate efforts were made to select a new site for the production of fuses by the firm. The advantage of having allotted to it the use of a concentration camp near Lublin because of the immediate availability of labor was considered . . . the possibility of locating the fuse production plant at Wüstegiersdorf in Silesia was discussed and considered. Production of fuses there was taken up and approximately 200 female concentration camp workers were assigned in the summer of 1944. All of these concentration camp inmates were Jewish. They were of Hungarian or Yugoslavian nationality. These women were not allocated by the local labor office; they were procured as a result of negotiations carried on by Weinhold and other plant leaders of the Krupp firm with the SS.[93]

On the railroad line from Breslau to Oppeln, which the Poles now call Wroclaw and Opole, on the eastern side of the Oder River, lie the towns of Markstädt and Fünfteichen. This area of the Silesian plain had been considered by I.G. Farben for its Buna rubber plant before Auschwitz was selected instead. Farben transferred its rights to 20 million square meters to Krupp, who had plans for an assembly line which could produce 600 light field howitzers per month. Krupp was ready to invest RM 70 million in the project. "The obstacles," said Krupp's secret report for 1941-1942, "could be overcome, partly through the personal intervention of Reich Minister Speer. The exceptional difficulty in obtaining workers for the new plant will presumably also be overcome thanks to the help of the Gauleiter [district leader] of Lower Silesia."[94]

Twelve hundred Jews in the area were herded into a *Judenlager*—a camp for Jews—at Markstädt, and their services made available to German industry. Alfried Krupp, still smarting over his eviction from Auschwitz, sent a memorandum to all of his plants: "We must now harness the entire strength of all the works combined . . . otherwise there is a risk that the works [at Markstädt] or parts thereof may be allocated to other firms."[95]

Krupp's new Bertha Works at Markstädt needed six thousand workers. The chairman of the board of directors wrote to his boss, Alfried Krupp, at the end of August 1943 and asked for permission to use concentration camp inmates and for help in getting them. The home office gave its prompt approval and contacted the WVHA, the SS Economic and Administrative Main Office, "to negotiate for the allocation of concentration camp labor."[96] The SS headquarters told the Krupp people to take it up directly with the commandant at Gross Rosen. The top SS men from Gross Rosen met with the Krupp officials at the Bertha Works, and plans were then made to convert an existing forced labor camp at Fünfteichen into a branch camp of Gross Rosen under the security supervision of the SS. The new concentration camp was scheduled to accommodate eight hundred inmates by October 10, 1943, fifteen hundred by October 15, and four thousand by December.[97]

As scheduled, fifteen hundred Jews were transported from Auschwitz in October 1943 to help with the construction. Their arms bore Auschwitz numbers between 130000 and 140000. Within a few months almost all of the twelve hundred forced laborers from Markstädt were also transferred to the Fünfteichen concentration camp. They discarded their civilian jackets with the Star of David. The German army guards were replaced by the more brutal SS. The prisoners had their hair clipped down the center, and in their blue and white stripes, with new numbers sewn under the left-hand jacket pocket and on the right trouser leg, they became full fledged concentration camp (KZ) inmates. The *Häftlinge* did not know that they could thank Krupp for their new status.

In its regular report to the main office in Essen, the Bertha Works management boasted: "In order to prevent a transfer of the Jews who work with the Speer Building Management the Bertha Works negotiated for having the Jews put in the concentration camp Fünfteichen. Thereby a better supervision of the allocation of labor [of the Jews] can be achieved in future."[98] Having thus arranged to put the Jews into a concentration camp, the Krupp firm was able to justify its request for more workers by arguing, "The chief thing is that there is a concentration camp ready to receive 4,000 to 5,000 concentration camp internees."[99]

In describing a meeting with Alfried Krupp and other members of the council of directors in October 1943, the Bertha Works manager, Heinrich Korschan, was later to state: "Nobody objected to the employment of concentration camp inmates which was announced at the time. On the contrary, it was accepted as an accomplished fact without any further comment."[100]

It was estimated that between ten and fifteen thousand laborers, mostly Ukrainians and Poles, worked for Krupp at Markstädt/Fünfteichen in one capacity or another.[101] How many Jews were employed was never precisely ascertained. A Czech witness, describing the camp, swore: "The Jews received the worst beatings . . . people were beaten to death or even thrown alive into the concrete which was used for new constructions."[102]

Krupp had a plant for the production of breeches for antiaircraft guns at Geisenheim on the Rhine. The Krupp managers requested and obtained two hundred Jewish women from the Natzweiler concentration camp to work in the Geisenheim plant from the summer of 1944 until they were evacuated toward Dachau as the war was drawing to a close.[103]

The Krupp firm had an interesting connection with another company in Neukölln, a suburb of Berlin. In 1934 the National Cash Register Company of Dayton, Ohio, set up a subsidiary in Germany. Shortly thereafter the NCR Company was changed into a joint venture with Krupp. Krupp contributed 20 percent of the capital, and the company was renamed the National-Krupp Registrierkassen GmbH—the National Krupp Cash Register Company. In 1942, the "commissioner to administer enemy property" placed the firm under complete German management, with Alfried Krupp as a member of the advisory board. The company was to manufacture timing devices for German bombs.

By the end of 1942 National Krupp Cash Register Company was procuring much of its labor from a forced labor camp which housed over six hundred Polish, French, and Russian women. In April 1943 the company set up a branch in the Jewish ghetto at Lodz, inside a textile factory that had been seized from its Jewish owner. By the end of 1943 the company had close to five hundred Jewish women working in the ghetto and that number was more than doubled by September 1944. Toward the end of 1944, as the noose around the Jews was tightened, the ghetto was emptied and the miserable inhabitants were shipped to Auschwitz to be selected for their fate. What happened to some of them can be seen from the description of one of the survivors:

On May 1, 1940 we were moved into the ghetto . . . In 1942 my two daughters, aged 10 and 7, were taken away by the SS to Auschwitz and killed. My husband and I stayed in the ghetto until August 1944 and then we were both taken to Auschwitz. There we were separated and he, too, was murdered by the SS. I stayed at Auschwitz for 4 or 5 days and then was transported in a freight car to Neukölln, near Berlin. There were but 500 women in the transport, almost all of them from Lodz but there were also some German Jews. There was one SS man on guard in each car and there were about 100 girls in each car. The trip took three days and three nights. There was nothing to eat on the way and only little water to drink . . . We were not allowed to leave the car. A pail served as our toilet . . . At Neukölln we were taken directly to three barracks surrounded by barbed wire. The barracks were near the railroad station and near a Krupp factory . . . I was sent to work for Krupp. We were guarded by many SS women who told us that it was a Krupp company and, if I remember correctly, the name Krupp also appeared on the outside of the building . . . It was impossible to do all that was demanded of us. I worked in a galvanizing section, dipping hot irons into cold water. The sparks flew into my eyes and burned and blistered my hands. It was terrible. I am unable to describe in detail all of our suffering. I can only say that it was a terrible thing and I can hardly believe that I am still alive today . . . The German civilian foreman of the Krupp company kept rushing us and we were all so terrified that if we stopped or slowed down we would be put in the crematorium that we worked to the last ounce of our strength. I endured this for nine months . . . I was then moved to Ravensbrück concentration camp . . . I was then removed by the Swedish Red Cross . . . I remained in Sweden for three years and then emigrated to join some members of my family in the United States . . . My poor health and my high blood pressure do not permit me to work. When I think of the time I had to work for Krupp it seems like another world.[104]

In the early summer of 1944, when the SS offered a large group of concentration camp inmates to the armaments industry, fifty to sixty thousand "Hungarian Jewesses" were put on the block and made available to any armaments firm that cared to make a bid.[105] Krupp representatives proceeded to Oranienburg to meet with the SS Main Economic Office and to request an allocation of slaves for work at the main Krupp plant in Essen. Approval in principle was obtained, and the Krupp people were told to arrange the details with the commandant of the concentration camp at Buchenwald, near Weimar.

Buchenwald's commandant, Colonel Hermann Pister, was most accommodating and came up to the Krupp main office to spend the night in Essen and work out the deal.[106] Krupp wanted two thousand men. Krupp already had seventy thousand employees, including twenty thousand foreigners.[107] Pister said he was sorry, but only women were available. He wanted to know where the inmates would be housed and how escape would be prevented. Krupp drew attention to a number of barracks that were being used to house Italian military internees and that might be suitable. It was located on Humboldtstrasse, 4.5 miles from Krupp's steel mill, where the inmates were to be employed.

There were two thousand Jewish females in a subcommando of Buchenwald at Gelsenkirchen, where they were being used by other German firms. Krupp, having higher priority, was invited to send his representatives to the Gelsenkirchen camp to see what was available. Krupp's advance scout reported back that the inmates were unsuitable, since they appeared too frail and weak for heavy work. It was apparently a take-it-or-leave-it proposition. Krupp was told that he could have five hundred of the Gelsenkirchen Jewesses, provided that he could find forty-five German women who would be trained at Ravensbrück to be the SS guards and that he would have the Humboldstrasse camp surrounded by barbed wire.[108] The Krupp personnel office called for volunteers, and the forty-five guards were recruited from Krupp's German staff.[109] Rubber truncheons and uniforms were provided by the SS.[110]

Krupp's foremen went shopping to Gelsenkirchen for a closer inspection of the goods. The girls, ranging in age from fifteen to twenty-five, had been rounded up in Hungary, Rumania, and Czechoslovakia in the spring of 1944. They had been through a selection once before. They and their families were all transported to Auschwitz, where they had seen old parents and weak relatives sent to the gas chambers. The "lucky ones" had their heads shaved, were stripped of their clothing and all their possessions, were issued a gray sacklike garb of burlap, were numbered and made ready for shipment as slaves of the Reich. They were not much to look at, but the Krupp men managed to pick out a batch of five hundred. Another twenty auxiliaries were thrown in for good measure.

The work in Krupp's *Walzwerke* II (rolling mill) and the *Anodenwerk* (electrode shop) did not last very long. On October 23, 1944, Essen was plastered with Allied bombs. Two days later another raid blasted the barracks on Humboldtstrasse. Amid the ruins the inmates huddled together like frightened animals on the straw.

The Nuremberg record was replete with evidence of brutal mistreatment of the Hungarian girls by Krupp foremen and the SS guards.[111] The girls, shivering and freezing, were driven away from the small fires that might have warmed them. Dog whips were used to goad them on as they plodded to work through the snow, their feet wrapped in rags and only a drenched blanket over their shoulders for protection. Jews were never allowed to enter an air-raid shelter. Instead they crouched in the narrow ditches outside, terrified but cheering in their hearts.

"We will kill you at the last moment," taunted the SS guards.[112] It was no idle threat. It was known to the Krupp officials that the SS was determined not to allow any of the prisoners to fall into Allied hands alive. A defense witness at Nuremberg testified: "Camp Commandant Rieck had made it understood that it was his strictest orders not to let them fall into the hands of the American army under any circumstances."[113]

As the British and American armies closed in on Essen, the Krupp management had to do something about the Hungarian girls. They could have opened the gates and set them free, or left them where they were and had them discovered by the Allied armies. With the full knowledge and approval of Alfried Krupp, another solution was found. It was decided, despite all of the logistical difficulties, to ship the girls back to the concentration camp at Buchenwald.[114]

The testimony about Krupp's decision to send the girls back to Buchenwald was elicited during a cross-examination which I con-

ducted of three Krupp defense witnesses. I mention that fact only because it may have made an undue impression on me. I had very little
to do with the Krupp prosecution, and it was only by chance that I was
asked to help out during the last stages of the trial. Those few cross-
examinations remained vividly in my memory, doubly so because my
own wife had narrowly escaped the fate of the slave laborers. She had
immigrated to America in time, but some of her schoolmates were
among the Hungarian girls working for Krupp.

No one can know what was in Krupp's mind at the time. It may be
that abandoning the girls to the SS and arranging the shipment to Buchenwald was as logical as returning any piece of borrowed equipment.
Surely no feeling of compassion entered into the deliberations. It must
have been obvious to every thinking person—if they gave it any
thought at all—that the girls, by being sent from Essen to Buchenwald,
were being moved from the frying pan literally into the fire.

When the Nuremberg tribunal rendered its judgment against the
Krupp directors in 1948, the judges were under the impression that
very few of the Hungarian girls from Humboldtstrasse had survived the
war. The judgment said: "On 17 March 1945, the girls were marched to
Bochum. There a train was made up for them and 1,500 male concentration camp inmates. They were shipped eastward under SS guards.
With the exception of a few who had escaped shortly before . . . nothing further had been discovered about the fate of the young 'Hungarian
Jewesses' of the Krupp firm."[115]

But there was more to the story than the Nuremberg court knew.
When the freight train reached the gates of Buchenwald, the fifteen
hundred male inmates who had been loaded on at Bochum were unloaded, Buchenwald commandant Pister had his hands full. The camp
was jammed with inmates, and the tanks of General Patton's Third
Army were racing in from the west. The freight train, still loaded with
the Hungarian girls, was rerouted north. After a few days travel, the
train finally arrived at Bergen-Belsen. There the girls from Essen—
what was left of them—were unloaded. Within a few weeks the British
army moved in, and those girls who were still alive were finally set
free. Many of them later came forward to hold Krupp to account.

### Dividing a Meager Loaf

Much of the information about Krupp's camps came from the more
than seven thousand concentration camp inmates who submitted applications for a share of the Krupp fund. The petitions came from
thirty-one countries ranging from New Zealand to Pakistan, and the
number was substantially higher than anyone had anticipated. Each
eligible applicant was given an initial grant of DM 3,000 ($750) and the

hope that more would follow after the total number of valid claims could be ascertained.

Certain applications could be approved quickly and beyond question. Where a complete transport list was discovered giving the names of the Krupp workers, all that was required was to verify the identity of the applicant. The two hundred women who went from Gross Rosen to Wüstergiersdorf were in that category. One had only to look down the list to see that prisoner 17055 was the sixteen-year-old student Magda Honig from Munkács, or that Klara Berger, number 17177, was a nineteen-year-old seamstress from Nagyvárad. Validating the claim was also relatively easy where the records showed that only Krupp had employed inmates in that particular place, such as Geisenheim, Neukölln, and Essen. Where many companies worked in the same region and there was a constant interchange of inmates, such as in the area of Langenbielau and Reichenbach, it was almost impossible to know from the records alone whether or not the applicant qualified for payment.

Once the number of approved claims exceeded two thousand, it was clear that, unless Krupp would augment the DM 10 million fund, the claimants would not be able to receive the full amount of DM 5,000 mentioned in the contract. There might not even be enough to continue to pay the DM 3,000 that had been advanced as a first installment. Pending clarification of the financial possibilities, it was necessary to call a temporary halt to further payments, and to tell the screening committee to follow as restrictive a policy as possible.

The moratorium came under immediate attack. Claimants could not understand why some of their comrades had been paid while others were told to wait. Having been conditioned in the camps to distrust everyone, they bombarded the Claims Conference with complaints, accusations, and threats. The Krupp company should have known better than anyone else how many inmates had worked for the firm, and it was considered appropriate, therefore, to apprise Krupp representatives of the predicament in which the conference found itself.

Nahum Goldmann arranged to meet Beitz in Bonn. According to Goldmann's report to Ernst Katzenstein, Beitz was willing to consider an additional payment, but he first wanted to have the views of his legal staff. After some time had elapsed and there was no further word Katzenstein sent Beitz a reminder. Beitz lost no time in replying: "I do not understand the implications in your letter regarding our compensation agreement. I must draw your attention to the fact that in my discussion with Dr. Goldmann he clearly confirmed that it was also his opinion that our agreement precludes the assertion of any additional claims. I therefore consider any discussion of this question as unnecessary."[116]

Katzenstein was astonished by Beitz's rebuff, and Goldmann was embarrassed and annoyed. Goldmann wrote to *"Lieber Herr Beitz"* saying, "I fear that you slightly misunderstood our talk in Bonn."[117] There was no *lieber* in Beitz's chilly two-paragraph reply, addressed in formal style to *Sehr geehrter Herr Dr. Goldmann;* Beitz explained that the payment by Krupp had been increased from DM 6 million to DM 10 million because of the uncertainty about the number of claims, and the contract had been fulfilled. "Despite all understanding for the difficult condition of the former concentration camp prisoners, which we solely for moral reasons expressed through our voluntary indemnification, we do not see ourselves in the position to make further sums available. I therefore do not consider even a discussion of this matter as appropriate.

With expression of high esteem [*Mit vorzüglicher Hochachtung*] Beitz."[118] The net worth of the Krupp holdings were reported to be one billion dollars, yet Krupp was not in a position, he said, to make any further sums available to the Jewish concentration camp survivors. It was not even a matter worth discussing.

Since pleading was obviously ineffective, it was decided to try prodding. Rheinhausen might still be Krupp's Achilles' heel. We felt that Krupp could hardly reject the camp survivors on the grounds that "a contract is a contract," and at the same time be insisting that the same principle did not apply to *his* contract with the Allies.

Rabbi Joachim Prinz, chairman of the American Jewish Congress, wrote to the United States Secretary of State: "We urge that the United States firmly press its demand that the divestiture order be carried out forthrightly and at once."[119] The ripples from the Prinz protest moved across the ocean to the Ruhr. Once again the Rheinhausen nerve proved to be a sensitive one. Beitz called for a new meeting with Goldmann.[120] When they met, Goldmann suggested an additional payment by Krupp of DM 5 million. In response, Krupp's lawyers demanded that Compensation Treuhand produce its records showing the exact status of all of the claims received.[121]

It was only five days before Christmas when Krupp's general manager wrote to the Claims Conference president. Despite his sympathy with the fact that the claimants could not receive the full amount they had expected, Krupp was, as a matter of principle, not in a position to increase the amount that had been agreed upon. He expressed his regrets, asked for Goldmann's understanding, hoped they would meet again, and conveyed his best wishes.[122] If the spirit of Christmas had reached Essen, it surely did not extend to the Jewish concentration camp inmates who had worked for Krupp.

Goldmann wrote back to Beitz, saying: "We must not forget that what we are trying to do is to provide a payment which the poor recipients will recognize as fair and which will not merely increase their bitterness." Goldmann asked that Mr. Krupp von Bohlen reconsider.[123]

Beitz snapped back a prompt: "No." The payment had, according to his reply, been a gesture of good will. Krupp had only agreed to the payment after Beitz had assured him that it would cost no more than DM 10 million. Both Goldmann and Blaustein had accepted that figure. Then Beitz went on the offensive, undoubtedly sparked by the reference to "bitterness" mentioned in the Goldmann letter.

We have seen from your report on claims that among the claimants are 400 Hungarian women who, according to the Nuremberg judgment, were surrendered by Krupp for execution. This error, together with other distortions, certainly contributed to the high term of imprisonment to which Herr von Bohlen was sentenced and which he to a considerable extent served. For this there is no restitution, not even a moral one in world public opinion. You will understand that in our House the awareness of this is felt with bitterness.[124]

Beitz's ringing rally to the flag of his chief had its effect. Goldmann replied that he was only trying to help the claimants, and he hoped to avoid any protests against Krupp that might arise if the Krupp workers received less than those who had worked for Farben. He agreed that legally Krupp had no obligation to pay anything more, and it was completely a matter of Krupp's discretion. As far as the Hungarian women were concerned, said Goldmann, "We are not responsible for what happened at Nuremberg," but if Krupp would provide the facts, Goldmann offered to seek some suitable way to correct whatever error had occurred.[125]

It was quite true that the Nuremberg judgment had referred to the shipment of the Hungarian girls to Buchenwald in the last days of the war, but that was only one small incident in a long record of Alfried Krupp's offenses that justified the verdict and the sentence. The court's statement that "nothing further has been discovered about the fate of the young Hungarian Jewesses of the Krupp firm" might well have implied that the girls were in fact killed.[126] That apparently was what Alfried Krupp believed, too, since it was only discovered later, when they submitted their claims, that they were still alive. What Krupp apparently forgot was that *he* was the one who had approved the transfer from Essen back to the concentration camp, knowing fully that the SS had said they would never allow the inmates to fall into Allied hands alive. The fact that the prisoners were not murdered in Buchenwald, as everyone who knew the circumstances might rightfully have expected, was not thanks to any effort on Krupp's part to save them. On the contrary, it took Krupp employees a great deal of effort to transport the girls off Krupp property and to the death camp just as the Allied armies were about to capture the city. It would have been so much easier to do nothing and allow the prisoners to be liberated on Humboldtstrasse. No one could really believe that it would be safer for Jewish girls inside the walls of an SS concentration camp than on the streets of Essen. Krupp's action had endangered the Jews and not protected them. Krupp could not know that the delivery would be aborted when the commandant at Buchenwald refused to accept the human cargo. Because many of the girls had somehow managed to survive, Krupp was considered, by the House of Krupp, to be the real victim, entitled to "moral restitution" in the eyes of the world.

It was more than clear that no matter what arguments were raised, Krupp would pay no more to his former concentration camp laborers. There was no choice for Compensation Treuhand but to divide the meager loaf, or whatever was left of the DM 10 million, among all of the eligible claimants in whatever manner seemed most equitable under the circumstances.

The Krupp company had reported that it used 270 inmates at Auschwitz. Only 87 survivors could be found. Of the 200 girls who were shipped to Geisenheim, 150 claims could be validated and it was not much different regarding the Wüstergiersdorf transport or the 500 girls who worked in Neukölln. Of the 520 girls who toiled for Krupp at Essen, only 365 were granted compensation. More than 25 percent of the original transport was never traced.

The most difficult validations arose regarding those who worked at Krupp's Bertha Works in Markstädt/Fünfteichen. The arbitrary distinctions, which the settlement with Krupp required, between forced labor camps and concentration camps, between *Bauarbeiter*—the construction workers—and production workers, and the fact that many other firms used forced labor in the same region, added to the difficulties of drawing a visible and rational line between those who qualified and those who did not. After very careful screening, over 1,700 Markstädt claims were finally approved. Only 120 claimants were able to prove that they had worked for Krupp at Langenbielau, (Bielawa) and Reichenbach, (Dzierzoniow) where many other firms used concentration camp labor.

The audit of Compensation Treuhand showed that 3,090 claimants from 33 different countries received a total of DM 10,050,900. (The amount over DM 10 million was interest earned by Compensation Treuhand.) Over DM 4 million went to claimants in Israel, over DM 3 million to claimants in the United States, and close to half a million to claimants in Sweden, West Germany, and Canada. Survivors in Australia and Hungary also received significant distributions. The maximum amount that each survivor was able to receive from the Krupp fund was DM 3,300, which was then $825.

In the forefront of the approximately 4,000 rejected cases were those who had helped to build a bridge over the Bug River at Trichati; 460

Trichati survivors had applied for a share of the Krupp fund, and they all had to be sent away empty-handed. They simply could not understand how a Jewish organization could turn them down. In fact, Compensation Treuhand was eager to pay them, but to do so would have required Krupp's consent and would have meant that the other claimants' shares would have had to be even further diminished. The least the Trichati survivors deserve, however, is that their story be mentioned.

Between the Dnieper and the Dniester the Bug River flows slowly toward the Black Sea. In 1941 the *Einsatzgruppen* reached the Moldavian Plain on their way to the Crimea in the region of the southern Ukraine, where Romania borders on the Soviet Union. Since Romania was an ally of Germany, the German military authorities in Berlin decided to assign certain occupation duties to the Romanian army. The German high command prohibited the deportation of Jews across the Bug into German operational territory, saying "they must be collected in concentration camps and set to work until a deportation to the East is possible." It was noted with annoyance that the Romanians had moved 110,000 Jews into two forests in the area of the Bug River and "the purpose of the action is the liquidation of these Jews."[127] *Einsatzgruppen* defendant SS Lt. Col. Gustav Nosske explained: "I assume that the Romanians wanted to get rid of them and sent them into German territory so that we would have to shoot them . . . We didn't want to do the work for the Romanians."[128]

Franz Rademacher of the German Foreign Office sent a formal complaint against the *Abschiebung*, or dumping, of Romanian Jews across the Bug River. His handwritten file note two days later stated: "28000 Jews had been brought over into German villages, in the meanwhile they were liquidated" *(Inzwischen wurden sie liquidiert)*.[129] The record was clear that all of the Jews trapped in that region were marked for death. The German army needed a railroad bridge to cross the Bug River. An attempt to build a bridge across the Dnieper had failed, as the foundation kept sliding into the rapids.[130] Krupp received the order for the steel structure. Labor would be provided by the Jews. There were about 1,500 of them being guarded by the Romanian gendarmerie in an old Russian cavalry barrack across the river, in a village called Trichati.

Krupp's engineer-in-charge, Rudolf Wegener, arrived on the scene in April 1942. From 150 to 400 Jews were handed over to him.[131] The Krupp work gang received metal identification tags bearing the name Krupp, and, like dogs, each prisoner wore the tag around his neck. Many of the Jews were beaten to death or died in the icy waters, but by October 1943 the bridge was ready for use.[132]

The Soviet armies launched their spring counteroffensive and captured the area in March 1944. Many of the Jews who were still left in the camp at Trichati were impressed into the Russian army to fight against the retreating Nazis. Years later, as men who had been through hell together, those who found themselves alive formed the Association of Trichati Survivors. When they heard that a settlement had been made with the Krupp company, they filed their claims and told the story of their suffering while they were working for Krupp on the bridge over the Bug River. Unfortunately, the claimants did not qualify under the terms of the contract. Technically they had not been concentration camp (KZ) inmates directly employed in a Krupp plant; Krupp was only a subcontractor. Engineer Wegener, who was still on the Krupp payroll in Berlin in 1962, and other Krupp supervisors who had been at Trichati confirmed all of the essential facts, but of course denied that there had been any mistreatment of the Jews.[133] When Krupp refused to make any additional funds available, it meant that the Trichati survivors would get nothing.

The absence of additional funds also precluded any supplementary payments for hardship cases. One such case was the claim of Abraham W., who had been at Markstädt/Fünfteichen beginning in June 1942. In January 1945 a Krupp crane ran over him and his right leg was amputated. His life was saved when the Russian troops entered the camp. He was most reluctant, in exchange for less than $1,000, to sign a waiver saying that he had no further claims against the Krupp company. Compensation Treuhand could do no more than offer him the same share offered to all others.

Abraham turned directly to Krupp in Essen for help: "I appeal to your conscience and your human feeling, and I am convinced that in your financial condition it should not be too difficult to provide an appropriate compensation to one who is damaged for life."[134] The Krupp lawyers replied: "May we in this context also draw your attention to the fact that the assignment of prisoners was the result of official orders, and that the firm which had to carry out the armaments orders of the Reich was forced to employ the KZ prisoners."[135] They recommended that he sign the waiver and take the money—from the Claims Conference.

It has been estimated that close to 70,000 foreign civilians and over 23,000 prisoners of war were employed in eighty-one different plants of the Krupp firm. As difficult as was the lot of all these forced laborers, those from the concentration camps, who probably never exceeded 10,000, were in a class apart. The Jewish inmates labored under the constant threat of death. They were denounced as vermin by the Reich and were treated accordingly by most Germans with whom they came in contact. All the Jews were marked for eventual extermination.

No one suggests that concentration camp labor was Krupp's first choice. But the decision to use the camp inmates was his. The only compulsion, if that term can be used, was his own desire to serve the Reich. No one forced Krupp to apply to the SS administration for an assignment of inmates. His will to use the inmates coincided with the will of the SS to make them available. No inmates were ever assigned to any Krupp company without the firm's prior specific request. All of the repeated and persistent declarations to the contrary by faithful Krupp employees are refuted by the unmistakable documentary record.

The treatment of concentration camp inmates who worked for Krupp companies is now well known. Certainly there were occasional surreptitious acts of kindness by some Krupp foremen who sympathized with the young Hungarian girls under their command. Some of the survivors tell of incidents when they were given a piece of bread or a potato by a compassionate German stranger. It also cannot be denied, as some employers have noted, that if the inmates had not been able to work, they would have been gassed by the SS. None of these truths can detract from the conclusion that being a concentration camp inmate working for Krupp, or any other German firm, was hell.

Alfried Krupp no doubt considered it an act of great generosity when he agreed to pay anything to his former slave laborers. The argument made repeatedly by Beitz and others that Krupp was quite prepared to do something, but that he did not want to be put under pressure and wanted to make a voluntary gesture on his own, after the German courts had destroyed the legal position of the claimants, leaves many questions unanswered. What prevented Krupp, who was the sole owner of a company worth a billion dollars, from coming forward with a payment long before he was approached by the Claims Conference? If Krupp was making a humanitarian gesture, why did he insist that, in exchange for his inadequate payment, the Jewish Claims Conference would have to guarantee to pay all Jewish claims against him and his subsidiaries? Why was there nothing from Krupp for the non-Jews? What prevented Krupp from settling the claim of Mordechai S., who only wanted a few hundred dollars for his crippled arm, or for making any payment to the impoverished Abraham W., who lost a leg while working for Krupp at the Bertha Works? What prevented Krupp from increasing the amount of the fund once it became clear that not even $1,000 would be available for each person who proved conclusively that he or she had worked for Krupp? Unfortunately, just as Krupp sat silent as evidence mounted against him in the Nuremberg court, these questions too will all remain unanswered. On Sunday, July 30, 1967, at the age of sixty, Alfried Felix Alwyn Krupp von Bohlen und Halbach died quietly in Essen. The era of the Krupp empire was over.

# The Electrical Companies See the Light

The staff managers of the big firms came to the camp to select women for their plants. It was an odd experience for us to see men in civilian clothes. They would arrive with somewhat embarrassed expressions on their faces. The women had to form up for their benefit, so that they could make sure of getting strong young girls; and it looked as if at any moment they would pinch their leg and arm muscles to test them. One manager would order 100 "pieces", another 500 or 1000, plus a few nurses or a couple of women doctors, and then another customer would turn up. We never felt sure whether it was an advantage or a disadvantage to be taken away.

Statement of a non-Jewish inmate,
Dr. Ella Lingens-Reisner[1]

# CHAPTER 4

## Keeping the Claims Afloat

No one can say for certain whether I.G. Farben or Krupp would have paid anything to camp survivors had the company directors not been confronted with a mass of incriminating evidence and the imminent threat of unfavorable publicity and court action. Judging by the arguments they raised in denying liability, one may reasonably surmise that the availability of embarrassing documentary proof had a persuasive impact. Nuremberg trial records had been the source of much of the proof against I.G. Farben and Krupp, but information about companies that had not been indicted was not readily accessible.

Germany's major electrical concerns, AEG, Telefunken, and Siemens, not only provided the electrical installations to the concentration camps but staffed some of their production lines with concentration camp inmates. The Allgemeine Elektricitäts-Gesellschaft was known as the "General Electric" of Germany, although it had no formal connection with its American namesake. In October 1957, five Jews who resided in Germany turned to Dr. Henry van Dam, the secretary-general of the Central Association of Jewish Congregations in Germany, and asked for help in obtaining compensation from AEG for labor they performed while interned in a concentration camp. Van Dam wrote to AEG and received a reply from its legal department in Frankfurt denying all knowledge or responsibility.[2] After receiving the names of three more claimants from the URO office in New York, van Dam sent a more comprehensive letter to AEG and offered to settle all of the known claims for a combined total of less than $10,000.[3] The modesty of the demand did not deter the company from again sending a completely negative response.[4]

Before the year was out, van Dam wrote to AEG for a third time and urged the company to reconsider.[5] The day before Christmas the AEG reiterated that it would make no payment.[6] That was enough to topple the secretay general of the Jewish communities. Van Dam handed the cases over to another Jewish attorney in Frankfurt, Martin Gur-Guttmann, who immediately filed a legal complaint against AEG in the labor court of Frankfurt. That court had no jurisdiction, but the emergency filing protected the claimants from AEG's possible defense that the claimants had filed too late.

Meanwhile, the Claims Conference arranged to have a young German lawyer on the staff of the JRSO in Berlin assigned to handle the claims against AEG, which had its legal situs in the former German capital. Dr. Karl-Heinz Schildbach was instructed to start a test case on behalf of Rivka W. of New York.

The plaintiff told a fairly typical story. She had been deported from Bavaria in November 1941 to a *Vernichtungslager,* or extermination camp, at Jungfernhof, near Riga, in German-occupied Latvia. She avoided being put to death, and in July of 1942 she was sent into the ghetto of Riga as a forced laborer. In November 1943 she was moved to a nearby concentration camp in an area known as Kaiserwald. From there, together with some 1,500 other concentration camp inmates, she was sent to work in one of AEG's factories which, ironically, was on the Grosse Freiheitstrasse, the Street of Great Freedom. There was no freedom for Rivka. She was told that if she did not lacquer the allotted quota of electrical wiring, she would be shot. According to her testimony, the Jewish girls were beaten by SS and Latvian supervisors and if there was some food left over by the Latvian workers, the Germans would throw it away with the remark, "Better to give it to the pigs than to the Jews." [7]

In September 1944 Rivka was moved westward to the Stutthof concentration camp near Danzig. A few weeks later she became part of a shipment of two hundred women sent to a camp which was about ninety minutes' march away from another AEG factory at Thorn (Torun). The conditions there were even worse than at Riga. The barracks were unheated, the food was inedible, and there was the long walk in the cold and darkness. As the Russian army approached, the women were herded out in the direction of a concentration camp at Bromberg (Bydgoszez), where they were finally abandoned to their fate.

Another major electrical concern whose former slaves demanded payment was the Telefunken company. Dr. Alfred Werner, a Jewish lawyer in Düsseldorf, filed a class-action suit, *Ellfers and 115 Others v. Telefunken,* just one day before what was generally regarded as the legal deadline set by German law.

Schildbach, acting on instructions from New York and armed only with the names of seven other claimants, asked the Telefunken attorneys whether they would be prepared to settle or at least agree to a six-month extension. Telefunken agreed to the extension for the seven cases, obviously believing there was little risk in accepting a slight delay. For the Claims Conference, the time gained was important since it was needed to gather the evidence to support a test case against the company.

The Berlin District Court *(Landgericht)* lost no time in throwing out all of the 116 claims against Telefunken that had been submitted by Dr. Werner. According to the judges, his complaint was procedurally defective because it had failed to itemize with sufficient particularity the individual damages which each of the plaintiffs had sustained.[8] Werner was outraged and embarrassed and said he would file an appeal.

Telefunken, having won the first round in the class action, waited until the extension they had granted to Schildbach was about to expire. They then informed him that the seven persons on his list could take their claims elsewhere. Said the company:

> During the war government agencies assigned workers to us—in addition to your clients—with whom we were not authorized to conclude any employment agreements and with whom no such agreements were made. No payment was due from us to these workers who were assigned to us. On the contrary we were obliged to pay the government agency which assigned such labor to us. If your clients believe that they are entitled to submit a claim may we suggest that they make such claims to the authorities competent to deal with it.[9]

Two days later Schildbach filed two new test cases against Telefunken. Rebecca F., the lead plaintiff, was born in 1931. When she was five years old her family fled to Holland. When the Germans overran Holland in 1943 the family was arrested, sent to a concentration camp at Vught in the Netherlands, and from there deported to Auschwitz, where Rebecca's parents were murdered because they were Jews. On June 12, 1944, when she was just thirteen years old, she was shipped to Reichenbach in Lower Silesia to work for Telefunken. Her co-plaintiff, Magda D., came to Auschwitz from Budapest in August 1944 and was also transferred to Reichenbach. She was then seventeen.

Their complaints alleged that upon arrival in the camp they were deprived of all their clothing and possessions, their hair was shorn, they were dressed in a pajama-like striped outergarment, given wooden shoes, and put to work for Telefunken twelve hours a day, seven days a week. They lived in overcrowded, lice-infested barracks. They suffered from mistreatment, beatings, hunger, and other inhumane working conditions. They were denied access to air-raid shelters. All of this, said the complaint, was known to the corporate directors, who were also familiar with, and accomplices to, the Nazi policy to exterminate all Jews. The plaintiffs cited the type of cursing to which the terrified girls were regularly subjected: "You damned Jews will finally understand what a Hitler-Germany means. Our Führer knows what he is doing and we are proud of him, that he will finally drive you Jews to your death. We Germans will finally get rid of you.''[10]

While the district court had the Schildbach cases under advisement, the Berlin Appellate Court, the *Kammergericht,* to which Werner had appealed the ruling against the 116 plaintiffs, handed down its decision. According to the court, it was not necessary to consider whether the complaint had been sufficiently precise, or whether it had been filed too late, since in the opinion of the appellate court, the action had really been commenced too soon. Telefunken was seen as merely an agency of the Reich and the slave labor claims were viewed as reparations that would have to be postponed until there was a final peace treaty with Germany.[11]

The claimants in the Ellfers case had taken a torpedo on one side with the district court's decision that the claims were filed too late, and a torpedo on the other side with the appellate court's decision that the claims were filed too soon. An appeal to the supreme court might provide a buoy to keep the claims afloat, at least for awhile, but the only hope to win the test cases handled by Schildbach was to find new evidence to prove that the German appellate court was wrong.

## Slaves Consigned Only on Demand

The position taken by the firms, and accepted without investigation by the Berlin appellate court, was that concentration camp inmates were assigned to work on armaments production and the companies had no choice or voice in the matter. The Claims Conference gradually assembled the evidence to show that the German firms were concealing the truth.

Lieutenant General Pohl, who was in charge of the Main Economic and Administrative Office—the WVHA—of the SS, provided a clear description:

This is how it worked. The enterprises would apply either to the camp commandant directly or to the office D II—it depended on their connections and on their situation. The camp commandant then had to visit the enterprise and discuss with the manager questions of billeting, feeding, and medical welfare of the laborers. In this respect he had to report to the office D II; office D II then would discuss these applications with the armament ministry and would receive a certificate confirming the necessity of the particular allocation. The applications having thus been prepared, Gluecks usually accompanied by Maurer, would see me about once a week, submit the applications to me, and I approved them. Only then would the camp commandant, through office D II, receive the order to furnish the inmates.[12]

Col. Gerhard Maurer was in charge of Department D II, which had to act on the applications for inmates submitted by the German firms. His sworn statement said:

The incoming post came to Glücks on arrival. Insofar as incoming mail concerned the labor allocation, it was given to D II where it was submitted to me by Sommer . . . Glücks and I went to Pohl on an average once a week for the purpose of discussing the current applications for assignment of prisoners . . . Pohl gave instructions that all applications for the assignment of prisoners had to be submitted to him for personal decision . . . Sommer was a specialized official for the labor allocation of prisoners in office D II . . . After me Sommer was the highest ranking SS leader in office D II . . . (He) received requests for allocation of prisoners in my absence.[13]

Captain *(Hauptsturmführer)* Karl Sommer joined the SS in January 1934 when he was barely nineteen. The responsibility acquired by the spring of 1944 attested to his dedication and ability. When asked to describe the official procedure for obtaining inmates, Sommer testified:

Originally, that is up to May or June 1944, the procedure which was followed was about the following: If any firm needed any inmates, it would write to the commander of a concentration camp or it would write to office D II in the WVHA. There it would request that these inmates should be furnished. If the commander of a concentration camp received such a request, then without having worked on it and without any notification to the firm, he had to pass it on to office D II. Whenever inmates were available, then the chief of office D II Maurer, personally went to see the firm. He would call the competent camp commander for a conference, and then he would discuss with that firm the intended assignment of inmates. He told the firm under what prerequisites inmates would be furnished for labor assignment. If the firm was ready and able to meet the necessary prerequisites—that is to say, to prepare security measures, accommodations, and so on—then Maurer would return to Berlin. He made a report then to Pohl. If Pohl agreed to this assignment of inmates, then the camp commander would receive the appropriate order. The firm was notified, and then it had to make the necessary preparations. As soon as the preparations had been completed, the inmates were furnished for labor. In the meantime the firm had to make the formal application.[14]

After May or June 1944, said Sommer, the Speer ministry would first have to confirm the priority of the request.[15]

Thus the three persons who must have known best—Pohl, Maurer, and Sommer—swore that concentration camp inmates could only be obtained by a German firm when and if it submitted a formal application requesting such labor and when the company established to the satisfaction of the SS that it was able to meet the SS requirements for security to avoid escape of the inmates.

Sommer's memory for details and his knowledge about every aspect of concentration camp labor had impressed the Nuremberg judges. Sommer had visited all the concentration camps and knew of the allocation of between 500,000 and 600,000 inmates which had been requested by various industries. The judges were also convinced that Sommer "was thoroughly familiar with the program for the annihilation of the Jews at Auschwitz."[16] The commander of Sachsenhausen, Anton Kaindl (affidavit reproduced in appendix 4), swore that Sommer was the best informed man about the overall picture regarding the employment of concentration camp inmates and that "all plants, employing concentration camp internees, applied to Division D for their assignment, and then I was charged by this agency which was my superior authority, to supply the manpower, as far as available, to the applying plants."[17]

Commandant Pister of Buchenwald confirmed the same procedures when he described how he had gone to Essen to see whether Krupp would qualify to receive the girls from Buchenwald.[18] Auschwitz commandant Höss (affidavit reproduced in appendix 3) corroborated the testimony of his Buchenwald counterpart: "The concentration camps have at no time offered labor to the industry. On the contrary, prisoners were sent to enterprises only after the enterprises had made a request for concentration camp prisoners. In their letters of request the enterprise had to state in detail which measures had been taken by them, even before the arrival of the prisoners, to guard them, etc. I visited officially many such establishments to verify such statements and this was always before the inmates would be sent."[19]

The statements made after the war by Pohl, Maurer, Sommer, Kaindl, Pister and Höss were sworn to at different times in different places and before different witnesses. The veracity and accuracy of their declarations was authenticated by official correspondence exchanged between the Nazis themselves while Hitler was still in power. On August 29, 1942, Maurer had issued an order (reproduced in appendix 1) to all of the concentration camp commanders, reminding them that no inmates could be assigned to a German firm without his permission and that a personally signed application was essential, together with an exact description of the number of guards who would be assigned, by the applicant, to prevent the escape of the prisoners.[20]

Albert Speer, Reich Minister for Armaments and War Production, issued an order in October 1944:

Subject: Requests for allocation and employment of concentration camp inmates.

. . . Newly received applications will be examined in collaboration with the Plenipotentiary General for the Allocation of Labor as to their justification and urgency, and will be forwarded to the SS Economic and Administrative Main Office by courier. Subsequently, the SS Economic and Administrative Main Office will send a representative to the applicants to examine conditions with a view to separate employment and escape-proof housing. Given these conditions, the requested labor will be allocated, subject to availability.

To ensure orderly proceedings and speedier completion, it is not permissible under any circumstances to communicate direct with the SS offices.[21]

Nowhere in the testimony of Pohl, Maurer, Sommer, Kaindl, Höss, nor in the 1942 order of Maurer, nor in the 1944 directive of Speer, was there any indication whatsoever that concentration camp inmates could be assigned to any company without the company's prior knowledge or consent. On the contrary, there was unanimous confirmation that it was quite impossible to get concentration camp labor without the company's specific request. The contention by German firms that these inmates were assigned to them or that they were coerced into using them was simply untrue.

Before any further settlements could be broached to any German employers of slave labor, it would be necessary to know which firms used which Jewish inmates and in which camps. Captain Sommer was the man who had most of the answers and he named names in a nine-page sworn statement (extracts in appendix 2) that listed close to two hundred German companies which had taken over half-a-million inmates from over a dozen different concentration camps.[22] Some of Germany's most prestigious firms were on the list, including the automobile manufacturers BMW, Volkswagen, Auto-Union, and Daimler-Benz.

The Sommer statement was obtained by an American investigator named Alfred Booth, an intellectual who had been forced to flee from Hitler Germany because of his anti-Nazi views. Educated as an economist, Booth had suffered a great deal before escaping to the United States, where he earned his living as a bricklayer until he could return to Germany after the war. He knew German industry and he knew Germans, and being an excellent interrogator, he was assigned to the war crimes research staff in Berlin. He confronted Karl Sommer with a batch of documents to make sure that Sommer's memory would not falter. That was in October 1946.

Several weeks thereafter, on a cold Sunday morning in Berlin, I received a phone call from the United States consul in Bern informing me, as head of the office, that my friend Alfred Booth was dying of cancer in a Swiss hospital and that his only hope was an immediate operation by Germany's most famous surgeon, Dr. Ferdinand Sauerbruch. Professor Sauerbruch was at that time operating in Luckenwalde, about 25 kilometers outside of Berlin in Soviet-occupied East Germany. The Swiss consul, whose permission would be needed for an entry visa to Switzerland, was skiing in Berlin's Grunewald Park. He was located and transported to his office, skis and all, to pick up his official seals. Sauerbruch was persuaded to return to Berlin immediately, and United States Army bulldozers were sent out to start clearing the snow from the highway. A Woman's Auxilliary Corps sergeant, on duty alone at the United States Air Force base in Wiesbaden, took it upon herself to release a rescue plane. The eminent German surgeon was brought in and, riding in the back seat of a United States military sedan, was whisked past the noses of saluting Russian guards standing at attention at the Charité Hospital in East Berlin. At the Templehof airport an American pilot was warming the engines and getting ready to fly through a snowstorm to deliver the German doctor to the Bircher-Benner Clinic in Zurich. The plane arrived in Switzerland within hours of the time I received the phone call in Berlin, but the all-out effort to save Alfred Booth's life was in vain.

One of Booth's last official acts had been his interrogation of Karl Sommer. The precious 1946 affidavit, uncovered again in 1960, seemed to be Alfred's way of saying "thank you" for that desperate attempt to save his life.

## The Secret Settlement with AEG and Telefunken

The time had come to talk to Germany's renowned electrical concern. After the test cases had been started against both AEG and Telefunken, we learned that in 1941 the Telefunken company had been acquired by AEG, and AEG's management could therefore speak for both firms. The main operational headquarters of AEG was located in a large new building in Frankfurt overlooking the river Main. At 10 a.m. on March 25, 1960, with the I.G. Farben agreement well on its way to being implemented and the agreement with Alfried Krupp safely signed, Ernst Katzenstein paid a visit to the AEG *Hochhaus*.[23]

AEG chairman Dr. Hans C. Boden was aided by his legal advisor Dr. Hellenbroich. Boden had been a Rhodes Scholar at Oxford and had served with the German diplomatic missions dealing with reparations after World War I. He had joined AEG in 1929 and had become a board member shortly thereafter. He had a reputation as an anti-Nazi, a diplomat, and a man who did not like to say no.[24]

After a cordial greeting, Boden lost no time in mentioning that in the spring of 1944 the Nazis had removed him from the board of AEG. During his tenure, he said, he had given instructions that as a matter of principle the company was not to employ concentration camp inmates. He conceded that his instructions were not always followed regarding plants in the oocupied territories, and that in those days Telefunken exercised a great deal of independence and could not be effectively controlled by its parent body. Boden expressed apprehension that a payment by AEG might be an acknowledgment of culpability, which would be detrimental not only to AEG but also to the reputation of German industry generally. According to his legal advisor Hellen-broich, AEG could not have employed more than 750 Jewish slave laborers at most.[25]

Hellenbroich, repeating the denials voiced by other German firms, was an adversary not to be taken lightly. He did not hesitate to go over Katzenstein's head to meet the Claims Conference president, Nahum Goldmann, in Zurich. There, Hellenbroich conceeded that a payment of one million marks was being considered by AEG. When Goldmann ridiculed that figure, Hellenbroich asked the conference president what he had in mind. Goldmann, never a man for details and apparently unmindful that Katzenstein had been advised to ask for DM 10 million, replied that the conference was thinking of about DM 5 million, or DM 6 million.[26]

At Katzenstein's next meeting with AEG, Hellenbroich continued to insist that the number of camp inmates who had been employed was insignificant and he reiterated all of the standard arguments to avoid a payment. Katzenstein handed over a list of 1,200 former inmates who had worked for AEG or Telefunken and drew attention to the fact that many more could be expected once a settlement was announced. Hellenbroich interjected that the DM 6 million which the Claims Conference hoped to receive was out of the question and demanded that the lists specify the camp in which each person was employed.[27]

Complying with AEG's request was not as simple as it sounded. Over a hundred persons, for example, writing independently from different parts of the world, swore that they had worked for AEG at "Ankers," yet that name did not appear on any map of the region and AEG absolutely denied that it had ever had a plant at such a location. The number of claimants was too large for the conference to dismiss the claims as fictitious, and after close interrogation of claimants, the mystery was unraveled. "Ankers" was neither a town nor a factory but was the German name for a part of a machine—a belt or *Anker*— which was being manufactured by AEG in Riga. The workers only knew that they worked at "Ankers," without knowing that it was a thing, not a place.

When Katzenstein next walked into the AEG building to resume negotiations, he decided to take the bull by the horns. After some heated skirmishing, he declared in exasperation that the Claims Conference, composed of leading Jewish organizations, could not be accused of fabricating lists of claimants or making unfounded demands. He called upon Boden to declare unequivocally whether he was prepared to settle the problem or not, and if so, on what basis. Somewhat to Katzenstein's surprise, Boden replied that he was prepared to pay DM 2 million at once. Katzenstein responded by assembling his papers and remarking that Boden had obviously failed to grasp the historical significance of the occasion. Before Katzenstein could leave the room, Boden, the diplomat, detained him. He was willing, he said, to increase his offer by another DM 2 million. Boden said firmly, however, that he could not possibly go beyond DM 4 million and even then certain conditions had to be met. He wanted no publicity whatsoever to the agreement, and he wanted the final answer from the Claims Conference within ten days.[28]

Katzenstein had been favorably impressed by what he perceived to be Boden's "inner readiness to come to an agreement." The sum offered came to a million dollars, an amount which, Katzenstein wrote, "could hardly be tossed to the winds if it is to provide some consolation for the poor victims of forced labor."[29] He was quite right, but no one knew at that time how many hungry mouths would have to share that modest sum. It might turn out to be quite inadequate. Furthermore, the acceptance of an insufficient payment might have an adverse impact on possible future settlements with other firms. If the Claims Conference accepted a payment that was very low, other firms might offer even less. If, on the other hand, the conference rejected the money and AEG got off free without feeling any adverse impact, other German firms would be encouraged to reject all of the slave labor demands.

The member organizations were polled, and it was the general consensus of the Claims Conference board that the AEG offer could not be turned down. "For the first time," reported Katzenstein, "Hellenbroich was very pleasant on the phone."[30] Nonetheless, AEG's lawyer did not fail to insist that certain conditions be met before the deal could be closed.

The agreement which was finally hammered out consisted of a simple exchange of letters. AEG, without recognizing any legal liability and without prejudice to any other German firms, was to pay DM 4 million "to ameliorate the suffering" of those Jewish concentration camp inmates who had been employed in factories of AEG or Telfunken. The Claims Conference guaranteed that the companies and their agents would be free of all further liability to Jewish inmates or their heirs. The conference was not obliged to render any accounting, no press release was to be issued, and the claimants were to keep the payments confidential. In order to alert the potential beneficiaries without disclosing the name of any AEG company, the conference was to publish an announcement calling upon all those who had performed slave labor for *any* German firm to submit an application.[31] The attempt to camouflage the AEG settlement by a public proclamation calling upon all Jewish slave laborers to make themselves known was like inviting bees to come to the honey. But that was only discovered later.

As soon as the agreement was signed, AEG remitted DM 4 million to the conference account with the Warburg bank and booked the item under "general expenses."[32] All the Claims Conference had to do was to see to it that all of the pending lawsuits were withdrawn, issue the general call-up, locate the beneficiaries wherever in the world they might be, verify the validity of their claims, divide the money among those entitled under the restrictive terms of the contract, and hope for the best.

Close to four thousand persons finally submitted claims for participation in the AEG/Telefunken fund. An effort was made to persuade Boden to increase the DM 4 million settlement sum, but Boden had reached retirement age and was leaving the company.[33] Katzenstein felt that there would be no purpose in trying to convince the legal advisor, Hellenbroich, who had been against the settlement in the first place.[34]

Just as in the Krupp case, the only way to deal with the problem of insufficient funds was to adopt the most restrictive rules before approving any claims. If the applicant could not show that as a concentration camp inmate he or she had worked in a factory of AEG or Telefunken, the claim was rejected. Those who did not work on the production line—such as clerical workers or kitchen help—were excluded. Those who worked on jobs where AEG was only a subcontractor were ineligible. A cutoff date was set. No hardship cases could be considered. There could be no appeals. There just was not enough money to go around.[35]

A total of 2,223 claims against the AEG/Telefunken companies was finally validated. Each award was for $500. Latecomers received only $375. The total amount paid out by Compensation Treuhand, including interest, amounted to DM 4,312,500 (see appendix 5). Of some 1,500 women who had worked at Riga/Kaiserwald, only 531 could be found. One hundred seventy-five survivors of AEG's Cable Works at Cracow/Plaszow were among the beneficiaries, as were 106 women who had been in Ravensbrück and had worked for AEG in Freiburg in Lower Silesia. Of the Gross Rosen inmates, 444 who had worked at Parschnitz were paid, 374 from the *Frieserwerke* at Weisswasser were located, and 515 who had been employed by Telefunken at the Sport School in Reichenbach received awards. Grants were given to smaller numbers from the concentration camps at Stutthof, Natzweiler, and Sachsenhausen.

Of the beneficiaries, 885 lived in Israel, 456 in the United States, 300 in Hungary, and nearly 200 in Holland. Survivors in Canada, Czechoslovakia, and twenty-nine other countries, from New Zealand to Brazil, all received their meager dole.[36] Five hundred dollars surely was not much, but at least it was a sign that somewhere somebody cared enough to insist upon a token payment for the scattered remnant of the Jews who had labored without wages in AEG or Telefunken factories. Those who had been forced to work for a much larger German electrical company—Siemens—would be next in line.

## Siemens Pays

The second largest electrical concern in the world is Siemens of Germany, which is made up of a multitude of companies.[37] The parent body Siemens & Halske (SH) was incorporated in Berlin but had its operational headquarters in Munich. The most important subsidiary was Siemens-Schuckert A.G., also known as the Siemens-Schuckert Werke (SSW), which operated out of Erlangen. Another major subsidiary, the Siemens-Bauunion GmbH (SBU) was also based in Munich. These were only a few of the leading branches of the vast electrical combine.

If Siemens had felt any strong compulsion to pay the former camp inmates, it could have taken the initiative to locate them. The company did not do so; on the contrary, the few individuals who had turned to the firm with a request for compensation had all been turned down cold.[38]

In January 1946 Hermann von Siemens gave his account of the use of slave labor by the Siemens company. He acknowedged that prisoners of the concentration camps at Oranienburg and Buchenwald did work in shops put at the company's disposal by the camp administration, but he could not recall how many persons were involved. He expressed the view that the prisoners welcomed the opportunity to work, and he was not aware of any undernourishment or ill treatment. He also mentioned that the Berlin Jewish women who worked for the company adapted themselves very well, and the company had protested when they were taken away by the Gestapo.[39]

This version was reiterated in the *History of the House of Siemens,* which was published after the war, by the company itself:

On the whole about 2000 Jews were employed during the first years
of the war and the firm as well as the Jews themselves believed
that it would remain so until the end of the war. But at the end of
January 1943 the Secret State Police started to remove all the Jews
from the Berlin factories and to transport them elsewhere. The
members of the Board of Siemens were horrified at these measures
for they knew what it meant for the victims. A member of the

Board of Directors went into the lion's den, in this case the Office of a first squad leader of the SS, and succeeded by urgently remonstrating with him and painting a picture of the collapse of vital war production, in obtaining authorization for the firm to keep the Jews for the time being. They could breathe again, but not for long, as four weeks later, just as work had started for the morning, a column of lorries appeared in front of the factories, police brought the Jews out and loaded them on the lorries and before anyone had time to do anything to stop them, the lorries and the victims were gone.[40]

Not a word appeared in the official company history about Auschwitz, Flossenberg, Sachsenhausen, Buchenwald, Gross Rosen, Ravensbrück, or Mauthausen. It was as if Siemens had nothing whatsoever to do with those dreaded camps. The evidence later uncovered as a result of the intensive searches by the Claims Conference and the reports of the survivors painted quite a different picture.

Auschwitz commandant Höss swore that he provided 1,200 females to Siemens in 1943 and about 1,500 in 1944. They bore tatoo numbers between 150000 and 200000 and worked in a former fertilizer factory which had been altered for the manufacture of electrical switches for aircraft. It was known as the *Kleinbauwerk* since it replaced the original SSW *Kleinbauwerk* that had been bombed out in September and November 1943. Some called it Bobrek, the name of the town 8 kilometers from Auschwitz.[41] When Göring complained to Himmler that not enough concentration camp inmates were being used for aircraft production, Himmler referred to Siemen's work at Auschwitz.[42]

Five hundred and fifty Jewish women, bearing tatoo numbers 55740 to 56290, were sent to Flossenberg concentration camp and from there were shipped to the Siemens factory in Nuremberg. The original invoices were found, showing that Siemens was charged RM 4 per day and received a credit of 65 pfennig per prisoner for having provided the food.[43]

Twelve hundred female prisoners had been taken from Sachsenhausen to work at the Werner Works in Siemenstadt Berlin,[44] and when the Werner Works was bombed out, Siemens transferred the operation to Buchenwald. Transport lists found in the archives of the International Tracing Service showed the identity of other inmates from Buchenwald who worked for Siemens at Neustadt bei Coburg in Bavaria. Another list showed the Gross Rosen inmates who had worked for Siemens at Christianstadt in Brandenburg. A letter was found which SS Lieutenant General Pohl had sent to Himmler on October 20, 1942, in which Pohl assured Himmler that the Siemens company was building new barracks at Ravensbrück to house 2,500 female inmates who would work on telecommunications equipment for the army.[45]

The Siemens-Bauunion was one of several companies building an underground factory for armaments production with the help of about eight thousand inmates from the Ebensee subcamp of Mauthausen. Women from Gross Rosen helped to dig trenches for SBU at Ober Altstadt, in the district of Trautenau. Large numbers of Jews were working for SBU in Cracow/Plaszow in Poland and in copper mines at a place called Bor, in Yugoslavia.[46]

It was learned that Siemens had prepared a special report shortly after the war in which the company had presumably described its use of concentration camp inmates. A search of libraries and archives throughout the world failed to produce the illusive record. The official Siemens archivist confirmed that such a report was on hand, but he refused to make it available on the grounds that it was an internal company matter.[47] Even the initial information assembled by the Claims Conference showed that Siemens' involvement with the concentration camps was massive. Despite the absence of a pending lawsuit, and despite the refusal by Siemens' legal department to consider any payment,[48] the Claims Conference decided to place the facts before the top men in the Siemens concern.

Adolf Lohse had never joined the Nazi party. He was on the board of both Siemens & Halske and Siemens-Schuckert and was a key figure in the company. When Ernst Katzenstein wrote for an appointment, he was referred, weeks later, to the head of the legal department, Dr. Walther Bottermann.[49] They agreed to meet at the Siemens building on the Wittelsbacher Platz in Munich.

Katzenstein began, as he had done with AEG, in a friendly vein by acknowledging the outstanding reputation of the Siemens company. He expressed the hope that an agreement could provide DM 5,000 for each surviving Jewish inmate who had worked without wages for a Siemens company and suggested that, following the pattern of the agreement with Krupp, an amount of DM 6 million be paid as a first installment to be followed, if necessary, by an additional payment of up to DM 4 million.

Bottermann responded in an equally friendly way and expressed surprise that the conference had even approached Siemens with the suggestion that any payment should be made. It was his contention that Siemens had employed very few camp inmates and the company had behaved well under the circumstances. Katzenstein had been well briefed, and when he presented evidence that the Siemens lawyer was badly mistaken, Bottermann beat a hasty retreat, explaining that he would have to verify the facts.[50]

At that particular time the trial against Adolf Eichmann was in full swing in Jerusalem and the press was replete with reminders of the Nazi crimes against the Jews. The Siemens company was planning to expand a subsidiary in New York to handle sales and services through-out the United States.[51] It may have occurred to some of the corporate representatives that an agreement with the New York Jewish organizations could do no harm and it might be good insurance. Rattling the skeletons in the corporate closet might be bad for business.

When the date for the next negotiation with Siemens arrived, both Saul Kagan and I happened to be in Europe and we joined the Munich meeting. Bottermann insisted that Siemens could not be compared with Farben or Krupp and that Siemens had been forced to employ concentration camp inmates. After the usual debate, with both sides making arguments that had almost become standardized, the Siemens lawyers were ready to make an offer. They said they could recommend a payment of DM 2 million. That was promptly rejected.[52]

Before the next meeting could be arranged there was a stroke of good luck which would have an important impact on the negotiations. For some time the Claims Conference had been trying to obtain the special report on camp labor which the Siemens archivist had refused to surrender. Katzenstein had asked for it during his first meeting with the Siemens lawyers, but they too had gone deaf and dumb in response to his request.[53] After a very intensive search, a copy of the document being hidden by Siemens was found. It was a forty-three-page report, dated October 31, 1945, entitled *Einsatz ausländischer Zivilarbeiter, Kriegsgefangener, Juden und KZ-Häftlinge im Hauses Siemens (The Use of Foreign Civilian Workers, Prisoners of War, Jews, and Concentration Camp Inmates in the House of Siemens)*. Although it was written by Siemens officials in order to exculpate the Siemens company, it contained a great deal of information that confirmed and supplemented what was known by the Claims Conference. It also refuted some important arguments made by the lawyers for Siemens, and its omissions were as impressive as its concessions. The Siemens report itself showed clearly that 3,900 concentration camp inmates were employed by the two principle Siemens companies—almost double the amount that Bottermann said was the maximum. At the next meeting, the Siemens lawyers would be in for a surprise.

However, it was not the objective of the Claims Conference to embarrass Siemens by unpleasant surprises but to induce the company to make a payment for the benefit of the surviving slaves. It was therefore considered advisable to "leak" the information to the Siemens people in advance of the next meeting. Eric Warburg was again called upon to play a middle-man's role. He was provided with copies of the leading documents, and he then arranged to meet with Siemen's director, Lohse, and his legal advisers.[54]

The gentlemen from Siemens were surprised and, according to Warburg, impressed with the fact that the Claims Conference had come into possession of the internal Siemens report.[55] Warburg hinted that the conference was also in possession of other documentary proof to support its contentions. Skillfully playing his role as an honest broker between two disputing factions, Warburg suggested that the conference might be persuaded to lower its demand from a maximum of DM 10 million to DM 8 million.[56] There was still a big gap between that and the DM 2 million offered as a possible payment by Siemens.

At the next meeting various drafts were considered and, after considerable debate, Bottermann increased the Siemens offer to DM 3 million. When Katzenstein turned it down, the offer went up to DM 4 million, which was also rejected. Having doubled the initial tender, the Siemens lawyers felt they had to go back for further instructions.[57]

A few months went by before the parties could meet again. This time, Bottermann increased the offer to DM 6 million. After further debate, Siemens put forth its final offer. The Claims Conference could have either a fixed sum of DM 6 million or an initial payment of DM 5 million which would be increased to DM 7 million if the number of claims warranted the increase.[58] There was no shortage of claimants, and it should have been clear which figure the conference would ultimately accept.

After several more drafts and counterdrafts were exchanged, the final meeting with the Siemens lawyers to draw up the contract was set. It lasted four hours and was most disagreeable. Bottermann reflected his conviction that his company had undertaken a completely voluntary and generous payment and was being confronted with demands and conditions by ungrateful representatives of the Jewish organizations. One point, of little substantive significance, reflected the atmosphere and attitudes. The Siemens draft contained an opening phrase to the effect that Siemens was making a payment without recognizing "any legal *or moral* obligation." I could understand and accept the exclusion of legal liability, but the exclusion of *moral* liability disturbed me. It seemed to be casting aside even a small sense of responsibility for what had happened to the Jews. Bottermann insisted that the phrase be retained. I asked, indignantly, why they were making the settlement at all if there was neither a legal nor a moral obligation. There was no answer. I suggested that if they were acting only under duress by the Jewish organizations, they should put *that* into the contract so the public would know what had motivated the payment. That too was refused. The Siemens lawyers insisted that the company could not avoid the employment of concentration camp inmates and had done everything in its power to alleviate the suffering of the slave laborers. The payment, they explained, was based on "moral contemplations" but not "moral obligations."[59]

The haggling and haranguing finally ended. The contract which was signed followed the general outline of the agreement with Krupp. It began with Siemens & Halske's declarations of readiness, without recognizing a "legal *or a moral* obligation," to make a payment to ameliorate the suffering endured by Jewish concentration camp inmates "as a result of National Socialist duress" while working for Siemens or its subsidiaries. Claimants could receive up to DM 5,000 ($1,250). Siemens agreed to pay an initial sum of DM 5 million (the equivalent of $1,250,000), but if this was not sufficient to provide each qualified applicant with DM 5,000, SH would add up to DM 2 million ($500,000) more. An auditor, who was to be mutually designated, would have to confirm that the petitions had been properly approved. The Claims Conference guaranteed that it would save Siemens and all of its agents forever harmless from all claims which might be brought by Jewish concentration camp inmates or their heirs in connection with forced labor for any of the Siemens companies.[60]

## Finding the Survivors

Almost 6,000 former camp inmates submitted claims against Siemens, but only about one-third could qualify for payment under the restrictive terms of the contract. They had worked for Siemens' firms in nearly a dozen different locations attached to half a dozen concentration camps.[61] The claims could be validated easily where a transport list had been located and could be compared with the application, but that was the exception rather than the rule. Three out of every five of the Jewish women who were on the transport list from Flossenberg to Siemens in Nuremberg survived the war and received a grant. Of the 500 Jewish girls listed who went from Buchenwald to work for Siemens at Neustadt bei Coburg, 333 were also paid. When there were no lists, the claimants had to prove eligibility by being familiar with the details of a particular camp and work done there.

A few descriptions will illustrate the nature of the facts assembled to serve as a guide in verifying the validity of the claims. It was learned, for example, that while the Siemens *Kleinbauwerk* at Bobrek was being readied for production, gangs of women were marched out of Auschwitz each day to do some of the dirty work. After Siemens engineer Bundzius chose several hundred Jewish machinists to work on the lathes and cutting machines, a small group were transferred to Bobrek to serve as helpers and charwomen. They were housed on the first floor of a stone building. Most of them were Polish Jews; of the four Czech Jews, one, Hanna S., was a *Kapo,* one of the inmates used by the SS to supervise the others, and another, nicknamed Anushka, did clerical work. Two of the four French Jewish women had been subjected to medical experiments in Auschwitz, and the other two were mother and daughter; the mother perished. The details of the work and an exact description of the camp grounds were provided by some of the survivors.[62] Less than half of the known Auschwitz workers ever appeared to make a claim.

The Sachsenhausen concentration camp provided inmates to firms in the Berlin area. In December 1944 a number of Hungarian Jews were taken by Siemens to a small camp at Haselhorst. The names of the Siemens engineers and foremen were known, as well as those of several of the *Kapos,* including one about twenty-four years of age known as Gypsy Franz the Rib Breaker. On March 28, 1945, the Haselhorst camp was bombed out and a number of prisoners and thirty-seven SS men were killed. The SS men were buried in the cemetery at Spandau; the inmates were sent back to Sachsenhausen.[63] Only a few survivors filed claims.

In the summer of 1944 a transport of Jewish women from the Polish town of Radom arrived at Auschwitz. Those who were not selected for the gas chambers were tatooed with numbers beginning with A24000. A Siemens foreman named Brandt came to Auschwitz and selected one hundred of these women to be transported to Ober Altstadt, where there was a subcamp of Gross Rosen. They were housed in one large wooden building and quartered about twenty-five women to a room. The Radomer Transport worked at the Siemens factory at Jungbuch, about an hour's march away. The SS guards were Frau Hoffman and Frau Biedermans. When the group was liberated by the Russians, many of the Jewish women returned to Radom to search for what was left of their families. Finding few survivors and encountering the hostility of their Polish neighbors of Kielce, they took refuge, like so many others, in the displaced-persons camps of Germany until they could find their way to Israel or other countries that would receive them. It was only when the story was pieced together from survivors in several countries that the claims of eighty-nine women of Radom who had worked for Siemens could be verified and honored.[64]

Ebensee is one of those beautiful little towns in Austria where tiny lakes lie cradled among the alpine mountains. It was also the location of a murderous camp attached to the main concentration camp of Mauthausen near Linz on the Danube. The hills and quarries were most suitable for the excavation of massive underground tunnels that could shelter German armaments industries from the incessant raids of Allied bombers. Siemens-Bauunion was constructing an underground factory near the railroad station Ebensee-Fingerleiten. The camp from which its workers came was about 200 meters from the tunnel entrance, where three to four hundred inmates wielded picks and shovels under SBU direction, but SBU was only one of about seventeen other building firms engaged in similar work in the area.[65]

The only lists of Ebensee/Mauthausen inmates which could be found were twenty-five folders of death registers and another list of the thousands of prisoners who had been in the camp when it was liberated by the United States Third Army. I had last seen the lists when I was a war crimes investigator working in the liberated Ebensee camp before the end of the war, but at that time no one thought to ask each ragged survivor for the name of the particular company under whose direction he was being worked to death. Even if the claimant against Siemens could be found on the Ebensee list, he still had to prove that he had worked for Siemens before his claim could be approved. Only seventy-four Ebensee survivors qualified for payment.

By September 1942 Siemens had a large factory in operation at Ravensbrück, consisting of at least twenty barracks or work halls fully equipped with machines for producing spare parts, microphones, relays, condensors, and other types of electrical equipment. It was located a short distance away from the main camp. Over two thousand prisoners were put to work on the Siemens machines. The first large transport of Jewish women arrived at Ravensbrück in September 1943. They came from Auschwitz, which meant that they qualified to survive as long as they were physically able to work for the country that was determined to annihilate them. The first transport was known as ''privileged Jews,'' since they came from large German cities and their deportation had been postponed, as discussed during Eichmann's Wannsee conference, because they were either of mixed lineage or had been married to Aryan husbands. In October another Jewish transport arrived and still another in December, which included Turkish and Spanish Jews who, since their countries were allied with Germany, were even allowed to bring their children with them. During 1944 more Jewish transports were received in Ravensbrück, including women who had managed to hide in Berlin. A large transport came from Auschwitz at the end of 1944 as that camp was being evacuated.[66]

The women of Ravensbrück had to undergo an aptitude test before being selected for work by Siemens. Their vision was tested by requiring them to read small print. To test the dexterity of their fingers, they had to bend a wire with a pliers and cut a paper into a specified pattern. The Siemens self-serving special report of 1945 described the working conditions in the various Siemens shops as being ideal, and also mentioned that the children were given light jobs as apprentices. Children were housed in a youth protection camp *(Jugendschutzlager)* at Uckermark right outside the concentration camp. The report alleged that about one hundred of the so-called apprentices worked for Siemens, and in some cases of good behavior the children could even be set free.[67] When the Claims Conference examiners began to screen the claims against Siemens for work at Ravensbrück no mention was found of that "youth protection camp" at Uckermark. Nor was it ever mentioned by any of the Siemens lawyers. All that could be uncovered was a reference in the International Tracing Service List of Camps which said that Uckermark had existed from January to April 1945 and that a portion of it was used as a *Vernichtungslager* to kill the women of Ravensbrück.[68] Only 350 Jewish women could be found who had survived their work for Siemens at Ravensbrück.

Cracow, one of the oldest and largest cities of Poland, sits astride the main railroad lines and was renowned as a trading center as well as a fountain of cultural and intellectual life. It was occupied by the Germans in 1939 and became the headquarters for the German army command, which preserved most of its ancient Romanesque and Gothic cathedrals and castles. The Vistula River, which the Germans call the Weichsel, winds around the city and joins the Sola at Auschwitz. It is an area of forests and streams which block the route from Germany into the Soviet Union. The German army needed to prepare the terrain for the *Blitzkrieg* of its tanks *(Panzers)* and their supply routes.

Around April 1942 Siemens-Bauunion undertook to build a railroad detour around the city and to erect at least seventeen bridges over the Vistula. By that time, all of the Jews from the surrounding region who were still alive had been impressed for forced labor. Some of them were assembled on Jewish cemeteries and forced to use sacred tombstones as building materials.[69] A camp exclusively for Jews (*Judenlager* or JULAG,) existed in a ghetto district called Plaszow. It was crowded with Jews from the adjoining villages, and Germans could come and pick up batches of the terrified captives for work in German military installations or other war-related activities.[70] Some of the men were put to work for SBU, until typhus broke out in the camp in the spring of 1943.[71] The governor general, Hans Frank, in a speech to a Nazi audience in Cracow on August 2, 1943, said: "We began here with 3-1/2 million Jews. Now only a few work companies are left. All of the others have—let us say—emigrated."[72] In one of his many pep talks to the German police units, Frank told them that it was laughable to argue about methods. The main thing was that they had carried out the difficult and unpleasant duty imposed by Hitler to assure the *Entjudung*, the "De-Judification" of Europe.[73] It was surprising that almost three hundred Jews who had worked for Siemens at Cracow could be found alive and their claims approved.

Another place where Jews faced *Vernichtung durch Arbeit*—destruction through work—was at Bor, in Yugoslavia. When that country was crushed in 1941, Germany retained control over the copper and coal mining districts of old Serbia. The Organization Todt was in charge of operating the copper mines to provide Germany with 50 percent of its copper needs. By 1943, with the German army stalled at

Stalingrad, the OT complained that they had only three thousand men available out of thirteen thousand needed. Reich Armaments Minister Speer, the OT, the Foreign Office, and the SS all agreed that it would be a good idea to take ten thousand Hungarian Jews, who were then in work battalions under guard of the Hungarian army, and put them to work in the mines.[74] The Hungarian government was less than enthusiastic, but under Nazi pressures, six thousand Hungarian Jews soon found themselves in the area of Bor not far from Belgrade. Hitler had explained to Adm. Miklos Horthy of Hungary on April 17, 1943, that Jews who refused to work should be shot and those who could not work should be eliminated in line with Hitler's overall view that all Jews were to be treated like contagious bacteria and wiped out.[75]

One of the Bor workers later confirmed that "about 6,000 men were dragged from Hungary to Bor where the forced laborers were sent to their death by SS and military units through inhuman tortures, starvation, horrible slave labor and killing through a shot in the back of the neck."[76] Another survivor, Istvan K. of Budapest, wrote that of the six thousand Hungarian Jews, only six hundred survived. "The main goal of the camp," he said, "was, if ever possible, to wear all the inmates out to destruction."[77]

Labor for the operations at Bor came from thirteen different camps. Each one had as a code the name of a German city. The largest camp was called Berlin. It was from here that Siemens-Bauunion drew its workers to carry out its assignments for the Organization Todt in partnership with another German construction firm. SBU undertook to build a drainage tunnel 3 kilometers long around the back of the mine, to build a dam against flooding, and to terrace the mountain in which the copper was located so as to allow strip mining of the valued metal. At least half a dozen other companies were responsible for the mining operations and for laying the tracks for the dump trucks. It was only by knowing the precise nature of his work that one could tell whether the claimant was employed by Siemens or some other company. Those who worked for SBU usually knew the names of the Siemens foremen or of Chief Engineer Tscheile.[78]

The Organization of Nazi Victims of Hungary petitioned Compensation Treuhand for consideration of the claims of nearly three hundred persons who had survived the grueling work at Bor.[79] There was no doubt that almost all of the Jews at Bor had been worked to death, but there was also no doubt that Bor was not a concentration camp within the classification of the Main Administrative Office of the SS and therefore the Bor workers did not qualify under the technical terms of the contract with Siemens. It was very much the same story as that of the Krupp workers who had built a bridge over the Bug River at Trichati in Transnistria in the winter of 1943. This time, however, Compensation Treuhand refused to exclude the Bor survivors. Siemens finally gave its necessary consent—after all, it was not going to cost Siemens anything if one group of Jews decided to share with another.

Siemens had paid DM 5 million but before the balance of DM 2 million would be made available, Siemens' legal department sent a team of auditors, of its own designation, to verify the validity of the awards and the fact that payments had actually been made. Under the contract, the auditors were to be designated by mutual consent, but the Claims Conference did not press the point. For five days the auditors asked questions and went through the files, journals, and financial statements of Compensation Treuhand. After a comprehensive examination, they issued a long report. They noted that Compensation Treuhand had its own internal audit as well as an independent audit through the firm of Loeb and Troper of Geneva and New York. In conclusion, they stated that all the proof had been shown to them and they were convinced that Compensation Treuhand's carrying out of the agreement with Siemens had been *sorgfältig und korreckt*—careful and correct.[80] After receiving the report of its own auditors confirming that DM 5 million had properly been paid out, the Siemens company transmitted the outstanding balance of DM 2 million.

Compensation Treuhand paid out, including accumulated interest, a total of DM 7,184,100. Among the claimants were 831 in Israel who received over DM 2,700,000; 474 claimants in Hungary, including the survivors of Bor, received over DM 1,500,000; and 371 claimants in the United States shared over DM 1,200,000. Czechoslovakian claimants divided close to half a million marks; claimants in Canada, Australia, Belgium, France, and West Germany all received over DM 100,000, while those in Yugoslavia, Austria, Sweden, and England received somewhat lesser sums. There were other awards to claimants in South Africa, Poland, Norway, Venezuela, Brazil, and other countries. All of them, dispersed like the wind around the globe, had one thing in common: they were all Jews who had toiled without pay for the Siemens company and had somehow managed to survive. For their services, their pain, and their suffering, they each received no more than DM 3,300—the equivalent of $825.[81]

# The Cannons of Rheinmetall

In the Name of the People

Mrs. Rachel B. of Brooklyn,
New York, Plaintiff,

against

Rheinmetall Berlin AG, Berlin,
Defendant

. . . Whether the specific armaments company went out of
its way to procure concentration camp prisoners is not
decisive since in every case the assignment—which
admittedly went beyond the permissible boundaries of
international law—was within the framework of the
governmentally-steered Armaments and War Planning
program . . . The substance of the complaint cannot now
be examined . . .

(Decision of the German Supreme Court, March 17,
1964)[1]

# CHAPTER 5

## Hanging On in the Courts

On the last day of December 1957 German attorney Karl-Heinz Schild-bach, acting on instructions from the Claims Conference, walked into the district court of Berlin-Charlottenberg and placed two cases on the docket. The plaintiffs were Helen R. and Rachel B., two Jewish women from New York. The defendant was the munitions firm of Rheinmetall Berlin A.G., the second largest armaments producer for the Third Reich.

The Rheinmetall company had been founded in 1889. After the Nazi rise to power, it had merged with another firm to become Rheinmetall-Borsig A.G. The parent company in Berlin was a holding company for a large number of armaments firms spread throughout the Reich, including plants in Berlin, Düsseldorf, and Unterlüss in the west, and Hundsfeld and Sömmerda in the east. In 1950, with many of its plants destroyed or dismantled, the firm was reorganized and the name changed to Rheinmetall Berlin A.G. By 1957 it was back in operation in the Ruhr with half of its production again devoted to armaments.[2]

The complaints of Helen and Rachel set forth that between July 1944 and March 1945, while they were inmates of a concentration camp, they had both been employed against their will by the Rheinmetall company at a place called Sömmerda, not far from Buchenwald. They had been forced to work twelve hours a day, seven days a week, without compensation of any kind. They suffered from hunger and exposure. They worked on drilling machines in the manufacture of shells for bombs and artillery and were subjected to inhuman mistreatment including beatings with sticks and rubber truncheons and kicks with hobnailed shoes. It was their contention that the Rheinmetall directors were aware of the plan to exterminate the Jews and supported the Nazi policy by showing no consideration whatsoever for the Jewish laborers.[3]

The defendant insisted that the inmates were forced upon it against its will and that it was ordered to pay the Reich for every inmate; the company denied that it had been in any way enriched. It disclaimed knowledge of any mistreatment and alleged that even if the girls had been abused, only the SS could be held accountable. It was clear that the company regarded the complaint of the Jewish women as an impertinence.[4]

The Berlin court ordered the plaintiffs to prove that the Sömmerda camp was the property of the Rheinmetall company, to name the Rheinmetall employees who had requested their services, to set forth the terms of the employment contracts, to identify all witnesses, to show what the company could have done to improve conditions, and to establish the comparable 1944 wage for unskilled workers in the metal industry.[5] The German judges were asking quite a bit, considering that when Helen had worked for Rheinmetall, she was not yet eighteen years old, and Rachel was not even twelve.

Schildbach was able to produce the 1944 wage scales from the Federation of German Labor Unions, but further information about Sömmerda was beyond him. At that time less than a dozen claimants from Sömmerda had made themselves known. In subsequent pleadings, the attorneys for Rheinmettal referred to the plaintiffs' complaint as a *Hassgesang* or song of hate, and referred to the claimants as "other Jewish imports."[6] This prompted Schildbach to demand an apology from the Berlin attorney for Rheinmetall, who explained that he had just taken over the language submitted to him by the firm's main office in Düsseldorf.[7] The published reports of the company showed that the vice-chairman of the board of supervisors in Düsseldorf was none other than Otto Kranzbühler, defender of major war criminals, who had also come to the aid of Farben, Krupp, and other industrialists.[8]

After hearing the oral arguments, the district court dismissed the complaints on the grounds that the litigation had been started too late. The deadline, according to the lower court, was not the end of 1957, as was generally believed, but the end of 1951.[9] The decision was contrary to an opinion rendered that very week by the next higher court, which held that other forced labor claims had not been filed too late but too soon.[10] Either way, the slave laborers would be out. The only hope was to appeal the two inconsistent decisions to the German Supreme Court (*Bundesgericht*). The Claims Conference had no illusions about the prospects for success, but delay was better than accepting defeat.

While the parties wrestled through protracted court proceedings, Ernst Katzenstein made repeated efforts to engage the Rheinmetall company in settlement talks, but to no avail. The company lawyers asked for the Claims Conference's views in writing, and Katzenstein conveyed the hope that purely legal considerations would not deter the company from entering into an agreement. He stressed the moral, humanitarian, and political aspects that had induced other companies to make a settlement.[11] In a politely worded letter the company graciously indicated that the only time a settlement might be considered would be if the highest German court finally decided that the company was legally liable.[12]

By that time, over eight hundred persons had turned to the Claims Conference with demands against Rheinmetall. They were survivors not only from Sömmerda but also from several other camps. The conference decided to try again, via new channels, to induce the company to come to an agreement.

Once more Eric Warburg was the intermediary. He succeeded in bringing Dr. Cornelius, head of Rheinmetall's legal department, together with Katzenstein in the office of the bank in Hamburg. Katzenstein put his cards on the table: the Claims Conference would settle all the Jewish claims against Rheinmetall for a pyament of between DM 3 million and DM 5 million, with each former forced laborer receiving up to DM 5,000. Cornelius said he would pass the information to his board. Two weeks later a brief letter from the firm to Eric Warburg conveyed the company's regrets that it saw "no possibility"—*keine Möglichkeit*—of coming to any understanding.[13]

Shortly thereafter the German Supreme Court rendered its decision in the case against I.G. Farben instituted by the Polish non-Jewish claimants with the support of Hermann Langbein's International Auschwitz Committee. The court held that the demands of the Polish nationals were in the nature of reparations claims and that the London Debt Agreement required that they be postponed.[14] The Jewish claimants soon became victims of the case lost by the Polish forced laborers. When the appeals of Helen R. and Rachel B. against the Rheinmetall company came before the supreme court, the *Bundesgericht* followed its own precedent, concluding that "die Klage als zur Zeit unbegründet abgewiesen wird"—"the complaint is dismissed as being unfounded at this time."[15] The use of concentration camp inmates was seen as part of the war effort planned by the government. In the opinion of Germany's highest court, the claims of foreign nationals who were employed as forced laborers could only be dealt with in a final peace treaty. When or if there would ever be such a treaty was not considered. The judges had forgotten that justice delayed is justice denied.

It so happened that shortly before the German Supreme Court rendered its negative decision in the Rheinmetall case, an appellate court in Stuttgart had held that a German national, Dr. Edmund Bartl, could validly assert a claim against the Heinkel aircraft company for which he had been forced to work as a concentration camp inmate.[16] As long as that decision in favor of a German claimant remained valid, there was a clear discrimination against all the non-German claimants who were being told by the supreme court that their claims could not be dealt with until there was a peace treaty. The Stuttgart decision provided the opening needed to appeal the cases of Rachel and Helen to the even higher German Constitutional Court on the grounds that the equality prescribed by the constitution was being denied to the Jewish women.[17] The constitutional court would eventually refuse to review the Rheinmetall decision, but before the court could even begin to act, the picture was changed by a development no one could have anticipated.

## Help from an Unexpected Quarter

When George Washington was president of the United States, a national armory was established in the town of Springfield, Massachusetts. Beginning with the colonial war, the armed forces of the United States were provided with weapons that came from Springfield. During World War II, fourteen thousand men and women of Springfield supplied the army with five thousand rifles a day. In 1964 the armory still employed some twenty five hundred persons in manufacturing small arms, rifles, machine guns, rocket launchers, and other armaments. The Department of Defense was then in the midst of one of its periodic economy drives and the Pentagon let it be known that the old armory at Springfield would have to be shut down.[18] But while preparations were being made to dismiss the workers of Springfield, the army was planning to place a large armaments order with the Rheinmetall company of Germany.

The *New York Times* reported that Secretary of Defense Robert S. McNamara and West German Defense Minister Kai-Ewe von Hassel had met, and the United States was considering the purchase of $50 million worth of guns from West Germany. The *Wall Street Journal* carried a similar story.[19] When Congressman Edward P. Boland of Springfield inquired of the Pentagon, he received a denial that any such contract was contemplated. Within a few days there was a correction, and the Pentagon confirmed what had been reported.[20] Congressman Boland promised to oppose it. The mayor of Springfield, Charles V. Ryan, was quoted as saying: "I think that this is disgraceful for the U.S. government to put 2,500 families out of jobs while at the same time planning to send a contract for $50 million to a country which right now is importing 20,000 foreign workers a month."[21] Going on nationwide television, Mayor Ryan called upon President Lyndon Johnson to give the armaments order to the Springfield armory. Headlines in all the local papers denounced the proposed contract, and officials of Springfield demanded that Secretary McNamara disclose the name of the German company that was to benefit from the $50 million American order.[22]

Stephen Ailes, Secretary of the Army, explained that the army had an urgent need for a weapon with more fire power than the .50 caliber machine gun then in use and that it had been determined that the HS 20 millimeter automatic gun produced by Rheinmetall was the best gun then available to meet the army requirement.[23] At the same time the president of the National Association of Government Employees stated publically that he had received information that the gun the Pentagon intended to buy from Germany had been tested at the United States Armaments Testing Ground at Aberdeen, Maryland, and had been found to be faulty.[24]

The diligent and energetic mayor of Springfield began to make inquiries about the German company with which the army felt it had to do business. It was not long thereafter that the mayor dropped in at my office in the Pan Am Building in New York. He wanted to know about the activities of the concern and its directors during the Nazi period.[25] He had come to the right address.

Official records indicated that Rheinmetall had employed over five thousand concentration camp inmates, Jews and non-Jews, and that Auschwitz commandant Höss as well as SS Lieutenant General Pohl had confirmed Rheinmetall's participation in the program to use inmate labor.[26] Rheinmetall's managing director, Otto Paul Caesar, had joined the Nazi party in 1937.[27] The second managing director, Ernst Blume, had become a party member in 1935 and also belonged to several other Nazi organizations.[28] The chairman of the supervisory board, Dr. Freiherr von Gemmingen-Hornberg, joined the Nazi party in November 1935 and had been convicted as a war criminal by the French.[29] Two other board members, Dr. Karl Guth and Dr. Curt Freiherr von Salmuth, had also joined the party.[30] Members of the Röchling family, which had acquired ownership of Rheinmetall after the war, had been convicted by a French war crimes court.[31]

Mayor Ryan was on his way to Washington to discuss the subject further and said he would appreciate whatever help he could get. I decided to put the facts before Deputy Secretary of Defense Cyrus Vance. My meeting with Vance was cordial and I indicated how helpful it might be if the Defense Department, as a potential customer, could express some support for a settlement between Rheinmetall and its former slaves. He expressed sympathy with the objective but said the State Department would have to be consulted.[32]

Rheinmetall was not without friends or agents in Washington, and word soon reached Düsseldorf that questions had been raised in the Pentagon regarding the proposed sale to the United States Army. It was not long before a counterattack was launched, led by retired Brig. Gen. Julius Klein, past commander of the Jewish War Veterans. Julius Klein Public Relations, Inc., who had handled publicity for

I.G. Farben, included among its German clients the firm of Rheinmetall. Klein sent a six-page letter with ten enclosures to State Department Assistant Secretary William Tyler saying:

My client, Rheinmetall GmbH of Duesseldorf, Germany, has informed me of a demand by a U.S. attorney for immediate payment of a substantial sum in "settlement" of an un-investigated and un-proven claim alleging use of "slave labor" by the company during World War II . . . The alternative to giving in to this demand is an implied threat to the agreement . . . A further threat is made that, if a purchase currently proposed by the Department of Defense of 20 mm cannon from Rheinmetall is consummated, "widespread publicity" unfavorable to the Defense Department and the State Department would ensue . . . During the post-war period, the technique of making allegations or implications of "Naziism" or "slave labor use" was employed against many substantial German firms . . . This is a naked threat to induce unfavorable publicity for the U.S. Departments of Defense and State if the purchase from Rheinmetall is completed unless the company pays the sum demanded.[33]

Klein denounced "persons attempting to use this familiar technique for personal gain" and referred to "this attorney," whom he failed to name, as making false allegations because he knew the facts could never be tested in a trial.

The letter from the Rheinmetall lobbyist revealed that the former general was working very hard for his German client but that he did not know, or chose to ignore, the facts. He even claimed that he personally assisted in the restitution negotiations and that he was one of the first members when the "Jewish Claims Conference" was formed "under the Chairmanship of Jacob Blaustein, a Director of Standard Oil of Indiana." I could understand Klein's having snubbed the actual chairman, Nahum Goldmann, for I recalled one of the first organizational meetings of the Claims Conference when Julius Klein had ineffectively demanded that the Jewish War Veterans be admitted to membership, only to be deflated by Goldmann's acid remark: "If we have to go to war with Germany, we'll call you."

Julius Klein had been a private and a field clerk with the United States Army at the end of World War I and had spent some time in Berlin in 1919. Thereafter, he worked as a newspaperman for the Hearst publications for several years. In 1933 he joined the Illinois National Guard and became a lieutenant colonel when World War II began. By 1943 he was the commander of a quartermaster truck regiment. After the war he transferred to the Army Reserve, where he was eventually retired with the rank of general. Known thereafter as "General Klein," he became active in Republican politics and in a number of veterans' organizations and fraternal societies. In 1947 and 1948 he was elected National Commander of the Jewish War Veterans of the United States of America. He opened a public relations firm with offices in Chicago, Washington, and Frankfurt as a consultant on national defense and as a policy consultant to industrial corporations. One Washington columnist described him as "a high pressure operator, claiming familiarity with the greatest of the great."[34] It was almost inevitable that some German firms having business interests in the United States should seek the services of a public-relations man who was a retired Jewish general and who said he was on intimate terms with many important members of Congress.

When I learned that Klein was acting for Rheinmetall and was apparently uninformed about the facts, I sent him a letter outlining the evidence that the Rheinmetall company had employed over twelve hundred young Jewish women from Buchenwald at its plant in Sömmerda under brutal conditions, and that the former Nazis on the Rheinmetall management had refused all compensation. I expressed the hope that it would be recognized to be in the interst of Rheinmetall to follow the example set by Farben, Krupp, Siemens, and other companies by settling the claims amicably. I offered to provide him with any further information he might desire.[35] I sent a copy of my letter to the State Department, where the man in charge, Richard B. Finn, acknowledged that the United States had informed the German Ministry of Defense that a solution of the problem of compensating the former Rheinmetall forced laborers would be desirable.[36] Julius Klein was then in Germany and, as I was also leaving for Europe, I took no further action until I arrived in Frankfurt. I then arranged to meet him at his hotel and offered to bring him up-to-date. I brought Ernst Katzenstein along and introduced him as the Claims Conference representative for Germany so that Klein would recognize that I was not acting on my own but on behalf of the Jewish organization.

Klein lost no time in proclaiming that we had bungled the job by applying an extortion-type approach rather than appealing to the moral conscience of the company. He did not seem to realize that for eight years we had been appealing to the corporate conscience and had made absolutely no impact. While we were talking, Klein received a phone call from Rheinmetall's managing director, Otto Paul Caesar, in Düsseldorf, who wanted to know whether he should meet with me and Katzenstein despite a negative recommendation from his *Syndicus* (company lawyer) Dr. Cornelius. I suspected that the timing of the call was staged (Klein, who had also been a motion picture executive in Hollywood, was a great showman), but he made his point, when in our presence he vociferously urged that Rheinmetall meet with us.[37] The next day Katzenstein received a call from Cornelius inviting us to come to Düsseldorf.

At the suggestion of the United States Embassy in Bonn, we first met with Ministerial Director Dr. Bode of the German Ministry of Defense. Bode promptly acknowledged the moral merit of the Claims Conference position and offered his assistance. He told us that twenty-nine of the Rheinmetall machine guns were then being tested by the United States and that the field tests would not be complete for several months. He offered to contact Otto Caesar, whom he knew, to stress the fact that there was more at stake than the initial Rheinmetall sale. This was the first order from the United States for German weapons, and if it started with a violent public reaction in the United States, it would cause great distress to all parties. Bode said he would also try to impress upon Caesar the economic foolishness of rejecting a small slave labor settlement and thereby jeopardizing a large arms order. We agreed to remain in touch and to refrain from any publicity until the situation could be further clarified.[38]

The next day Katzenstein and I went on to Düsseldorf, where we met with Caesar. The meeting was to no avail. The Rheinmetall manager insisted that because the ownership of the Rheinmetall firm had changed hands, the Röchling family, which had acquired the company after the war, owed nothing for any possible misdeeds before their time. He agreed, however, to discuss the problem with the new owners.[39]

Ten weeks later a formal one-paragraph letter was received: "After careful consideration of all the circumstances, our Board of Directors came to the conclusion that our company cannot recognize the merits of your demands."[40] The quiet diplomacy that the Claims Conference had tried to pursue had failed. There was only one alternative left and that was to take the issue to the American public.

### The Power of the Press

The Claims Conference was not an organization that liked to "go public." It had a continuing relationship with the German government and was hesitant about doing anything that might jeopardize the larger Jewish interests. But B'nai B'rith, the largest Jewish fraternal order in the United States and one of the twenty-three member organizations of the Claims Conference, had half a million members who were deeply concerned about all Jewish problems; this group could act independently and was willing to come to the aid of the concentration camp survivors by mobilizing American public and political support, even if that might create displeasure in certain German circles.

The story B'nai B'rith set out to tell was that of Rachel, a Czech Jewish girl, eleven years old, who was seized by the Germans and sent to Auschwitz with her whole family. Her parents and all of her seven brothers and sisters were murdered. Rachel was sent to Buchenwald and was taken from there as a slave to work under unspeakable conditions for Rheinmetall, Hitler's second largest armaments producer. After the war she searched in vain for some trace of her family and wandered through the displaced-persons camps of Germany until, assisted by Jewish charities, she found a new home in the United States. Meanwhile, the Rheinmetall company changed its name and began to prosper. Whereas some German firms made funds available for forced laborers, Rheinmetall adamantly refused to consider any payment.

Philip Klutznick, the past president of B'nai B'rith, recommended that before releasing the story to the press, the problem be discussed with German Ambassador Heinrich Knappstein. The ambassador asked that nothing be done until he could take up the matter during a forthcoming trip to Bonn. In the meanwhile, his staff was studying German expert opinions, which concluded that despite the corporate alterations, the new Rheinmetall company was legally identical with its predecessor.[41]

Mayor Ryan of Springfield, in the interim, had learned that the testing of the Rheinmetall cannon was to be completed by the end of January 1966 and a decision on the gun made in February. He had seen a secret intelligence report showing that the gun, described as "Cannon, 20mm, Automatic, M139 (H.S.820/L85) Modified," had been phased out of use by the West German army five years before because it was defective.[42] According to his information, what Rheinmetall was trying to sell and what the United States Army was about to buy was a cannon that the German army considered unusable.

When the German ambassador returning from Bonn reported that the Rheinmetall company denied having ever employed slave laborers and refused any payment, the restraint that had been exercised by B'nai B'rith came to an end. On February 3 the president, William Wexler, sent telegrams to Secretary of State Dean Rusk and to Defense Secretary McNamara protesting the planned purchase from Rheinmetall "or any other former exploiter of slave labor that refuses to assume responsibility for its actions." A few days later all of the information was given to the press.

On Sunday, February 6, 1966, the *New York Times* carried a front-page article, "Pentagon Scored on Gun Purchase—Pentagon Denounced for Plans to Buy Guns in West Germany." A Springfield paper ran a two-inch caption in large block letters, "Former Plant of Nazis Said Rival of Armory—Mayor Scores Any Order to German Firm." The *Christian Science Monitor* quoted cables to President Lyndon Johnson alleging that the army intended to buy the gun even though it had failed its tests at the Aberdeen proving grounds. All the press services—American, German, and international—picked up the story, which received widespread media coverage across the country.[43]

No sooner had the story hit the newsstands and the air waves than various members of the Senate and the House began to ask for an explanation from the Pentagon and the State Department. Senator Jacob K. Javits of New York called for a full report. Congressman Leonard Farbstein of New York announced plans to introduce new legislation that would deny the use of government funds for the purchase of materials from German companies which had denied compensation to slave laborers. Congressman Jonathan Bingham of the Bronx planned to review the whole situation, and Senator Edward Kennedy of Massachusetts asked for more facts.[44] Congressman Boland introduced a bill "to prohibit the purchase by the United States of arms or ammunition from foreign firms which have used slave labor unless compensation had been made to the individuals involved or their heirs."[45] A similar bill was introduced a few days later by Congressman Joseph Y. Resnick.[46]

In response to the public criticism, an information sheet was sent out by "Rheinmetall AG Washington Information Office." It sought to refute the Associated Press reports by maintaining that the Rheinmetall company was a new firm unrelated to the one that employed the concentration camp inmates. It said that only two claimants had come forward and the German courts had concluded that the claims were legally unfounded. It contended that "inquiries to obtain supporting records for the claimants alleged to have worked in the plants located in West Germany have never been answered," and characterized the protest of the mayor of Springfield as incorrect and misleading. It asserted that the Rheinmetall cannon was the most suitable weapon for American military requirements, according to "the consensus of the military experts." The next sentence concluded: "For additional information, telephone *Major General Kenneth Buchanan*" (name underlined). The implication was that military authorities would refute the unfounded allegations against Rheinmetall. What it failed to mention was that Major General Kenneth Buchanan had retired from the army and was in fact the paid employee of Julius Klein; the release had come from the address of the public relations firm of Julius Klein, registered agents for Rheinmetall.[47]

Congressman Jonathan B. Bingham, joined by Congressman Emanuel Celler of Brooklyn, the "Dean of the House," protested to Secretary of Defense McNamara: "We are very disturbed to learn of the contract negotiations between the United States and the Rheinmetall Company of Düsseldorf . . . It is impossible for us to understand why a company which not only utilized slave labor but which, even now, refuses to acknowledge the wrongdoing involved, should be favored by the U.S. Government." The congressmen urged that no contract be given to Rheinmetall "so long as that company maintains its intransigent policy regarding those who were slave laborers in its plants."[48]

The Jewish War Veterans of the United States of America issued a press release disassociating itself from its former commander, Julius Klein, and opposing the transaction with Rheinmetall. Said Milton A. Waldor, the national commander, "Such an order should be given to the Springfield Armory . . . both on the military and economic merits and also on the basis of the fact that Rheinmetall has refused to make even token payments for financial claims of former slave laborers during the Nazi era." Commander Walder, who described Julius Klein as "a representative or a lobbyist for Rheinmetall . . . acting in his private and public relations capacity," was quoted as saying, "All thinking people must realize that General Klein does not speak for the Jewish War Veterans."[49]

Assistant Secretary of Defense John T. McNaughton sent an assurance to President Wexler of B'nai B'rith that no final procurement decision had yet been made on the Rheinmetall gun and that the United States would give appropriate consideration to the questions raised in Wexler's protest to the secretarys of state and defense.[50]

In response to the news that Congressman Leonard Farbstein had introduced legislation to block the purchase from Rheinmetall, Klein sent the legislator a copy of the long letter he had submitted to Assistant Secretary of State Tyler the year before. Said Klein,

Mr. Benjamin Ferencz, member of a New York law firm, has stirred up the Rheinmetall controversy by unethical means, choosing to sidestep the true facts in the case . . . The entire picture has been distorted in its presentation to you. Mr. Ferencz is attempting to pursue these alleged claims against Rheinmetall for a legal fee from his clients. He has also misrepresented the facts to the president of B'nai B'rith, Dr. William A. Wexler and our good friend, Philip Klutznick . . . Mr. Ferencz encouraged the labor unions there [in Springfield] to make protests to our government against Rheinmetall which failed . . . As I said above, the 20mm cannon is a weapon our Armed Forces need.[51]

What Julius Klein could not know, and perhaps would not believe or understand, was that I had never requested or accepted a fee from any concentration camp survivor, nor would I derive any personal financial benefit whatsoever whether or not a settlement was reached on behalf of the slave laborers.

The stories in the press and the ensuing protest had their first visible impact when an unexpected emissary arrived at my New York office. An attractive lady of regal appearance, wearing a mink coat with matching mink hat and carrying an alligator handbag over her arm, said she wanted to talk to me about the Rheinmetall guns. She introduced herself as Mrs. John R. Hecht of Vancouver, British Columbia, and said she had some information that I might find of interest.

By way of credentials, Mrs. Hecht explained that her father and one grandfather had been members of B'nai B'rith. Her husband, she said, had been the principal shareholder of the Hispano-Suiza company, which owned the patents on the 20 millimeter gun. He was then in Geneva trying to expedite the purchase of the guns by the Pentagon. He was, said Mrs. Hecht, acting on behalf of Hispano-Suiza's new Swiss owner. Her knowledge of the details about the cannon and the Pentagon order showed that she was very well informed.

After we had reviewed the situation, Mrs. Hecht informed me that she had been authorized to transmit an offer from the Rheinmetall company. The firm was willing, she said, to pay $2,000 to each inmate who had worked in a Rheinmetall plant in West Germany. Although ·she probably meant DM 2,000, since the claimants had only asked for $1,250, her information tended to give credence to an article that had appeared in the German press quoting a representative of Rheinmetall as saying, "We admit that we are the legal successors of the firm of Rheinmetall-Borsig which used concentration camp inmates. We are also willing to satisfy claims arising from that time but of course the claims must be proved."[52] I suggested to Mrs. Hecht that she pass the word back to her husband, who could relay it to Düsseldorf, that if the company was really serious about reaching a settlement at this late stage, contact had to be made immediately with Katzenstein in Frankfurt.[53]

The next day Mrs. Hecht phoned and told me that she had been in touch with her husband in Geneva, who had been in communication with the Rheinmetall company in Düsseldorf. She disclosed what I had long suspected. The man calling the tune was the vice-chairman of the Rheinmetall board and an old adversary from the Nuremberg trials, Otto Kranzbühler, the staunch defender of German industrialists. Kranzbühler had suggested that Rheinmetall might pay DM 3 million ($750,000) in trust to the United States Embassy. The fund would be controlled by three Americans, three Germans, and one neutral national. They would pay it out to those forced laborers who could prove that they had been employed by the Rheinmetall company, and payment would vary according to the length of the employment.[54]

My response was that the Claims Conference had requested DM 5 million but could consider a compromise. I doubted that the mixed claims commission was feasible and suggested that Rheinmetall apprise itself of the techniques used by Compensation Treuhand to verify claims. I told her that time was running out, since forces had been set in motion that would be difficult to reverse.

A few days later Mrs. Hecht reported that Kranzbühler was eager to settle, since he had been urged to do so by the German Ministry of Defense. Otto Caesar had been called back from vacation and the matter was being reconsidered in Düsseldorf.[55] The State Department confirmed to the B'nai B'rith president that "the Ministry of Defense brought this matter to the attention of the current management of Rheinmetall" and gave its assurance that the State Department was interested in "an equitable solution of this problem."[56]

The mayor of Springfield, continuing his effort, sent a strong letter to President Johnson: "We're wondering what's going on down there. The gun is unreliable and the Defense Department knows it is unreliable. (Ask to see the Aberdeen evaluations, Mr. President.) The German government knows it's unreliable. And yet, the Pentagon pushes on ahead with the contract and willfully continues to misrepresent the Rheinmetall gun as the best 20 millimeter available in the whole world."[57]

Mrs. Hecht reported that the information the company was receiving from its advisors in Washington was that the protests were not to be taken too seriously.[58] The date of the scheduled Rheinmetall board meeting came and went, yet no word was heard from Mrs. Hecht and not a sound from the Rheinmetall company. Katzenstein finally broke the silence by phoning attorney Kranzbühler. The Rheinmetall answer came back loud and clear: "No deal!" There had been a meeting of the Rheinmetall board and, according to Kranzbühler, they were enraged by what they considered to be a systematic and organized press campaign directed against the company and its agents. A series of syndicated articles by the columnists Drew Pearson and Jack Anderson criticizing Julius Klein for alleged improper conduct in another matter was seen, in the words of Kranzbühler, as a *Vorgeplänkel* or preliminary skirmish which was then followed by an orchestrated series of attacks in the *Washington Post,* the *New York Times,* the *Chicago Tribune,* and other papers. Whether the United States acquired the gun was a matter to be settled between the two governments, declared Kranzbühler defiantly, and his company was not going to surrender to what it considered to be blackmail tactics.[59]

Katzenstein suggested to Kranzbühler that they meet personally in order to reexamine the problem from a purely humanitarian point of view. Kranzbühler rejected the suggestion as a waste of time and asked Katzenstein to inform the people in New York that they could expect nothing.[60]

B'nai B'rith President Wexler addressed a new communication to the secretary of state criticizing "the continued intransigence of Rheinmetall." Wexler also appealed to the secretary of defense, stating that "a firm which remains unrepentant toward slave laborers it had exploited did not deserve a purchase order" and that "action consonent with the principles of human rights that are fundamental to our national integrity must be an overriding consideration." The *Denver Post* carried an article under the headline "Ex-Nazi Magnates Won't Pay Debts." Members of Jewish communities across the country began to call for action against the German firm.[61]

The German side did not remain silent. *Der Spiegel,* Germany's leading news magazine, carried a long article under the caption, "Shots against the Wonder Weapon." The author made no secret of where his sympathies lay. "Organizer of the campaign against Rheinmetall," said *Der Spiegel,* "is the New York restitution lawyer, Benjamin (Ben) Ferencz. He represents, according to his own admission, around 1,000 American citizens who—although they have received indemnification payments under Bonn's Federal Indemnification Law—demand additional grants . . . Rheinmetall (Ltd.) in Düsseldorf rejected the unreasonable request." The article went on to repeat the arguments put forth by Julius Klein and other Rheinmetall representatives and quoted the words of the company, which described the gun as "the wonder weapon without competition in the whole world." It said that McNamara's promise to buy 2,500 guns and 10 million rounds of ammunition was in exchange for a German purchase of over $2 billion worth of arms from the United States. According to the author, while Rheinmetall was getting ready to carry out its part of the bargain, "Ben Ferencz, who had been laid low in the courtroom, began to voice a canonical song against the slave drivers of the Rhein" by conducting "a massive public campaign to move Rheinmetall toward payments which are neither legally nor morally justified."[62]

In an attempt to correct the false impression created by *Der Spiegel* that I was simply a self-serving blackmailer acting for my own enrichment, I sent translations of the article, as well as some corrective comments, to members of the Congress, the United States government, and others who had been concerned with the subject. In an accompanying letter to Congressman Celler and Congressman Bingham I stated that a complete congressional investigation of all of the facts would indeed be a public service.[63] The office of Senator Javits called upon the State Department for a clear statement of the truth, and Assistant Secretary for Congressional Relations Douglas MacArthur II sent a comprehensive reply to the senator from New York. In it, the State Department accurately reviewed the situation and gave its conclusion regarding "certain facts and legal matters":

1. During the war the predecessor company of the present Rheinmetall AG was called Rheinmetall Borsig AG . . . The majority interest in Rheinmetall Borsig AG was acquired by the Roechling family in 1956, and the company was at that time renamed Rheinmetall AG. The company was then only in possession of the plants

in West Germany, namely the plants in Duesseldorf, Lower Saxony and West Berlin; the plants in East Germany had been nationalized and were under the control of the East German regime.

2. It appears that of the five present principal officers of the Rheinmetall AG, three were members of the Nazi Party during World War II. Of these five officers, two, including one of the Nazi Party members, were plant directors of Rheinmetall Borsig AG during the war. The degree of active involvement in Nazi Party activities by the three wartime members of the NSDAP is not known.[64]

The Synagogue Council of America sent letters protesting the purchase to the president, to the secretarys of state and defense, and to leading members of Congress.[65] The Jewish Nazi Victims Organization of America joined the protesters.[66] It was reported that a past national commander of the Jewish War Veterans addressed some 190 members from posts throughout Massachusetts and denounced Julius Klein in strong terms for having discredited the Jewish veterans organization.[67]

In Bonn the German Ministry of Defense was caught in the cross fire between Rheinmetall and the Jewish organizations. Ministerial Director Dr. Knieper discussed the problem with Rheinmetall vice-chairman Kranzbühler. In an attempt to break the impasse, Knieper sent a note to the military attaché at the German Embassy in Washington in which he suggested that a joint German–American committee be established to deal with the problem. That sounded suspiciously like the proposal for a mixed claims commission mentioned by Mrs. Hecht in my office about a month before. Cyrus Vance made it clear that no direct United States government involvement was desired. Vance suggested that his German counterpart come up with a better idea.

Knieper discussed the problem again with Kranzbühler and a few days later was able to confide to Katzenstein that "Rheinmetall had declared that it was ready to pay something."[68] He was reluctant to disclose what "something" meant, but he did say that Rheinmetall would be in touch with Katzenstein directly and he had reason to believe that some notificaton would go out of Washington to the Jewish organizations in America. When Katzenstein asked whether he should contact Knieper again after he had heard from Rheinmetall, the German official replied, "Preferably not." With all the verbal shooting taking place, the defense departments of both governments obviously preferred to remain far behind the lines of combat.


## A Most Unusual Deal

The Pentagon was eager to buy the Rheinmetall cannon, but there was considerable concern about political backfire if the purchase was concluded before the Jewish claims issue was settled. The Defense Department had begun to probe the possibility of acquiring an alternate weapon, and it was hoped that Rheinmetall's awareness that the United States was beginning to look elsewhere might inspire the company to change its mind. The Defense Department and the German Ministry were working on some way to overcome the impasse, but the details were shrouded in secrecy.[69] It seemed prudent under the circumstances to try to damp down the fires of indignation which were still burning fiercely.

The German ambassador felt that a cup of tea might help to douse the flames, and so he invited Rabbi Jay Kaufman, the executive head of B'nai B'rith, to drop in. While the distinguished representative of the Federal Republic of Germany poured tea for the Jewish rabbi, he casually let it "slip out" that consideration was being given to the idea of setting up a trust with DM 2 million ($500,000) which could be used for the Jewish claims. He thought that his friend Phil Klutznick, who had recently been designated by the American president to be an ambassador at the United Nations, would be just the right man to serve as trustee.[70] Klutznick was then on duty in Geneva and he would soon be approached by a Rheinmetall representative, a lawyer and former minister named Hans Wilhelmi.

Ambassador Klutznick found himself in the middle of a problem that was not of his making nor to his taste. He had been drawn in because he enjoyed the confidence of all of the parties. He was the past president of B'nai B'rith, was a director of the Claims Conference, was respected by the German ambassador and the United States government, and, through Julius Klein, whom he had known for many years, was also acceptable to Rheinmetall. He was in an ideal position to play the middleman role, but it was a thankless task he did not welcome. When approached by Wilhelmi, Klutznick suggested that the German emissary place his plan before the Claims Conference representative in Germany. The advice that Klutznick gave to the Claims Conference was to get the problem out of everyone's hair.[71]

Dr. Hans Wilhelmi, senior partner of the Frankfurt law firm of Wilhelmi, Wilhelmi and Wilhelmi, appeared at the Grüneburgweg office of Katzenstein. He disclosed that as a result of negotiations between Rheinmetall, the United States State Department, the German Ministry of Defense, and the German Embassy in Washington, it had been agreed some six weeks before that $500,000 would be paid by the three partners involved in the weapons sale. Apparently the three companies were Rheinmetall, which would manufacture the gun, Hispano-Suiza of Switzerland, which held the patent rights, and the Heinrich Diehl firm of Nuremberg, which would make the ammunition. According to the plan, the money would have to be held in trust, with Katzenstein and Wilhelmi serving as the joint trustees. If the United States failed to purchase the Rheinmetall cannons, the money was to be returned to Wilhelmi.[72]

There were three basic objections to what Wilhelmi proposed. Under no circumstances could the Claims Conference enter into an arrangement on behalf of slave laborers that was conditional upon the United States government's buying cannons from a German company. Second, the amount of DM 2 million which was being offered was clearly inadequate, and further, the conference would not accept a payment from uninvolved companies against which the slave laborers had no complaint. (It was not known at that time that Diehl had also used concentration camp inmates.)

Katzenstein explained the three difficulties to Wilhelmi, who left the office in order to relay the information privately to his clients. Within the hour he returned to report that all he could do was to increase the offer from DM 2 million to DM 2.5 million—a supplement of $125,000. Katzenstein was disgusted with the purely commercial approach to what should have been recognized as a moral problem. He was inclined to break off the negotiations, but it was not that easy.

The Pentagon wanted to buy the Rheinmetall guns. The criticism against the purchase had been justified by the moral argument that the United States should not do business with a former Nazi firm that was evasive and unrepentent. If the company's image remained unaltered and the army nevertheless bought the guns, members of the Congress would be annoyed and the United States government might appear to be unconcerned about moral or humanitarian considerations. If the United States refused to buy the gun, the German government would be annoyed, the army would feel frustrated, and the American defense capabilities might even be impaired. In any case, the Jewish organizations were bound to catch the blame. The Claims Conference had a tiger by the tail and the problem was how to let go.

Wilhelmi was anxious to find some way to break the impasse. The first proposal, for a mixed German–American claims commission, had been turned down by Assistant Secretary Vance. The next suggestion that a special trust be administered by Klutznick had been turned down by the new ambassador. A Katzenstein–Wilhelmi joint trust had been refused by Katzenstein. Then Wilhelmi suggested that he alone would serve as trustee. He agreed to drop any reference to the other two companies.[73]

The Jewish organizations were also eager to find a way out. The form of the settlement and even the inadequate amount was not the real stumbling block. The main difficulty arose from the fact that the Claims Conference could not and would not under any circumstances enter into an agreement which was dependent upon the United States buying guns from a German firm. Wilhelmi accepted the point and his final proposal was that there would be no written agreement of any kind but only a tacit understanding. He gave his personal committment that he would place the DM 2.5 million in a separate account and if the guns were purchased by the United States Army, he would immediately hand the money over to Katzenstein. No committment from the Claims Conference was required. Under the circumstances, the conference agreed to "wait and see." Wilhelmi was astute enough to recognize that if the Jewish organizations accepted the money, the voices of protest would become muted or stilled.

Time was of the essence. The top German and American defense officials were meeting in Washington and the item of the Rheinmetall cannon was high on the agenda. If a settlement was going to be made, the Germans wanted that fact communicated to the Americans immediately to make sure that the purchase did not fall through. The Claims Conference officers whose approval would have to be obtained were in various parts of the world. I was standing by in Frankfurt; Kagan was in New York; Goldmann was somewhere between Israel and London; Blaustein was in Baltimore or Chicago; Rabbi Kaufman was in Washington; and Klutznick, who was being kept informed, was in Aix-les-Bains. It would be necessary to pull all the strings together before the deal could be wrapped up.

As soon as the discussions in Frankfurt had gone as far as they could go, I proceeded to Bonn to report to the United States Army liaison people at the American Embassy. They had been kept constantly informed of the ebb and flow of the negotiations and were relaying the information to the Pentagon. The final decision about the cannons was to be made at a meeting in Washington between the German minister and the American secretary of defense on Friday, the 13th, of May, 1966.

Nestled in the woods less than an hour's drive from the German capital of Bonn lies the village of Maria Laach. It has a small lake, pleasant walks, and an inn run by a local monastic order. It seemed an ideal place to stay, since I was eager to avoid the prying inquiries of reporters who were also eagerly awaiting the outcome of the conference in Washington. Early Saturday morning I tuned into the Armed Forces radio network to hear the news. It was announced that in a meeting between German Minister von Hassel and Secretary McNamara "the controversial weapon" had been acquired by the United States Army. By Monday morning the story was in all the German papers. *Die Welt* carried a long report from its Washington correspondent:

The signing of a binder agreement for the delivery of a two-centimeter-rapid-fire cannon to the American army ended a controversy which arose when Jewish organizations protested against doing business with the firm of Rheinmetall. The Jewish organizations criticized the firm for having exploited concentration camp inmates during the war.

Von Hassel expressed his satisfaction that the differences had been overcome. He did not exclude the possibility that the signing would release new protests. The tests of the rapid-fire cannon, which can be used for land as well as air combat, had completely satisfied the American experts. The contract amounts to about DM 80 million. It is the first time that the United States has given a large armaments order to Germany.[74]

The *Frankfurter Rundschau* quoted von Hassel as commenting that the American purchase of DM 300 million worth of Rheinmetall cannons showed that armaments collaboration was not a "one-way street."[75]

The *Wall Street Journal* on May 16 carried a United Press International dispatch under the headline "U.S. to Buy German Gun":

In a rare move, the U.S. turned to a foreign source for weapons, agreeing to buy a German gun for U.S. Army use. Defense Secretary McNamara and Germany's Defense Minister Kai-Uwe von Hassel announced the agreement at the end of a 5-1/2 hour Pentagon meeting covering a wide range of U.S. and North Atlantic Treaty Organization problems.

The gun is the Hispano-Suiza 820, a 20-millimeter weapon to be mounted on the Army's M-114 armored command and reconnaissance vehicle used by scout squads of tank platoons.

Defense Department officials said a contract is yet to be worked out, but that eventually the Army expects to spend a total of $74.2 million for the guns, ammunition, spare parts, technical data and royalties. Rheinmetall G.m.b.H. is the gun's German manufacturer.

Army officials said there was no similar weapon available for production in the U.S.

By 9 a.m. Monday morning, Knieper was back in Bonn and was meeting with Rheinmetall's managing director. By 11 a.m. Wilhelmi had received his clearances and had, by special messenger, instructed the Deutsche Effecten-und Wechselbank to pay over DM 2.5 million to an account in the name of Ernst Katzenstein. Wilhelmi, acting for clients whose identity was never clearly established, had arranged to deliver $625,000 to Katzenstein without the exchange of a single piece of paper.[76]

Most newspapers simply reported that the United States government had agreed to buy the German guns. No reference was made to any settlement or payment for the slave labor survivors. This put B'nai B'rith in a rather unfavorable light, since it gave the false impression that the Jewish service organization had been ineffective. Bernard Simon, B'nai B'rith's conscientious public relations director, felt impelled to correct the erroneous image of his employer. B'nai B'rith issued a one-page release disclosing that Rheinmetall had deposited DM 2.5 million to an account of the Claims Conference in order to provide some compensation for an estimated one thousand forced labor survivors of Rheinmetall factories.[77] The *New York Times* picked up the story under the headline: "Nazi Victims Win Pay with U.S. Help—Arms Maker to Reimburse Jews Used as Slave Labor." The international edition of the *New York Times* used the heading: "Jews To Be Paid for Slave Labor—Washington and Bonn Force Compensation by Company."[78]

The extreme right wing *National Zeitung und Soldatenzeitung* placed the story under a headline saying: "Rheinmetall Gave In to B'nai B'rith, 3% of the Armaments Contract Went to a Zionist Organization."[79] *Wehrdienst*, a publication dealing with German army matters, wrote, "There is no cause to break out in rejoicing over the first American armaments order from Germany." The article confirmed that DM 2.5 million had been paid but said the money had not come from Rheinmetall alone, nor was it a payment to former camp inmates. It was, said *Wehrdienst*, a 1 percent commission paid by the three partners to the deal. The article stated that Rheinmetall, under pressure by Bonn, had paid one million deutsche marks, Hispano had matched that amount, and Diehl had thrown half a million into the pot.[80]

It was a most unusual deal.


## Dividing the Fund

When Wilhelmi dropped $625,000 into the lap of Ernst Katzenstein, there were no strings attached. The conference had a completely free hand, but the amount was so inadequate that only a most restricted distribution would be possible. The International Tracing Service had a list of more than a thousand women who had been taken from Buchenwald to work for Rheinmetall at Sömmerda. A great deal of information was available about two other Rheinmetall plants at Unterlüss and Hundsfeld near Breslau. It was decided by Compensation Treuhand that only those three camps could be considered. Those concentration camp inmates who had been in Rheinmetall camps about which very little was known would have to be sent away empty handed. The alternative would have been to have a long and costly screening procedure, at the end of which the beneficiaries might have received only a pittance.

An important document was uncovered which turned out to be the missing piece needed to complete a sad picture. It was part of the story of what had happened to two thousand Jewish girls who had been rounded up by the Nazis in Hungary and Czechoslovakia in 1944, taken to Auschwitz, sorted to determine whether they should be sent to the gas chambers or to work, and then, having passed the test of fitness for slave labor in the German munitions factories, shipped to the special Buchenwald subcamp at Gelsenkirchen in the Ruhr. The camp commandant, SS First Lieutenant Dietrich, meticulously kept a precise inventory of his stock. His status report of November 26, 1944, accounted for each of the two thousand women originally under his charge:[81]

| | |
|---|---:|
| Pregnant prisoners sent to Auschwitz | 8 |
| Work detail to Krupp-Essen | 520 |
| Natural death | 3 |
| Killed in bombing raid | 138 |
| Wounded in bombing raid | 94 |
| Left behind in hospitals | 21 |
| | 784 |
| Balance of prisoners transferred to Sömmerda | 1,216 |
| Died in Sömmerda | 2 |
| (Balance on Hand) | 1,214 |

This official SS record showed the transfer to Krupp of the 520 Hungarian Jewish girls whom Krupp had sent back to Buchenwald when the Allied armies marched on Essen. It showed that those who were not killed or assigned to Krupp's work detail had gone to Sömmerda to work for Rheinmetall. On the date of the report, 1,214 of them were reported to be alive. It was up to Compensation Treuhand to try to find them—if they were still among the living.

Many of the applications sent to Compensation Treuhand described work for a munitions factory at Unterlüss, about 60 kilometers northeast of Hannover in West Germany. Some of the claimants knew it was a Rheinmetall plant. The mayor of Unterlüss confirmed that there were four labor camps in the town which provided Russian and Polish women to a number of German firms. Camp I had three hundred Jewish women. Other sources disclosed that in September 1944 a group of women from the ghetto at Lodz were shipped via Auschwitz and Bergen-Belsen and from there to work at Unterlüss. They were already in the camp, which consisted of two large wooden barracks capable of housing about four hundred persons each, when a similarly selected shipment of five to six hundred Hungarian Jewesses arrived. Rheinmetall had the only factory in Unterlüss, and Rheinmetall's work camps, with constant replacements coming in from Auschwitz, housed an estimated nine hundred women.

The Unterlüss inmates were put to work digging trenches, building air-raid shelters and roads, and making the grounds ready for a new plant to supplement another Rheinmetall factory at Neulüss about 12 kilometers away. Many of the girls worked on the assembly line filling shells and grenades with an explosive powder that caused their skin to change color. To counteract the poison and the bitter taste left by inhaling the fumes, the girls received a ration of milk. If the name Unterlüss or Tannenberg/Unterlüss was mentioned, or there was reference to the cup of milk or to the discoloration of the skin, Compensation Treuhand had no difficulty in recognizing that the applicant must have worked for Rheinmetall and the claim was approved without delay.[82]

Information about other Rheinmetall camps came from records of criminal prosecutions conducted by German authorities. For example, an SS female guard, Eva Kowa, who was in charge of the Jewish women employed by Rheinmetall-Borsig at Hundsfeld near Breslau, was suspected of murder, and a number of Rheinmetall directors and supervisors were called to testify in a German court about conditions at Hundsfeld.[83] Their testimony revealed that there were three slave labor camps at Hundsfeld. One was for men, one was for French women, and the third was for Jews. The inmates were employed by Rheinmetall in the manufacture of condensors, electrical instruments, and small parts for the V-2 rockets being launched against England. The Jewish camp was opened in July 1944 in a barren industrial area. The first transport of inmates to arrive consisted of 360 Polish Jewish women from Auschwitz. On August 20 a similar transport arrived. They had been picked out by Rheinmetall's man in charge of labor procurement, Herr Möller, who admitted that he made repeated journeys to the concentration camp to choose suitable workers. Additional transports arrived regularly. In September a shipment included women from Lodz and Warsaw and 14 Hungarians. In October, November, and January more Jews arrived.

Alfred Hecker was the Rheinmetall director in charge of the Hundsfeld operations. The women worked in three different departments. Richard Richter's department had two sections for the manufacture of condensors. Plant engineer Schönherr supervised 400 Jewish women in Department I and another 250 or 300 were employed in "Richter II." A section under Karl Lusche used another 300 Jewish women. In all there were about 1,000 Jewish women out of a total of 2,000 camp inmates employed by Rheinmetall at Hundsfeld. There was no other German munitions firm in Hundsfeld, and the inmates who worked for Rheinmetall stayed together as a group.

On January 25, 1945, the camps at Hundsfeld were evacuated. For three days and three nights the inmates were driven on foot through the snow and cold toward Gross Rosen. Those who stumbled or fell on the way were shot. From Gross Rosen, the Jewish women were taken south in cattle cars to Mauthausen and from there they were shipped northwest to Bergen-Belsen, where those who were still alive were set free by British troops on April 15, 1945.[84]

Of the 1,214 women who were alive in Sömmerda on November 26, 1944, 992 were located and paid by Compensation Treuhand. Only 261 of the approximately 900 who were at Unterlüss ever appeared to receive a share of the fund. Of the estimated 1,000 Jewish inmates at Hundsfeld, only 262 could be found.

One of the girls who was on the Sömmerda list, Bimbi Grosz, explained that some of those who had worked with her at Sömmerda might still be alive within the Soviet Union. Compensation Treuhand received no claims from East Germany or the USSR and the suspicion could not be avoided that the Jews in those areas may have been politically constrained from submitting an application to an office in West Germany. Bimbi Grosz, her family, and her friends had been seized by the Germans in a raid on a small village in Hungary. They were sent to Auschwitz, "selected," sorted, and shipped to Buchenwald, and some were assigned to work for Rheinmetall at Sömmerda. After the war Bimbi Grosz returned home to her Carpathian town to find that her relatives were all gone and the area had been annexed by the Soviet Union. After many years of effort she managed to obtain an exit visa to join her sister in New York. She brought with her the names of thirteen neighborhood friends who had worked with her in the German munitions factory.[85] Their names were all confirmed by the International Tracing Service's Sömmerda list. Bimbi Grosz described the conditions of hardship under which the Sömmerda survivors in the USSR still lived. Compensation Treuhand was eager to help.

Russian rubles would be of very little value to the Sömmerda girls who were still alive in the Soviet Union. They would derive a greater benefit from a useful gift parcel. A dedicated member of the Compensation Treuhand staff, Gerda Lippman, went shopping in Frankfurt to see what was available to bring the greatest joy to the recipients in Munkacs (Mukachevo), Bergszasz, and other little Hungarian villages in what is now Transcarparthian Oblast, USSR. Each parcel was matched to the known age of the recipient, as scarves, bolts of cloth, coats, sweaters, ball-point pens, and other items were shipped, duty paid in advance, from Germany to the Jewish women in Russia. The receipts that the beneficiaries had to sign for the "gifts" implied that the parcels had come from Bimbi Grosz in the United States, who, of course, had only supplied the names.[86] The surprised recipients must have been very impressed with the sudden prosperity that had apparently befallen their recently emigrated friend Bimbi in the *Goldene Medina* — the golden land of promise.

Other concentration camp inmates who worked for Rheinmetall

could not be given even a gift parcel. Applications from persons who said they worked for Rheinmetall in Düsseldorf or Berlin had to be rejected simply because it would have been too difficult to confirm all of the facts and there just was not enough money available to allow any further dilution of the payments.

Those who had been together as slave laborers for the Rheinmetall firm in 1944 and 1945 had been dispersed across the globe to whatever lands would give them refuge. The $625,000 received from Rheinmetall was sent to twenty different countries: 806 recipients were in Israel, 380 were in the United States, 65 in Canada, and 29 in Sweden. Only 80 of the Rheinmetall slave laborers could be found in their native land of Hungary, while 33 were traced to Romania and·29 to Czechoslovakia. The others had found new homes in Australia, Brazil, Mexico, Chile, Great Britain, and other lands. The total amount distributed to the claimants was DM 2,546,095.74 (appendix 5). The amount that each surviving Rheinmetall slave received was DM 1,700—$425.[87] The payment from Rheinmetall was only a token. It was also the last payment to be made by any German firm to its former forced laborers.

After the payment to the Claims Conference had been delivered, the Rheinmetall company renewed its posture of complete innocence by denying that it had ever made any payment to benefit its concentration camp workers. Company representatives were quoted as saying: "The press reports that we have recognized claims by the concentration camp inmates who were assigned to us or to our legal predecessor by the former Reich and have made an agreement to compensate them are incorrect. We are also not under any obligation to recognize such claims since in two test cases which were taken all the way to the Federal Supreme Court the complaints were dismissed."[88]

When a few years later Hermann Langbein of the International Auschwitz Committee appealed to Rheinmetall for a payment for the non-Jewish workers, his repeated requests were rejected with the argument that there was neither a legal nor a moral obligation to pay for deeds for which the Reich may have been responsible. To his observation that Rheinmetall had made a payment for the Jewish survivors the Rheinmetall officers replied: "On this occasion we consider it useful once more to point out specifically that the payment to the Jewish Claims Conference which you know about came about in consideration of an order which we expected to receive . . . The company payments were therefore balanced against counterpayments."[89]

Some correspondents and congressmen were not convinced that the United Sates had done so well with the purchase of the cannons from Rheinmetall. The respected *New York Times* military analyst Hanson W. Baldwin published a long report under the headline "Army Orders Gun from Bonn That Officers Call Substandard." It explained that the gun was manufactured by Rheinmetall and that the total cost including guns and ammunition would run about $150 million. Said the *New York Times,* "A number of Congressmen are interested in discovering why the contract was awarded for a gun that admittedly does not meet normal specifications."[90] The *Times* reported that the army vice-chief of staff, General Creighton Abrams, had opposed the purchase of "substandard" 20 millimeter guns from the West German government after a conference with the Combat Development Command and the Army Materiel Command. Congressman Paul Findley, who was described as an articulate Phi Beta Kappa man with a wide range of investigative and legislative interests, led the congressional criticism against the purchase from Rheinmetall.

On December 18, 1967, a report out of Washington carried the story: "Army Cancels Its Order of German Guns. The Army has quietly cancelled the last half of the $150,000,000 procurement of German-made 20 mm cannons and ammunition which Rep. Paul Findley last year disclosed did not work properly."[91]

Years later the army officer who had been the procurement manager maintained that the cutback had been purely for reasons of economy. He mentioned, however, that it had been necessary to make about eighty modifications to turn the German gun into a usable weapon.[92]

In 1978 the press announced that the United States Army was prepared to spend $4.5 billion for tanks whose 120 mm cannons were to be manufactured, not by the American or British bidders, but by the German firm of Rheinmetall.[93]

# The Shark Who Got Away

Nothing will convince us that we are war criminals.

> Final Statement by Defendant Friedrich Flick on behalf of all defendants. *The United States of America v. Flick, et al.* Nuremberg, Germany, November 1947.[1]

# CHAPTER 6

## "Frederick the Great"

Friedrich Flick, facetiously called *Friedrich der Grosse,* was surely also called a shark by investors on Wall Street. Flick's manipulations of stock and his ruthless acquisitions made him the sole owner of one of the largest conglomerates in the world. The Flick concern manufactured everything from toilet paper to dynamite. He controlled over three hundred companies, including Daimler-Benz, whose 150,000 employees produced the luxurious Mercedes automobiles. In 1972 Flick was described as "the most important industrialist of his time."[2] This was quite an impressive achievement for a man who started out as a farm boy, grew wealthy, under questionable circumstances, before Hitler, and was convicted in 1947 of major war crimes during the Third Reich.

Flick's father was a farmer in the Siegerland, an area east of the Rhine and south of the Ruhr that contained deposits of high-grade iron ore. Upon completing two years of commercial training, Friedrich found a position with a small mining firm. A few years later he moved to the board of a hometown mining company, and this brought him into contact with the coal and steel barons of the Ruhr. The ambitious young man began to acquire some shares, to suggest mergers, and to expand his operations across Germany and into Upper Silesia, with its rich deposits of bituminous coal. By 1921 he had managed to gain control of iron ore mines and steel plants in Silesia, and in 1923 he moved on to Berlin. Flick then traded his Silesian holdings for shares in some of the leading steel companies of the Ruhr, and soon maneuvered himself into a position of control.

It did not take Flick long to strike up a friendship with Adolf Hitler. He was rewarded when Göring gave Flick exclusive "aryanization" rights to Jewish coal interests in Czechoslovakia, as well as iron resources in Lorraine. When the German army occupied the territories in the east, Flick had easy access to the industrial riches of the area, and to the slaves who could be seized there.[3]

Flick met regularly with Himmler to discuss economics and to put some money into the SS collection box, part of which went regularly to high ranking SS officers.[4] There was no bigger contributor than faithful Friedrich Flick. The DM 100,000 which was turned over to Himmler each year was transmitted via Flick's cousin, Konrad Kaletsch, who assured the SS that there was more where that came from.[5] Kaletsch, who joined the Nazi party in 1937,[6] could be relied upon to be a discreet adjutant to the *Konzern Herr*—the top man in the company.

To the Nazis, Flick was a loyal comrade. When *Einsatzgruppen* General Ohlendorf returned from the eastern front to report to Himmler's "Circle of Friends," Flick was a member of the select audience.[7] Flick and cousin Kaletsch were high on the distribution list of a secret report dated November 19, 1941, describing the elimination of all of the Jews of Kiev, Krivoy Rog, and other towns in which "those who did not escape were liquidated [*liquidiert*]."[8] Himmler also invited Flick to join in a visit to some concentration camps. As far as Hitler, Himmler, and Ohlendorf were concerned, Flick was a man who could be trusted.

After the war, six members of the Flick concern, including Friedrich Flick and Konrad Kaletsch, were tried at Nuremberg for war crimes and crimes against humanity, including the enslavement and abuse of concentration camp inmates, and plunder in occupied territories. The tribunal was presided over by the Hon. Charles B. Sears, formerly an associate judge of the Court of Appeals of the State of New York. He was joined on the bench by Judge William Christianson of the Supreme Court of Minnesota and Judge Frank Richman of the Supreme Court of Indiana. The trial lasted over six months and the record covered more than ten thousand pages. The accused were represented by fourteen German lawyers.[9]

Defense counsel Otto Kranzbühler carried the burden of the main defense against the slave labor charge, arguing that the defendants had done no more than what any other persons in their positions would have done in defense of home and country. He pictured the deeds of the German industrialists as acts of military and economic necessity against "the Red flood." The employment of forced labor was explained away as something beyond the defendant's control in a society where production was ordered by the state and supervised by the SS. Failure to meet production quotas or to reject assigned labor was to risk imprisonment or death, said Kranzbühler, and his views were echoed by Flick's main counsel, Dr. Rudolf Dix. The Hague Conventions were dismissed by Kranzbühler as an anachronism that the Allies had themselves repudiated.[10]

In rebuttal General Taylor took up the challenge, denying Kranzbühler's thesis that deportation of foreign workers was an act of German self-defense and that the wholesale deportation of millions of civilians was lawful under international law. Taylor warned the court that it was being "led down the garden path."[11]

The judges were sympathetic to the plight of the accused, but the evidence could not be denied. Flick was found guilty of spoliation, of using slave labor, and of supporting the SS through his contributions; he was sentenced to seven years of imprisonment. Half of the defendants, including Konrad Kaletsch, were acquitted. Flick's sentence was reviewed by General Lucius D. Clay and confirmed, and strenuous efforts by the defendants to have the decisions overturned by the courts in the United States did not succeed.[12]

By January 1951, when United States High Commissioner McCloy released all of the imprisoned industrialists who were still in the Landsberg jail, the Flick directors, having been given time off for good behavior, were already at liberty and busy rebuilding the empire of Friedrich Flick. Documentary proof assembled at Nuremberg showed that many of the companies Flick owned or acquired had been users of concentration camp labor. Dynamit Nobel Aktiengesellschaft (DAG) was such a company.

In the year 1865 a young Swedish chemist and engineer, having traveled around Europe and the United States, decided to form a company in Hamburg that might put to good use the knowledge he had acquired about the qualities of nitroglycerin. The company bore his name: Alfred Nobel & Co. Nobel acquired international patents for dynamite, and his firm grew rapidly. It was not long before he became known as "the dynamite king."

Alfred Nobel died unmarried and childless in 1896. The bulk of his massive fortune was left in trust to be used for awards based on outstanding accomplishments in the fields of physics, chemistry, medicine, literature, and peace. The Nobel Prize became world renowned and the name Nobel was often linked with the word "peace." It also continued to be associated with dynamite.

By 1941 DAG had consolidated dozens of different munitions companies all over Germany and held majority interests in nineteen other firms engaged in related activities. The main administrative office was in Troisdorf near Cologne, and one of the directors was Friedrich Flick.[13] A subsidiary of DAG—GmbH zur Verwertung chemische Erzeugnisse (Corporation to Exploit Chemical Products)—known by its abbreviated name Verwert Chemie, became one of the largest munitions producers for the German army.[14]

In August 1944, a transport of a thousand young Jewish women who had been seized in Hungary and Czechoslovakia was assembled in Auschwitz, sorted, and quickly transshipped to the Nobel firm in Allendorf near Kassel. The prisoners were herded from their barracks to an underground munitions factory concealed in a wooded area about an hour's march away. The inmates, working in two shifts of twelve hours each, had to measure out a predetermined amount of multicolored explosive powder which was then poured into shells and grenades.[15]

Another thousand Hungarian Jewish women were sent to Hessisch Lichtenau near Leipzig. Each day they were taken by cattle car to Fürstenhagen, which was about half an hour's ride away, and from there on foot for about forty-five minutes until they reached an underground munitions factory hidden in the woods. The company was called Fabrik Hessisch-Lichtenau der GmbH zur Verwertung chemische Erzeugnisse, and it too was a subsidiary of Dynamit Nobel. Both camps were attached to Buchenwald.[16]

At Ludwigsdorf in Lower Silesia, near Wüstergiersdorf, another munitions plant employed about six hundred Polish Jewish women from the concentration camp at Gross Rosen. They came in three transports of about two hundred each, beginning around May 1944, and their working conditions were the same as those endured by the two thousand Buchenwald inmates who worked in the other Dynamit Nobel companies. After the war was over, those who had survived felt that they were entitled to payment from their former masters.

By 1963 Dynamit Nobel was again busy producing munitions for Germany and many other countries. It reported sales of close to DM one billion, and Friedrich Flick, who owned 80 percent of the company, was chairman of the board.[17] With thousands of persons petitioning the Jewish organizations for help in obtaining compensation from the German munitions firms, it seemed appropriate for the Claims Conference to tactfully approach the Dynamit Nobel chief in the hope that he might be persuaded to follow the example set by a few of the other users of concentration camp labor.

## The Agreement That Never Was

Eric Warburg was called upon to establish the right connection to the Flick concern. The man whom Warburg introduced as the representative of Dynamit Nobel had acquired a reputation as an anti-Nazi. Dr. Fabian von Schlabrendorff, a lawyer from Wiesbaden, had written a book in which he described his participation in various attempts by German officers to do away with Adolf Hitler. According to von Schlabrendorff, in March 1943 he had handed a parcel to an officer on Hitler's plane, with a request that the "two bottles of brandy" be delivered to a certain general of the Army High Command. The bottles actually contained dynamite. A corrosive acid was supposed to eat through a wire and release a detonator that would ignite the explosive, and that, according to the plan, was to be the end of Adolf Hitler. Unfortunately, nothing happened. Von Schlabrendorff managed to retrieve the parcel only to discover that the detonator had not fired.[18]

Again according to von Schlabrendorff's account, he was brought before the People's Court by the Gestapo on February 3, 1945, but, as luck would have it, at just that moment an American bomb fell directly on the courthouse, killing the notorious Nazi Judge Roland Freisler and destroying the records against the accused. There had thus been several very dramatic incidents in von Schlabrendorff's life that had been associated with explosives before he appeared as the intermediary for Dynamit Nobel.

The meeting took place in Hamburg around a table that had been used by several generations of the prominent Warburg banking family. The anti-Nazi lawyer who appeared for the Nazi munitions firm was very accommodating, as he asked Ernst Katzenstein, the Claims Conference representative, to set forth the Jewish demands. Katzenstein replied that the conference hoped to pay each of the approximately 1,300 known claimants against Dynamit Nobel an amount of DM 5,000.

Much to Katzenstein's pleasant surprise, von Schlabrendorff promptly agreed to draft an agreement that he promised to put before the owners of Dynamit Nobel for consideration. The proposed contract, which was worked out jointly on the spot, provided that any claimant who could show that he or she worked in any of the three designated DAG plants would be entitled to receive DM 5,000. The conference would screen the claims and would receive an initial sum of DM 5 million as a minimum and DM 8 million as the maximum. Von Schlabrendorff declared that within the week he would submit the proposed contract to Flick, who held 82 percent of the shares of Dynamit Nobel, and to Bührle and Company of Switzerland, which held the remaining 18 percent. Katzenstein described the meeting as "the most satisfactory negotiation I have ever had in a slave labor matter."[19]

Shortly thereafter von Schlabrendorff suffered a heart attack. By the time he got around to setting up another meeting with Katzenstein, more than half a year had passed from the date of their first optimistic encounter. Von Schlabrendorff reported that he had held two meetings with the owners of Dynamit Nobel, whose position he described as being "neither yes nor no." From his detailed explanation it was difficult to detect where the "yes" came in, since he recited all of the standard reasons advanced by the other industrialists as justification for their refusal to pay.[20]

Katzenstein expressed his keen disappointment. He reminded von Schlabrendorff of the moral and political arguments and told him that if Dynamit Nobel was in fact rejecting the idea of an amicable settlement, it should say so unequivocably. Von Schlabrendorff replied that Flick was not opposed to the idea but the minority shareholder, Bührle, was against it.

The next day Eric Warburg phoned Katzenstein in Frankfurt to say that the company was toying with the idea of a one-time grant of $1 million (DM 4 million). Warburg asked for authority to suggest that a payment of DM 5 million would be acceptable.[21]

When the senior officers considered the latest proposal, they reached the conclusion that it would be advisable to accept the lesser sum if that proved necessary in order to reach an early settlement. Warburg then informed von Schlabrendorff that DM 5 million·was the conference's last word. Von Schlabrendorff reported to Warburg that he had discussed the problem with Friedrich Flick for two hours in Düsseldorf but no conclusion had been reached.[22]

There may have been reason to hope that Flick would do something for his former slaves. On his eightieth birthday the German tycoon, who was still actively in charge of the Mercedes company and the other firms in his domain, announced that he was donating more than a million dollars to German charities.[23] But the former concentration camp survivors had yet to see a sign of Flick's generosity.

More than a year went by, during which either von Schlabrendorff or Warburg repeatedly relayed some technical or legal question which, they said, required clarification and which Katzenstein then provided. By the start of 1964 Katzenstein handed over a batch of twenty-nine pages of documentary evidence, showing all the wartime subsidiaries of Dynamit Nobel, including Verwert Chemie and its plants in different locations. SS documents showed that the plants at Allendorf and Hessisch Lichtenau had used inmates from Buchenwald. The bills from the commandant showed how many had been employed on specific dates. Newly discovered evidence disclosed that there were plants at Christianstadt and Ludwigsdorf that drew inmates from Gross Rosen and a plant at Kaufering near Landsberg that received concentration camp laborers from Dachau. Other official SS records left no doubt that camp inmates could only have been obtained by German firms upon specific request. Flick's own affidavit was submitted to prove that he was on the board of DAG through 1945.[24]

Von Schlabrendorff continued to negotiate with Katzenstein, but Friedrich Flick gave free power of attorney to a personal representative, just as Alfried Krupp had appointed Berthold Beitz. Von Schlabrendorff stated that he had succeeded in winning over Flick's new man, a German lawyer who had joined the Nazi party in 1933 and had been associate defense counsel to Kranzbühler during the Flick trial at Nuremberg.[25] He was Dr. Wolfgang Pohle, who, when he was not working for Flick, was serving as a leading member of the German

*Bundestag.* Von Schlabrendorff and Warburg promised to meet with Pohle and asked Katzenstein to phone the next day to receive the good news. "Let us wait and see," declared a more cautious Katzenstein.[26]

About a month later von Schlabrendorff reported that he had finally presented Pohle with a draft settlement of the slave labor claims and that, although Pohle had posed a few questions and had some minor suggestions, he had raised no substantive objections. Von Schlabrendorff and Katzenstein then agreed upon a revised version of the contract which took into account the relatively minor points raised by Pohle. The contract stipulated that a final payment of DM 5 million would be made by May 1, 1964.

No sooner was the meeting over than Katzenstein was on the phone to New York with the long-awaited announcement, which he then confirmed in writing: "At last Flick has agreed to pay a fixed amount of DM 5 million to the Claims Conference." Within three days he had obtained approvals from the senior officers, had signed the agreement on behalf of the Claims Conference, and had sent it to von Schlabrendorff with a request that the DM 5 million be deposited to an account with Brinckman-Wirtz and Company in Hamburg.[27]

It had been agreed that no ratification by the Dynamit Nobel board of directors was needed. All that was still required was a resolution by the executive board of directors (*Vorstand*) and a transfer of the money. It looked as if an agreement between Flick and the Claims Conference was about to be concluded.

### Dangling in the Wind

By May 1, 1964, the money had not yet arrived. Von Schlabrendorff phoned to say that the meeting of the executive board had been postponed, but he had spoken to Flick and "he was optimistic about the outcome."[28] That optimism was not in evidence when he volunteered to come to Frankfurt to report personally to Katzenstein; a personal visit was always an omen of bad news.

According to von Schlabrendorff, during the meeting in Düsseldorf doubts had been expressed about an agreement which was restricted only to Jews and which failed to cover other Flick companies such as Daimler-Benz and Auto-Union. Further assurances were requested regarding the value and durability of a guarantee from the Claims Conference.

Von Schlabrendorff reported that he had replied that there was no reason to deny compensation to one group of entitled persons just because others were not covered, that the agreement might be expanded to cover other Flick plants, and that Warburg's confirmation of the reliability of the Claims Conference should suffice. He was convinced that since the owners of the company had both come out unequivocally in favor of a settlement, they would overrule the management at the next board meeting. Von Schlabrendorff gave his assurance that Flick was eager to dispose of the whole problem quietly, and might put up another DM 2 million for that purpose.[29]

Katzenstein, who had by that time also become skeptical about von Schlabrendorff's optimism, reported: "I am very doubtful indeed whether the matter will come to a positive end on July 22/23, 1964 and I do not know whether I can take seriously Flick's alleged eagerness to settle this matter, and in addition thereto to supply money in respect of other companies of his concern. After my meeting with von Schlabrendorff was over, I informed Eric thereof; he shared my apprehensions."[30] The fears were justified. The board meeting was again inconclusive, although von Schlabrendorff remained confident that "the matter would be brought to a good end."[31]

Two years of vacillation by Flick had convinced me that the Jewish organizations had been used in a cat and mouse game in which the Claims Conference was not the cat. I urged that a "white paper" be prepared to expose the truth to the public. It was my conviction that Flick had no desire or intention to pay anything, and that the agreement prepared by von Schlabrendorff as attorney for Flick and signed by Katzenstein on behalf of the world's leading Jewish organizations would never be honored.[32]

As there was no indication in 1965 that a public protest against Flick would have had any useful effect, the Claims Conference decided that the only viable alternative was not to break off the negotiations which, von Schlabrendorff repeatedly assured Katzenstein, were still very much alive. The attorney for Dynamit Nobel continued to pass on requests for additional documentation to prove the connection between Flick's company and the munitions plants that had employed concentration camp inmates, and Katzenstein invariably supplied additional evidence that left no room for doubt. Yet the new submissions were followed only by new delays and reports of new meetings where new problems were raised.[33]

Around the middle of 1965 von Schlabrendorff reported that the legal aspects of the case were being studied by Professor Heinrich Kronstein, who would render an expert opinion.[34] By the beginning of 1966 von Schlabrendorff explained that Flick's staff lawyers had objected to the opinion rendered by Kronstein in support of the Jewish claims and that a second *Gutachten*—expert opinion–had been requested. Von Schlabrendorff urged Katzenstein to avoid any public attacks that might jeopardize the settlement with Dynamit Nobel, which, according to him, was imminent.[35]

Kronstein issued a second opinion, which von Schlabrendorff described as very impressive. After Warburg read the opinion he "was pretty sure that there would be a positive settlement."[36] A few months later, when he informed Katzenstein that the deal was about to be confirmed, a wiser Katzenstein wrote: "I hear the calling but I lack the faith."[37]

Reports were received from Eric Warburg or von Schlabrendorff that the forced labor problem would be considered by the board of Dynamit Nobel in November 1966, then in December, then "some time in January," then "on January 5th," and then "on January 25th." Finally, on January 26, 1967, fifteen representatives of Dynamit Nobel met to consider what should be done about the claims of the former Jewish concentration camp inmates. Von Schlabrendorff was present, and reported the outcome of the meeting to Ernst Katzenstein. What he described was simply incredible.

All of the doubts were resolved and even the majority shareholder group, according to von Schlabrendorff, concurred that payment should be made. For the first time, therefore, all of the shareholders were in complete agreement. "In my opinion and that of Kronstein," said von Schlabrendorff, "the settlement was in the bag." There was only one little catch that prevented von Schlabrendorff from confirming the agreement in a legally binding way—he said the company was short of cash![38]

The German financial pages had reported that Friedrich Flick's personal fortune was estimated at over DM 2 billion. Just a few months before he had given his fifty-year-old son, Otto-Ernst, a cash payment that was well over the total amount being requested for the thousands of Jewish claimants who had survived work in companies controlled by Flick. He had given his sixteen-year-old granddaughter, Dagmar, more than the total amount required to satisfy the Claims Conference.[39] The argument that Flick or Dynamit Nobel could not raise DM 5 million to pay off the Jewish claims would have been almost laughable were the subject matter not so serious. The conference was expected to believe that Flick was a billionaire with no money.

The reason given for not concluding the settlement was an obvious pretense. Flick could pay the money out of his vest pocket—an opinion which Eric Warburg, a banker, later confirmed.[40] Katzenstein challenged von Schlabrendorff to show Flick's good faith by entering into an immediately binding contract according to which Dynamit Nobel acknowledged its obligation and agreed to pay the DM 5 million in installments at a later date. Von Schlabrendorff said he had no such authority, but it was a good idea which he promised to explore with the company. Undaunted, he assured Katzenstein that the whole matter would be finally settled in a matter of months.[41]

My own response was to suggest that Katzenstein give the company a fixed date to wind up the deal, and if there was no contract on that day, without any threats or requests, to release all of the facts to the press and give the public the whole truth regarding the many years of fruitless and frustrating effort by the Claims Conference to reach an amicable agreement with the convicted war criminal.[42]

Von Schlabrendorff came to New York in the spring and met there with Saul Kagan and Eric Warburg. He stated officially on behalf of his client that the Jewish claims would be settled at the latest by the end of the year.[43]

In the middle of the summer, it was announced that Dr. Fabian von Schlabrendorff had been nominated to fill a vacancy on the German Constitutional Court, beginning September 1, 1967. Von Schlabrendorff again promised to settle the Dynamit Nobel matter before that time, and Warburg reported that there was every reason to expect that the matter would be settled within the next three or four weeks.[44] By the time that von Schlabrendorff assumed his new duties on the court, nothing had happened to move Dynamit Nobel nearer to a settlement, and von Schlabrendorff's new duties barred him from any further dealings with the matter.

## To the Bitter End

The senior officers of the Claims Conference were still reluctant to criticize Flick publicly unless there was some reasonable assurance that it might produce positive results. New approaches would have to be tried first.

At the start of 1968 Nahum Goldmann wrote to Hermann Abs, an influential German banker, and asked him to intervene with Flick.[45] Abs informed Goldmann that a report from Konrad Kaletsch confirmed that the claims of forced laborers had been discussed by von Schlabrendorff as attorney for Dynamit Nobel since 1962 but the company was convinced that it had neither a legal nor a moral obligation to make any payments. Abs recommended that the Claims Conference be in touch with Eberhard von Brauchitsch, a forty-year-old lawyer who was acting for the aging Flick.[46]

Warburg warned against an approach to von Brauchitsch, whom he knew to be a staunch opponent of any settlement. I urged that an approach be made to Friedrich Flick directly, for I feared that Flick's death would mean an end to any chance for a payment. Katzenstein felt that neither he nor Goldmann could meet personally with a convicted war criminal.[47]

For many months nothing of significance happened and the Claims Conference senior officers, on the suggestion of Jacob Blaustein, decided to seek the intervention of former United States High Commissioner McCloy, who had played such an important role in persuading Alfried Krupp to come to an understanding with the Jewish organizations.

John McCloy, a very cautious and able lawyer, thought it prudent to seek advice from friends in Germany before he sent a letter directly to Friedrich Flick, and he wrote to von Schlabrendorff for guidance. Von Schlabrendorff replied that since he was on the bench, he could no longer act in the Flick matter, but he informed the former high commissioner that the letter had been passed on to Heinrich Kronstein. Within the week, Kronstein sent McCloy a concise outline of all of the legal arguments that had been raised by Dynamit Nobel in opposition to any settlement, including the fact that there was no proof that any member of the management had "participated in any act of torture." Kronstein suggested that McCloy seek further assistance from Hermann Abs.[48]

On April 9, 1969, McCloy wrote to Abs saying:

I find the legal position of the firm to be unbearably legalistic and really irrelevant to the main moral issue. It is not a matter of "claims" and "time of filing." It is a fact that the firm did employ Jewish slave labor and certainly no proof of "torture" is now needed to show that injustice was done and unjust returns from the labor were enjoyed . . . I know that I do not need to repeat that I have absolutely no interest in these claims other than a purely humanitarian one and one which I believe is in the interest of Germany.

When Kronstein returned to Germany, he contacted Flick's faithful cousin, Konrad Kaletsch, and told him about the interest in a settlement shown in the United States. Kaletsch was apparently sufficiently impressed to pass the word along that he would be prepared to discuss the subject with McCloy.[49]

Flick's youngest son, Friedrich-Karl, was in the United States on company business, and McCloy arranged to meet him at a reception held by Flick in New York. While they discussed the Dynamit Nobel problem, McCloy hardly noticed Flick's friend who joined in the conversation. He was Eberhard von Brauchitsch, nephew of Field Marshal von Brauchitsch, Commander in Chief of the German army under Hitler. Young Brauchitsch would make a stronger impression on McCloy the next time they met. McCloy made it clear that he thought a settlement of the Jewish claims was in order. The younger Flick thought the matter should be reconsidered, and suggested that McCloy should review the situation in Germany with Kaletsch.[50]

McCloy arranged to meet with Konrad Kaletsch and other leading officials of the Flick concern in Düsseldorf. The elder Flick was not present. But Konrad Kaletsch, who had been with his cousin in the dock at Nuremberg and who knew what McCloy had done for German industrialists, was in the chair. Wolfgang Pohle was there and sat quietly. The energetic young Eberhard von Brauchitsch, who had not been noticed by McCloy when they met at the party in New York, had come, brief in hand, poised to rebut any argument that the American lawyer McCloy might make.

McCloy had been up late the night before and his stomach was upset by his travels, so he was not in a fighting mood, although he put forth his moral arguments as best he could. Kaletsch responded that McCloy was asking them to overrule a negative decision that had been reached unanimously by all members of the board. Von Brauchitsch pounded out his legal arguments in an effort to persuade the former high commissioner that the rejection of the claims was justified. When McCloy returned to New York, he informed Blaustein of the disappointing Düsseldorf meeting. What he recalled most vividly was that during the course of the von Brauchitsch tirade, McCloy asked to be excused, "having to run out of the room several times to vomit."[51]

After some time had elapsed, McCloy phoned and asked me to come to his Wall Street office, where he cross-examined me on many of the legal details. When we were through, he felt that the time had come for him to address a personal letter to Friedrich Flick.[52]

McCloy was then engaged in disarmament negotiations on behalf of the United States government, and it was almost two months before he could find the time to sit down and put his thoughts to paper. The problem of dealing with Nazi criminals and restitution to the victims of oppression was a subject which moved McCloy deeply, and he needed repose in order to adequately convey his innermost feelings.

In his November 13 letter to "Dear Dr. Flick," McCloy referred to the meeting in Düsseldorf in which he had not been successful in persuading the Flick people to consider any payment to surviving victims of the German slave labor policy. He recalled his own role in moderating the sentences of some of those who had been convicted at Nuremberg, and said that his act of clemency had been coupled with the hope that, in due course, compensation would be provided by firms which had made use of slave labor. He reminded Flick that several of the leading German companies had already done so. McCloy wrote:

I feel deeply that a legalistic approach to this matter entirely misses
the point. Therefore as one last effort on my part to urge that
amends along the lines of the Schlabrendorff proposal be made, I
am writing to you as a major factor in the control of Dynamit Nobel that you use your influence to clear up, as far as now may be
possible, this old wrong.

Most of the Jewish concentration camp inmates who managed to survive the horrors of the camps, some of which I myself witnessed at the close of the war, are old women broken in health and living in straightened circumstances. I hesitate naturally to impose on anyone my personal views as to a proper course for another to take in a matter of moral obligation, but I do feel that for you to exert your influence to see that this step is taken would inure to the benefit of the Company, the Federal Republic and your own reputation as a sensitive humanitarian. I trust you will forgive me for writing you personally in this vein, but my conscience has impelled me to do so in spite of the attitude taken by your representatives in Dusseldorf whom I was received by last June.

Katzenstein sent copies to Eric Warburg, von Schlabrendorff, Abs, and Kronstein in the hope that they would lend support to the McCloy initiative. Judge von Schlabrendorff conveyed to Katzenstein his hopes for success. The only substantive comment he had was to suggest that McCloy be advised—in a discreet way—that it was not appropriate, even for an American, to omit the "von" from his title.[53]

More than a month passed and there was no sign of a reply to the McCloy letter. Katzenstein phoned the Flick company and learned that the letter was being dealt with by von Brauchitsch, who was on vacation in Arosa. The young German executive was known to travel in the company jet, to have a phone in his Mercedes limousine, and to act with dispatch.[54] Obviously, the letter from America was not high on his list of priorities.

When von Brauchitsch returned from holiday, he wrote to McCloy on January 7 "on behalf of Dr. Friedrich Flick." The German text was followed by an English translation:

Dr. Flick repeats and confirms fully the opinion expressed by Messrs. Kaletsch, Dr. Pohle and the undersigned in the discussion with you in Düsseldorf on June 18, 1969, and the various reasons which have been stated to justify this view. To his regret Dr. Flick feels unable to urge Dynamit Nobel AG to take a different course with regard to this matter . . . Dr. Flick is of the opinion that under no aspect, nor under a moral aspect either, it would be indicated or justifiable for Dynamit Nobel AG or the Flick group to fulfill the demand of the Claims Conference.

Dr. Flick asks for your comprehension of his final decision in this affair . . . Dr. Flick sends you his best regards, in which I join.

Sincerely,
von Brauchitsch

Friedrich Flick had already been released from Landsberg prison by the time McCloy demonstrated his compassion by releasing other convicted war criminals. Unlike Alfried Krupp, who was given back his freedom and his fortune by McCloy, Flick owed the former high commissioner nothing. The letter to McCloy was replete with arguments and observations that were completely erroneous. Ernst Katzenstein sent von Brauchtisch a detailed rebuttal. Von Brauchitsch was not content to allow the Claims Conference to have the last word. Said he, "I stand by every point of the letter." The contrary evidence was brushed aside as "political documents from the Nuremberg trials."[55]

A last ditch effort led by the new German ambassador in Washington, Rolf Pauls, produced nothing more than a vague hope that if any former Jewish employee of Flick could prove that he was indigent, the company might consider the individual case.[56] The Claims Conference had the names of over 3,500 persons who said they had been slaves in a Flick company. Most of them were sorely in need, but to tell Jewish slave laborers to submit proof of their poverty to their former exploiters, in the hope that they might receive some unspecified grant, was not a procedure that any respectable Jewish organization could accept. Even if Dynamit Nobel paid a few people—which was doubtful—no one could explain to the others who had survived that they would receive nothing because in the eyes of some German administrator they were not needy enough.[57]

For over nine years, every effort had been made to persuade Flick and his assistants that they owed something to those who had worked in Flick companies without pay under the most inhumane conditions. The courts had left the determination of legal liability in suspense. Efforts to use moral persuasion had been made by Fabian von Schlabrendorff, Eric Warburg, Heinrich Kronstein, Hermann Abs, John McCloy, Rolf Pauls, the Claims Conference representatives, and others. The urgings had been made to Kaletsch, to von Brauchitsch, to Pohle, to Flick's son, and to the owner, Friedrich Flick himself. Every effort had met with nothing but excuses, delays and frustration.

Toward the end of 1970 Jacob Blaustein passed away at the age of seventy-eight. He had been a courageous fighter for human rights, and his inability to persuade Flick, a fellow industrialist, to do something for the Jewish slaves was one of Blaustein's last great disappointments. The Claims Conference representatives were finally convinced that Flick had no intention of paying anything. Flick's defiant peroration at Nuremberg—"Nothing will convince us that we are war criminals"— still echoed in my ears.

I turned my complete file over to B'nai B'rith, which prepared to give the whole truth to the press. A B'nai B'rith article labeled Flick an "unrepentant slave master." The story recounted the vast wealth he had amassed under Hitler, and after Hitler, and outlined Flick's friendship with mass murderer Himmler. Car buyers were told that "the man who profits most from the sales of Mercedes cars is a convicted war criminal who has not yet paid off his debt to society." The report showed that Flick's actions were a violation of many international laws. It recited all the dodges and excuses the company had advanced over the years to avoid a payment to the former slaves.[58]

Just as the report was ready to go to press, I asked B'nai B'rith to withhold publication. On July 20, 1972; in his ninetieth year, Friedrich Flick died in his home on Lake Constance. The *New York Times* obituary described him as "an industrialist who aided Hitler" and one "who built a vast fortune" while remaining a mystery man who shunned the limelight.[59] One biographer said that in 1971 Flick got richer by $360,000 every day.[60] Some of the most prominent people in Germany attended his funeral.[61] "Am I right," asked Katzenstein, "in my assumption that the Dynamit Nobel case will be laid to rest with Flick's body?" The answer which I sent back was yes.[62] Nothing could have been gained for the former slaves by disclosing the bitter story.

Although Friedrich Flick was reputedly the richest man in Germany and the fifth richest man in the world and left assets worth over one billion dollars to a playboy son, when he went to his grave he had paid the Jewish concentration camp inmates not one single cent.[63]

# A Medley of Disappointments

The managers were under a duty to do what was possible to ameliorate the suffering [of the inmates] and to avoid making their burden unnecessarily heavier. This obvious humane duty toward those prisoners who were given over to their custody is not only a moral but also a legal obligation.

Decision of the Appellate Court of Stuttgart in the case of *Bartl v. Heinkel,* May 19, 1965.[1]

# CHAPTER 7

## A Pyrrhic Victory

At first he was afraid to give his name. He was a Jew who was born in Chemnitz, had been in the camps, had immigrated to Israel, and had then returned to Germany to live in Frankfurt. Someone had thrown a rock through his car window when he had exposed a former Nazi, and the Auschwitz survivor was frightened. He would have preferred to remain anonymous, but he became so bitter and enraged that he could no longer contain his anger.[2]

In the summer of 1944, when Adolf Diamant was twenty, he was transferred from the ghetto at Lodz, to which he had been deported, to the concentration camp at Auschwitz/Birkenau. His parents went straight to the gas chambers. One September day, two civilians appeared at the morning roll call, including one who was identified as an engineer by the name of Pfender, and demanded that all metal workers step forward. Diamant was one of about two thousand young men who were taken away. He was assigned, under control of the concentration camp at Neuengamme, to work in Braunschweig (Brunswick) for the Büssing Company, which was busy manufacturing trucks for the army. In April 1945 he was liberated.

In 1957 Diamant visited his former employer, whose trucks and busses could be seen all over Germany. He had no difficulty in obtaining a certificate from the Büssing Company confirming that he had worked for the firm and that the company had made a payment for his services to the account of the concentration camp at Neuengamme. Similar declarations were given to several other former camp inmates.[3] The certificates were issued every time a former inmate wrote to the company and asked for compensation. It was attached to a polite letter explaining to the former prisoners that the company had no choice but to accept the concentration camp laborers against the company's will, that the company had done all it could to ameliorate the suffering of the prisoners, and that the firm had already paid the SS for the services, hence the claim should be directed against the German government. At the same time the company warned that, if sued, it would have to plead the statute of limitations as one of its defenses.

Adolf Diamant, having heard about the decision of the Frankfurt court in the Wollheim case against I.G. Farben and of the subsequent settlement, started a lawsuit against Büssing in Braunschweig. The tone of the defensive arguments raised by the company got sharper as the proceedings continued. The firm even challenged the identity of the complainant and said he was an Israeli citizen who could not, under a cited Nazi law, be treated as a German. It was suggested that the plaintiff from Tel Aviv was really a Marxist whose Frankfurt residence was a subterfuge.[4] This so annoyed Adolf Diamant that he called in the press, gave them the full story, and repeated it on German television.[5]

Compensation Treuhand had registered a few hundred claims of former Büssing workers, but no action had been taken by the Claims Conference on their behalf. The most that could have been done would have been to start a test case, but the energetic Mr. Diamant had already done that on his own. Ernst Katzenstein simply asked Diamant's German attorneys to keep him informed of further progress.[6]

When the decision of the district court was handed down, it was found by the court that Büssing had a complete list of all of their former concentration camp workers, and that Diamant's name was on the list. The fact that the company had paid the SS was held to be no defense since, according to the judge, no one was entitled to sell the labor of a person who had been unlawfully deprived of his freedom, and the contract between Büssing and the SS was therefore null and void. Furthermore, the German indemnification law could not absolve the defendant of liability since the law provided no compensation for the services rendered by the plaintiff to the defendant. A traditional German juridical principle—*Geschäftsführung ohne Auftrag*—required that payment be made by anyone knowingly accepting another's labor and deriving a benefit from it. Claims of that type, said the court, had a thirty-year filing period.

The Braunschweig court carefully computed the time the plaintiff had worked for the defendant. It came to 1,778 hours of labor. The court concluded that, according to the wartime wage controls, the appropriate pay scale was RM 1 per hour, and therefore the plaintiff was entitled to RM 1,778, which, under the currency conversion law of 1948, had to be revalued into deutsche marks at the rate of RM 10 = DM 1. The plaintiff was accordingly entitled to only DM 177.80, which, at the prevailing rate of exchange amounted to precisely \$44.45.[7] As far as is known, the Büssing company did not file an appeal and the decision became final. The plaintiff slave laborer had won his case.

## The Courageous Dr. Bartl and the Aircraft Companies

There would have been no German air force without the private aircraft companies of Junkers, Messerschmidt, and Heinkel. Each of them employed thousands of concentration camp inmates. Junkers reached into Buchenwald, Messerschmidt absorbed thousands of inmates from Mauthausen and Dachau, and Heinkel took Jews from the ghetto of Cracow/Plaszow and the camps of Sachsenhausen, Oranienburg, Ravensbrück, and Mauthausen. Himmler reported to Göring that he had about 36,000 inmates working for the aircraft industry on March 9, 1944, and that the amount would be increased to 90,000. A top-secret SS chart gave the breakdown for each concentration camp and company.[8] None of the firms ever paid anything to any of the camp survivors.

Many of the camp inmates who had toiled in the underground factories, caves, salt mines, and quarries, where the aircraft producers tried to hide from Allied bombs, asked the Claims Conference for assistance with their claims. I could not forget what I had seen when Mauthausen and its subcamps, including Gusen, had been liberated. A mound of human bones surrounded the quarry that hid the aircraft factory of Messerschmidt.

By 1960 Messerschmidt A.G., located at Augsburg, was back in business and employed over two thousand people. It had assets of over DM 30 million. The Messerschmidt family controlled the company and held options to acquire most of the shares held by the Bavarian government, which had helped to finance the firm's reconstruction.[9]

In the spring of 1962, Ernst Katzenstein and I were in Munich to negotiate the conclusion of the settlement with the Siemens company. We paid a visit to the Bavarian Ministry of Finance and discussed the possibility of a similar agreement with Messerschmidt. It was suggested that the subject be broached at the Federal Ministry of Defense in Bonn, which was trying to build up the German aircraft industries. Shortly thereafter, Katzenstein visited Ministerial Director Dr. Knieper at the ministry, who suggested that Katzenstein talk to Director Fritz Rudorf, of the Dresdner Bank, who sat on the Messerschmidt board. Rudorf suggested that Katzenstein talk to the personal representative of the Messerschmidt family, Dr. H. Ritter von Srbik.[10]

Von Srbik made it quite clear that it was simply out of the question to provide, as Katzenstein had suggested, up to DM 5,000 for each surviving Jewish concentration camp inmate who had worked for Messerschmidt. Although Messerschmidt owned its own airport right outside of Munich, and it was a rather valuable piece of real estate, the company could not be compared in wealth with Farben, Krupp, Siemens, or any of the others that had settled the Jewish claims. Von Srbik promised, however, to discuss it with the board and the other aircraft producers.[11]

It was not long before Rudorf reported that the board of Messer-schmidt had declined to make any payment. The reasons given were that the company had no control over the employment of the inmates, and "the financial situation of the firm was bad."[12] A few days later, on December 19, the *Frankfurter Allgemeine Zeitung* quoted the retir-ing board chairman as saying that "things at Messerschmidt are again going very well." Knieper and Rudorf both explained the inconsis-tency to Katzenstein by saying that while it was true that the financial position was good, it was going to get bad![13]

Press reports showed that Willy Messerschmidt was at that time busy advising the Egyptian government on building rockets, which Egypt's President Gemal Abdul Nasser declared would be used to de-stroy Israel. The *New York Times* reported that Willy Messerschmidt had developed an aircraft that he was prohibited from building in West Germany and he had therefore designed the plane for the Hispano-Suiza Company, which produced it in prototype. A large staff of Ger-mans, including former designers for Junkers and Messerschmidt, were in Cairo helping President Nasser develop his own aircraft, which the Israelis feared could carry high-explosive rocket warheads. "A Munich physician wanted on charges of medical atrocities in concen-tration camps" was reported to be employed as a company doctor at the Messerschmidt factory near Cairo.[14]

With the Messerschmidt family again in complete control of the com-pany, and with Willy Messerschmidt and his colleagues helping a coun-try that had publicly declared its intention to destroy the survivors of the Holocaust, Katzenstein was not surprised to be finally informed that the Messerschmidt company "does not see itself in a position to grant your wish for an agreement."[15]

No test case had been started against Messerschmidt in the German courts, nor was any such case likely to succeed. The leading challenge to the aircraft industry came from a non-Jewish anti-Nazi German law-yer who sued the Heinkel aircraft company. The sad case of Dr. Ed-mund Bartl, former prisoner of the Sachsenhausen concentration camp, against his former employer Ernst Heinkel A.G. made legal his-tory.

Bartl was arrested by the Gestapo in 1941, taken before a special tribunal, charged with opposition to the Nazi regime, and sentenced to two years in prison. When his term expired, the Gestapo took him into "protective custody" and shipped him to the concentration camp at Sachsenhausen. The Heinkel company had a large aircraft factory in the nearby town of Oranienburg, and Bartl soon found himself living in a camp inside the factory grounds and, side by side with six thousand other prisoners, doing heavy manual labor under threat of being exe-cuted if he failed to meet the quotas set by the Heinkel foreman.[16] He was beaten regularly and suffered constantly from hunger and thirst.

His eyes were seared by sparks from a welding machine he was forced to operate without protective goggles. When he was liberated, the former lawyer from Sudetenland was nearly blind, he weighed only eighty-six pounds, and his health was permanently ruined.[17]

As soon as his strength would allow, Bartl moved to West Germany. Years later he discovered that the Heinkel company had also relocated in the west and had its main office in a suburb of Stuttgart. In 1959 he commenced a lawsuit in the Augsburg District Court, alleging that Heinkel had been enriched by his labor, that for twenty-four months he had received no wages, that the company's negligence in failing to provide proper working conditions had caused him great injury, pain, and suffering, and that he was entitled to compensation. He asked for a partial judgment of DM 10,000 ($2,500).

The district court held that since the Heinkel company had paid the SS the inadequate sum of only RM 132 ($44) per month for Bartl's services, the firm had been unjustly enriched, and the plaintiff was entitled to compensation on that ground. All the other claims were dismissed for having been filed too late.[18] Both parties appealed to the appellate court in Stuttgart.

The higher court rendered a thirty-eight-page opinion. It concluded that the lower court had not gone far enough. Not only was the plaintiff Bartl entitled to a payment for Heinkel's unjust enrichment, but he was also entitled to his unpaid wages and for the damages caused by the company's negligence. According to the Stuttgart Appellate Court, the company was legally responsible for what were the foreseeable acts of its agents. Since Bartl had been reasonably diligent in locating the company after the war, and in commencing his action, the court concluded that he was not barred by any of the time limits.

The appellate court reasoned that the Heinkel company had the power and therefore the duty to prevent inmate supervisors from beating other inmate laborers, and that the management was obliged to do what it could to minimize the suffering of the workers and to prevent the addition of any unnecessary burdens. "This obvious humane duty toward those prisoners who were given over to their custody is not only a moral but also a legal obligation. In both directions, in making things easier and in preventing additional burden, the managers of the company did next to nothing."[19]

The decision in favor of Edmund Bartl attracted wide public attention. *Der Spiegel* carried the story under the title "Slaves and the Reich" and showed a picture of Himmler at Auschwitz and a photograph of Bartl over the caption *Schmerz nicht verjährt*—which meant that his pain and suffering were not barred by any time limits.[20] The article also listed many of the principal German firms that had been extensive users of slave labor, and no doubt gave rise to considerable apprehension in some corporate board rooms. The Heinkel company appealed to the German Supreme Court.

The federal court had already ruled that forced labor claims of Allied nationals were in the nature of reparations and would have to await a final peace treaty with Germany. To grant the claim of a German national like Bartl might validate the allegation raised by the Czech claimants in the case against Rheinmetall that the German courts were discriminating, in violation of the German constitution. Besides, if Bartl prevailed, where would one draw the line, and what would be the consequences to German industry if the companies had to pay all of their surviving forced laborers? Bartl's lawyer feared that the Finance Ministry, pressured by the Federal Associatoin of German Industries, was unduly influencing the court.[21] The supreme court found a way out.

Bartl's claims were all dismissed because, according to the supreme court, he had filed too late. A *German* national should have known his rights, and Bartl had failed to assert them within the normal time period. Non-German nationals would have to wait for a peace treaty. As long as no slave laborer was entitled to payment, there was complete equality—even if the rejections were on completely inconsistent procedural grounds—and a constitutional challenge alleging discrimination would not prevail. The German firms were completely protected by the shield of the supreme court, and Bartl, facing financial ruin, was ordered to pay all the court and attorney fees for both sides.[22] The German judges had succumbed to the temptation to temper justice not with mercy but with expediency.

## Brown Coal and Gasoline

Shortly after Hitler came to power, he began to move Germany toward a war economy. One of his goals was to make the Reich as independent as possible of imported foreign oil. Synthetic fuel could be manufactured from lignite, which was known as brown coal. A number of collieries merged to form Braunkohle-Benzin A.G., for the purpose of producing synthetic fuel in four big plants. BRABAG, with its top-priority war mission, became one of the biggest users of slave labor.[23] Fritz Kranefuss, an SS brigadier general, was on the executive board. He was on intimate terms with Himmler, and the WVHA was ready to give him any laborers he wanted.[24]

When BRABAG asked the Buchenwald commandant for 1,000 prisoners and 120 SS guards for work at Magdeburg, it took only four days for the guards to be dispatched, and the "Commando Magda" prisoners arrived within three weeks. The Buchenwald strength reports showed that over 5,000 Jews, in what was called "Commando Wille," were working for BRABAG at Zeitz. The plant at Böhlen received a

Buchenwald transport of 1,000 men, and commandant Pister teletyped a warning against increasing the number since there was not enough food to keep them alive. Another batch of 1,000 prisoners from Auschwitz went to work for BRABAG at Schwarzheide under the supervision of the concentration camp at Sachsenhausen.[25]

BRABAG factories were prime targets for the Strategic Air Command of the United States and Great Britian. The raids took a heavy toll, particularly among the Jews, who "were driven like dogs into the countryside and those people who didn't go along were shot."[26] Vengeful beatings followed every Allied bombardment, and the Jews were forced to remove unexploded shells and dredge the craters that had filled with poisonous coal gasses. Within nine months 75 percent of the prisoners were dead or disabled as a result of overwork, famine, and disease. Jews who were *verbraucht* (used up) were assembled, shipped back to Buchenwald and from there to Auschwitz, to be gassed, burned, and replaced by another shipment.[27] Most of those thousands of Jewish concentration camp inmates who worked for BRABAG were "exterminated through labor," but over 500 survivors turned to the Claims Conference for help.

Dr. Karl-Heinz Schildbach, acting on instructions from the conference, met with BRABAG's managing director, Dr. Erich Würzner, who had been in charge of the BRABAG plant at Magdeburg during the war.[28] Würzner denied that he had any personal knowledge of what had happened to the concentration camp inmates and pointed out that his company had lost all of its plants in the east and was almost without funds. He politely declined Schildbach's offer that an agreement be reached in principle, with payments deferred until the company could acquire adequate resources to meet its obligations.[29] Schildbach was not convinced that BRABAG was without funds, since he had read that very day that BRABAG was acquiring a 25 percent interest in Caltex GmbH, which had a capital of DM 13.2 million.[30] He immediately filed four test cases against BRABAG with the district court in Berlin.[31]

The plaintiffs described the murderous conditions under which they had worked, and gave the names of sixty-one witnesses who had been with them in the BRABAG camp. The complaint of Herman B. recounted his futile efforts to persuade the camp authorities to acquire essential surgical instruments. Others swore that they had personally seen the leg of an injured Jew cut off with an ordinary wood saw and without any anesthesia.[32] A witness from Israel testified that only 300 out of 1,300 of his group survived the back-breaking BRABAG work assignments. He cited a BRABAG foreman who specifically acknowledged that the Jews were deliberately being worked to death. He described a scene wherein a Jew named Bachner complained that the members of his work gang could not carry on the strenuous pace, and, for daring to speak out, Bachner was shot and killed on the spot.[33]

Despite the particularly appalling circumstances under which the Jews had to toil for BRABAG, every effort to reach some understanding with the firm proved futile. For five years the company consistently refused to reach an accommodation with the former forced laborers. BRABAG made settlements with bondholders and other creditors, but no money could be found to pay any of the Jewish claims.[34]

The Claims Conference, confronted with the negative and evasive decisions of the German Supreme Court, concluded that no useful purpose would be served by spending additional Jewish funds in pursuit of a hopeless cause.[35] The four test cases against BRABAG, in whose service thousands of Jewish laborers died, were allowed to lie dormant in the district court in Berlin, where they may still be dangling to this very day.

## Construction Companies as Slavemasters

The Estonian port of Reval (Tallinn), not far from Leningrad, was severely damaged when the German armies drove out the Russians who had occupied the area at the outbreak of the war. There were about a thousand Jews still living in Reval when the Germans entered. The SS *Einsatzgruppen* soon reported: "There were no spontaneous pogroms. Only by the Security Police and the SD were the Jews gradually executed as they became no longer required for work. Today there are no longer any Jews in Estonia."[36] By 1942 German Jews were being shipped in as replacements. Girls who could understand the German commands were considered more reliable, and as long as they were able to work they could stay alive.

It was in the winter of 1942 that the shipment of slaves for the German construction firm of Philipp Holzmann arrived in Reval. Some of the prisoners were only thirteen years old. They were all crowded into the local prison, where they were assigned ten to a cell, which meant that four of them had to sleep on the cold stone floor. At 5:30 each morning they were assembled for roll call and then marched out to the construction company to help repair the damaged wharf. They were forced to carry heavy bags of cement and loads of building materials. They were threatened that they would be allowed to live only if they worked harder. Beatings by Holzmann foremen and starvation was part of the routine. The women were warned by a Holzmann supervisor: "If any of you escape, 10 other women will be held responsible and will be shot on the spot." When the Russians started their counteroffensive in the summer of 1944, the Holzmann workers of Reval were evacuated to the concentration camp at Stutthof.[37]

Most of the major German construction companies used inmates from many concentration camps. [38] The building firms became prosperous again after the war by helping to rebuild the destroyed German cities, but none of them acknowedged any responsibility to the camp survivors. By 1960 Philipp Holzmann employed about 16,000 men, had a balance sheet showing over DM 100 million, was paying dividends of 16 percent to its shareholders, and had a substantial interest in over a dozen other construction companies. Its supervisory board of directors included Hermann Abs. The chairman of the executive board was Dr. Walter Kesselheim.[39]

Eric Warburg helped to arrange a meeting between Ernst Katzenstein and Walter Kesselheim to see if anything could be done to work out a settlement on behalf of the former forced laborers. The atmosphere was pleasant, but Kesselheim insisted that all of the company's records had been destroyed and he could not consider the problem without further clarification of the facts and the law.[40] Two years later there still was no progress. Finally, it was made very clear by the Holzmann company that there was no possibility for a settlement and there was no purpose in continuing the discussions. The press reported that Holzmann had a turnover that year of over half a billion deutsch marks.[41]

Two test cases against Holzmann, initiated by the Claims Conference, came before the Frankfurt District Court. Although the judges were bound by the supreme court's negative ruling, they did not hesitate to call upon Holzmann to settle the claims of the slave laborers, and they drew attention to the high dividend Holzmann was paying to its shareholders.[42] Holzmann refused. The court could not find it in its heart to render a judgment against the plaintiffs and thereby compel the girls to pay all the court costs to their former German employer. Instead, the court issued a one-paragraph decision saying that since no money had been posted as security for costs, the court would treat the claims as if they had been withdrawn.[43]

The claims against the large construction firm of Leonhard Moll, of Munich, followed the route of the Holzmann and other slave labor demands. The company, which had been established in 1894 as a family concern, denied all liability, pleaded that the claims were filed too late, and flatly rejected any possibility of a settlement.[44]

All of the big construction companies had more orders in Germany after the war than they could handle. They needed no foreign markets and they were impervious to any pressures that an American Jewish organization might try to bring against them. Some of them even argued that they had been victimized when they used the concentration camp inmates. That attitude was best reflected in a decision of an Austrian court regarding claims against Austrian construction companies that had worked in close cooperation with Siemens-Bauunion and other leading German firms.

The Austrian firms of H. Rella and A. Porr were, like Siemens-

Bau-Union, engaged in the building of railroad bridges and other construction work in Bor, Yugoslavia. The Hungarian Jews from Auschwitz who were digging the ditches and toiling in the copper mines in the spring of 1944 were being worked to death. One of the survivors, Jacob S., a tailor from Budapest who had emigrated to Haifa, sued the companies in the courts of Austria. The claims were finally rejected. One of the grounds given to justify the dismissal of the claims was that the SS was paid more than what the starving workers were worth. According to the Austrian judge, it was the construction company rather than the concentration camp inmate that was the real victim.[45]

## A Global Approach Fails

One of the objectives of the Nuremberg trials had been to disclose the facts so that all the world would know what had actually happened in Germany under the Nazis. The primary goal of the Claims Conference in supporting test cases against German firms had been to obtain some measure of redress for the camp survivors. Litigation was costly and hazardous and an effort was therefore made to find some easier way to achieve the desired end. The plan was to reach an overall agreement with the nongovernmental Federal Association of German Industries, the Bundesverband der Deutschen Industrie, whereby the BDI, using funds provided by the former users of concentration camp inmates, would make a payment that could be divided among the forced laborers in accordance with some mutually acceptable formula.

Soon after the agreement was reached with I.G. Farben, I arranged to have dinner with Dr. Werner Veith, a representative of the BDI's legal department. I drew his attention to the favorable publicity that had resulted from the Farben settlement and suggested that it might be in the interest of German industry and its reputation abroad if other firms could see their way clear to making a similar payment. I noted the moral arguments but also reasoned that an overall settlement would diffuse any possible stigma and would also diminish the prospects of a substantial number of lawsuits against many German firms.[46]

A few weeks later the head of the BDI's legal department, Dr. Wolfgang Froehlich, informed me that he had discussed the suggestion with a number of firms, but the circumstances in each case were so diverse that they could not see how the problem could be disposed of in one overall agreement. I then outlined a more specific plan which Froehlich again discussed with the companies, but again the answer came back that a global approach was not considered feasible.[47]

In the meantime, test cases had been commenced to safeguard the position of the claimants, and the Claims Conference reached the conclusion that taking on one company at a time might be easier to handle than trying to insist upon a package deal. I advised Froehlich that the pending legal actions would have to take their course and that an overall agreement might be reconsidered at a later date.[48]

In the spring of 1962, after the settlements with Farben, Krupp, and AEG had been concluded, Nahum Goldmann suggested that Ernst Katzenstein sound out Chancellor Adenauer's state-secretary, Dr. Hans Globke, on how the slave labor problem could best be wound up. Although Globke had written a commentary on the Nazi racial laws during the Hitler period and was frequently the object of criticism by anti-Nazi groups, he had repeatedly been helpful in connection with Goldmann's efforts to have the indemnification legislation improved. Globke discussed the problem with Dr. Fritz Berg, president of BDI, and then informed Katzenstein that any further effort to reach a global accord would be a mistake. It was his conclusion that any such agreement would be viewed as a confession of guilt by German industry, and efforts to pursue a global approach would only unite the companies in a solid front of opposition.[49]

The idea of an overall final accord was toyed with for a number of years thereafter, but got nowhere. At one point Krupp's general manager, Berthold Beitz, offered to talk to Berg about it, since, after all, the more firms which acknowledged that they had employed slave labor, the less odious would Krupp appear. But Beitz's intervention had no visible impact.[50]

The Claims Conference dropped its efforts to reach some amicable accord that would serve as a symbol of German industry's willingness to help the former slaves. Only the sense of deep injustice felt by some of the survivors kept the idea alive. Years later, an organization called The World Jewish Federation of Victims of the Nazi Regime demanded to know from Compensation Treuhand why so few companies had paid the former forced laborers and what was being done about it. The letter, dated May 19, 1970, was signed by Tuvia Friedmann, Chairman. On June 7 the *Jerusalem Post* carried a story, "Survivors of Nazi Slave Labour Press Claims," and Friedmann was quoted as saying, "Of the two million Jews who were used as slaves in the German war production only 200,000 survived." He planned to demand DM 1,000 for every month of slave labor, and the payment received for those who perished would be used to encourage new births to compensate for the two million Jewish children who were murdered by the Nazis.

The World Jewish Federation of Victims published ads in Israeli newspapers calling upon forced laborers to register. The ads implied that West German President Heinemann and the BDI had encouraged the victims' federation to pursue its demands for payment. The figure mentioned was DM 72 billion.[51] The World Federation wrote to me for assistance, but I refused, pointing out that in my view there was no hope whatsoever of obtaining any further payment, and to encourage the former slaves to believe the contrary was doing them a disservice.[52]

But Tuvia Friedmann had come out of the camps a very determined man. A delegation from the World Federation arrived in Germany, and, according to the press, demanded one billion dollars.[53] Shortly thereafter it was announced that the mission had been a complete failure. The BDI had refused to receive the delegation and efforts to induce the German government to intervene were equally fruitless.[54] The frustrated efforts of Tuvia Friedmann and his World Federation were no more than a feeble reflection of the continued unhappiness and desperation felt by many camp inmates who had been forced to slave for German firms without compensation of any kind.

# The Last Word

*Hass ist nie das letzte Wort.*
　　Rolf Hochhuth, *Der Stellvertreter*

# CHAPTER 8

## "Hate Is Never the Last Word"

There is a touching scene in Rolf Hochhuth's play *The Deputy (Der Stellvertreter)* which takes place in August 1942 in the Berlin apartment of First Lieutenant Kurt Gerstein, an anti-Nazi who has infiltrated the SS. Horrified by what he sees happening to the Jews in the concentration camps, Gerstein has personally appealed to the Pope, "the deputy," to intervene to stop the deportations. Gerstein is visited by a Vatican priest, Father Riccardo, who offers his help. Gerstein asks the priest to give his frock and passport to a Jew, Jacobson, who is hiding in the next room, so that the Jew may flee the country. Father Riccardo gladly agrees. Before Jacobson can leave, he learns from Gerstein that both his mother and his old father, a German war veteran, have been deported and are on their way to death in Auschwitz. Jacobson explodes in a fit of grief and fury. He warns the SS man Gerstein, who had risked his own life to help him, to reconsider allowing him to escape. He swears that he no longer considers himself a German and he will live only to return for his revenge against all Germans, to meet "murder with murder" and "fire with fire." Father Riccardo asks the distraught Jacobson whether he would wreak his vengeance even on the children of those Germans who tried to help his brethren, and adds the gentle reminder, "Hate is never the last word."[1] Eventually all three of them—the Jew, the German SS man, and the Catholic priest—die in the Nazi gas chambers.

The last word should not be spoken here without some review of the overall picture. The Jews were not alone in the concentration camps, nor were they the only forced laborers in Germany. Before the war was over there were more than ten million foreigners employed on German soil. One out of every five workers in the Reich had come from Russia, Poland, France, Holland, Czechoslovakia, Belgium, or other occupied territories. During 1939 and 1940 millions of men and women came voluntarily to work in German agriculture, industry, or domestic service. As the needs for manpower increased—in mining, building, and war production—voluntary recruitment was replaced by coercion and terror. In the early days fairly decent working conditions were ordered as a means of ensuring adequate production, but the Nazi racial doctrines, which regarded Slavs, as well as Jews and Gypsies, as subhumans, was soon reflected in the treatment accorded the Polish and Russian workers. Three million Soviet prisoners of war died or disappeared while in German custody.[2] There were Germans who were drafted for work in war production, there were foreigners deported to work for Germany, there were forced labor camps which no one was allowed to leave without strict controls, there was work in the ghettos, and finally, at the bottom of the ladder, there was work in the concentration camps.

I have not spoken in detail of the extermination factories like Auschwitz/Birkenau, Belzec, Chelmno, Sobibor, Maidanek, or Treblinka, whose primary function was to destroy those who were physically unable to work for Germany.[3] Nor have I dwelt on the SS *Einsatzgruppen,* whose mission was to kill without mercy or pity every Gypsy, Jew, or Communist official who fell within their grasp.[4] My focus has been on the Nazi program of forced labor that began with compulsory work decrees inside Germany, was then extended to the occupied territories, then to the ghettos, and finally to the forced labor camps which soon became branches of the main concentration camps run by the SS. The official tabulation published by the Federal Republic of Germany in 1977 showed that there were no less than 1,634 such subcamps. All of them contained slaves whose primary function was to serve the German war effort. Prisoners were put to work by the SS itself, by other agencies of the Reich such as the Hermann Göring Works and Organization Todt's construction battalions, by the army, the air force, and the local police. Requests for workers came from thousands of private German firms engaged in war production that needed help to meet their own work schedules. The demand exceeded the supply, and those companies with the highest priority or the best connections were given preference.

Well over half a million inmates were leased out by the SS to hundreds of German firms by the end of 1944.[5] The workers included Germans who might have committed some minor infraction, Communists, Socialists, other political opponents of the Nazi regime, priests, Seventh Day Adventists, as well as homosexuals, "asocials," and common criminals. Each group had its own distinctive color and triangle worn on the striped blue pajama uniform of the KZ *Häftlinge.* All of them shared the suffering, the brutality, and the dehumanization to which concentration camp inmates were subjected. Large numbers of Christians perished as a direct consequence of the arduous tasks and working conditions in the camps. As a class, there can be no doubt that the Jews suffered most of all, but in focusing on their claims, I have not wished to minimize the suffering of all the others.

Regardless of their nationality, the Jews were segregated in the camps and considered, even by many of their compatriots from France, Belgium, Poland, and other lands, to be outcasts and a group apart. They were frequently the target of anti-Semitic abuse by other prisoners and mistreatment even by fellow Jews and *Kapos* who sought to curry favor with the German masters. Jews were regarded as contagious vermin by their Nazi oppressors and were treated accordingly. They were given the most strenuous and most dangerous work.[6] Jews who could not work were either dead or about to die.

Of the hundreds of German firms that used concentration camp inmates, the number that paid anything to camp survivors could be counted on the fingers of one hand. Less than 15,000 Jews received any share of the combined total of under $13 million paid by the few German companies. Even the severe hardship cases of those who had survived work for I.G. Farben at Auschwitz got no more than $1,700 each. Krupp's Jewish slaves and those who toiled for Siemens had to settle for $825. The AEG/Telefunken slaves each received no more than $500, and the Jews who worked for Rheinmetall received even less.

Most of the beneficiaries, scattered in all parts of the world, never really understood the nature of the payments. They could not comprehend why one company paid something while another paid nothing. Almost all of the recipients saw the small funds as just another part of the mysterious and vastly larger panorama known as Restitution— *Wiedergutmachung*. To those camp survivors who had seen their families wantonly annihilated, no amount of money could ever erase their memories.

Many German industrialists saw things quite differently. In their eyes, Germany had been at war and needed all the labor it could get. Conscription of workers was justified as a military necessity. During the last days of the war, with the German armies in retreat, even German citizens faced hunger or starvation. When German towns were bombarded by Allied planes, everyone had to work hard to dig out of the rubble. Even moderate Germans rationalized that the camp inmates and certainly the Jews, who Hitler had told them were responsible for the war, could not expect any favors. The extermination camps were something about which the average German knew little and wanted to know less.

The leaders of German industry should have seen the truth more clearly than the man in the street. Surely those who were tried and convicted as war criminals on the open records of the Nuremberg proceedings could hardly convince any objective person that they were unaware of what was happening to the Jews. They did not have to know precise details—although many of them did. Everyone could see that the Jews had disappeared from Germany and only some of the able-bodied workers returned as concentration camp inmates to labor in the armaments factories. The conditions of work could not possibly have been a secret. One out of every five inmates engaged in heavy labor perished each month and had to be replaced.[7] Those engaged in lighter work were not treated very much better. Yet no German company came forward after the war and volunteered to do anything for any survivor. Even those few companies that made a payment did so under circumstances which indicated that their motivation was not to help the former slaves but rather to obtain some benefit for the company itself.

I.G. Farben was eager to eliminate a cloud on the corporate assets in order to free valuable shares for distribution to the stockholders. Alfried Krupp's eagerness to sidestep the Allied order to sell his Rheinhausen coal and steel operations, and his feeling of indebtedness to his liberator, John McCloy, surely influenced his decision to settle the Jewish claims. Krupp resented what he perceived to be the injustice of his having been imprisoned partly because the court believed that his Jewish female slaves from Buchenwald had perished, whereas it turned out that (no thanks to Krupp) most of them had managed to escape destruction. The agreement with Krupp spoke about "ameliorating the suffering" of the former camp inmates, but Krupp's unwillingness to go beyond the inadequate original sum raised serious doubts about the sincerity of that clause copied from the Farben contract. The electrical companies, which bargained to keep the cost of compensation down, must have given some consideration to their image and their sales abroad. Siemens rejected even the mention of a moral obligation. Rheinmetall left no doubt that it never wanted to pay the former camp inmates and later denied that its payment was for such a purpose. It shared the opinion of Friedrich Flick that the demands of the Jewish camp survivors were nothing short of blackmail. In every case the companies tried to minimize the number of claims and to do as little as they could rather than as much as they could.

The persistent denial by all German firms, without exception, that they had requisitioned the concentration camp inmates cannot be reconciled with the overwhelming documentary evidence to the contrary. The consistent testimony given independently by such SS leaders as Pohl, Maurer, and Sommer, the camp commanders Höss, Kaindl, and Pister, and the testimony of Albert Speer, all supported by the correspondence and documents issued during the war, suggest very strongly that the German denials are a distortion of the truth.[8]

This is not to imply that during the early days some forced laborers were not assigned by local labor offices without the specific request for such laborers by the company concerned. Nor is it to suggest that concentration camp labor was preferred to ordinary German workers— although Pohl testified that "the work performed by the concentration camp prisoners was very cheap."[9] Surely the companies were under pressure to complete their accepted or assigned production goals, but beyond that there is no evidence of compulsion of any kind that could have forced companies to take concentration camp prisoners if they had not wanted them. All of the evidence supports the conclusion that the companies were eager to get help from any source and that the firms competed to get as many concentration camp inmates as they could. The testimony of hundreds of inmates describing how they were selected and even tested by company recruiters cannot be denied.

It has been argued in defense of the German firms that the working conditions for the prisoners were as good as could be expected under the circumstances and that the inmates were eager to work for the munitions companies because their lives were thereby saved. There is some merit in the argument—but not much. Surely there were difficult times for all Germans during the last years of the war and surely there were differences in the degrees of mistreatment of forced laborers. Persons who worked in light industry inside Germany, such as some of the girls employed by the electrical companies, had it easier than prisoners in the quarries or the mines. Those who had acquired a skill in an essential industry were less expendable than those who were unskilled or readily replaceable by a new shipment. The threats and the beatings varied with the particular foremen. There were occasional acts of individual kindness, such as a word of consolation or the gift of an extra crust of bread—gestures so rare that they were gratefully recalled by some of the privileged survivors. It is true that many of the inmates were eager to leave the concentration camp to work in war production. But it was not because they desired to help Hitler's war effort or to enjoy the benefits of such employment. It was because their only alternative was the gas chamber.

It cannot be denied that the lives of many inmates were indirectly saved by virtue of the fact that they were employed in vital war work. But there is very little moral credit due to a company whose motivation in using the inmates was not to save the prisoners' lives but to serve corporate or national purposes. Had Germany won the war, the fate of the Jews would have been sealed. Concentration camp inmates were put to work by German industry not to save them but to save Germany. Victory for Germany meant defeat for the inmates and death for the Jews. The postwar argument that the German industrialists saved the Jews by providing labor opportunities for them is an invented and unpersuasive rationalization. Under typical conditions "exploitation was combined with extermination.''[10] Under the most favorable circumstances, keeping the Jews from being annihilated was a temporary necessity rather than the ultimate objective.

All generalizations regarding the conduct of a people or a country must be false. Nations are composed of individuals with different perspectives, different moral conceptions, different opportunities, pressures, and degrees of courage. There can be no doubt that there were some Germans who felt compassion for the concentration camp inmates, including the Jews, and some who went out of their way to offer assistance even at risk to themselves. Men like Kurt Gerstein have become the deserving subjects of books written in their honor.[11] The description given by the German engineer Hermann Graebe, as he witnessed a massacre of Jews, shows by its poignancy that he was ashamed, and suffered to see man's inhumanity to man.[12] There are cases of individual courage on the part of Germans in their contact with Jews. The story of Oskar Schindler has almost become a legend.

Oskar Schindler came from a Catholic family that had been engaged in the manufacture of enamelware in the Sudetenland. Soon after Germany occupied Poland, Schindler took over a factory in the neighborhood of Cracow and began to produce utensils needed by the German army. In 1940 he had 150 Jewish workers, and by 1942 the number had increased to over 500. As the SS moved in and tried to deport his workers to the extermination camps, Schindler took steps to protect them. Although he was required to pay the SS for every person he employed, he managed to bring and keep whole families together, including many who were old and nonproductive. Jews with a work card were exempt from deportation, and by 1944 Schindler had more than a thousand Jews in his care. He bribed the SS to leave those whom he regarded as his flock alone, and he purchased supplementary rations on the black market to keep his Jewish workers from starving. Even Jews who worked nearby for Siemens-Bauunion at Cracow/Plaszow described how they could sometimes warm their hands by the fire in the Schindler work hall, where they dared to cook a potato that they had managed to hide or steal. When the Germans retreated from Cracow, Schindler, with great difficulty, established another factory in the Sudetenland and transfered all of his Jewish workers as a group. The initiative and courage shown by Oskar Schindler and his wife, Emilie, is credited with saving over a thousand Jewish lives.[13]

After the war the Schindler family fell upon hard times and the Jews whom he had saved came to his aid. The needy Schindler family became the beneficiaries of grants from various Jewish organizations, including the Claims Conference under a special program to assist non-Jews who had helped save Jewish lives. When Schindler died in October 1974 the *New York Times* (November 7) reported the story of his courage under the Nazis. The Jewish grants were continued to his widow, who left Germany for Argentina. A tree-lined lane leading to the entrance of Yad Vashem, Israel's document center to memorialize the Holocaust, is called The Avenue of Righteous Gentiles. A plaque at the base of one of the trees bears the name of Oskar Schindler, a Christian whose heroism in defense of his fellowman has not been forgotten. Unfortunately, there were, and are, too few heroes anywhere.

In a dictatorial state like Nazi Germany, where terror and violence reigned supreme, it would have been asking too much to expect the average citizen to take a militant or open stand against government policy. But the restraint born of fear was eliminated when the Nazi regime was toppled, and after the war there was nothing to prevent those who had known about the mistreatment of other human beings from acknowledging that there was a responsibility on the part of every accomplice. Some German courts, such as the appellate tribunal in Stuttgart and the district court of Frankfurt, had no hesitation in rendering forceful decisions in favor of the former slave laborers. Some German lawyers, like Otto Küster and Walter Schmidt, were ready to speak out; but too often it was only those who had nothing to be ashamed of who expressed a sense of guilt and culpability.

German industry showed no sign of remorse. Could it be that nothing could ever convince them that what they did was wrong? If German firms feared to make a payment to their slave laborers lest it be taken as a confession, they failed to recognize that it would also have been welcomed as a gesture of atonement. They failed to realize that there is no such thing as a benevolent slavemaster and that slavery in any form is intolerable. The feeling of solidarity among German companies outweighed any sense of obligation to the camp survivors. Otto Kranzbühler, the German lawyer who advised many of the large companies regarding the demands of the forced laborers, expressed the view in 1975 that McCloy's clemency was influenced by the need to rearm Germany and, according to Kranzbühler, showed McCloy's recognition that no punishable acts had been committed by the German industrialists. In reaffirming the innocence of his clients who, he acknowledged proudly, rewarded him well for his loyalty, Kranzbühler also expressed his own conviction that Nuremberg was both premature and wrong in trying to change anything.[14] He was not alone in his opinion.

SS General Otto Ohlendorf, who was one of the more outspoken of the Nazi mass murderers and was closely associated with the industrialists who supported Hitler, did not hesitate to admit that his *Einsatzgruppen* killed ninety thousand Jews. After his conviction I went to visit him in his Nuremberg death cell, hoping to find some sign of regret. There was none. He was convinced that what he had done was right, and he warned, "The Jews in America will suffer for what you have done to me."

It is not uncommon for a criminal to see himself as the victim and to see the real victim as the oppressor. There can be no doubt that Flick and many other German industrialists who declared their innocence considered the demands of the surviving Jews to be little less than extortion. Krupp considered himself unjustly imprisoned because more Jewish girls survived than was originally believed. Siemens would sign no contract that suggested an indebtedness of any kind. The Federal Association of German Industries never spoke out publically on behalf of the camp survivors. The users of forced labor remained silent. Silence is often a sign of shame, but in the case of the German firms, that would be a misinterpretation. There was no shame, for in the words of Friedrich Flick, "You will never convince us."

Not all supporters of Hitler adhered steadfastly to the Nazi views. Albert Speer, Hitler's friend, architect, and minister for armaments and war production, was sentenced to twenty years in Spandau prison, under the control of the four occupation powers, for having aided Nazi crimes. When his term was fully served and he was released, he published his memoirs.[15] Speer, who knew as much about the use of slave labor as anyone in Germany, said very little in his book about the Jews and practically nothing about the concentration camps. Despite the omission, the book revealed that Speer was a man who felt, if not repentence, at least contrition for what he had done. He acknowledged that "a feeling of profound involvement and personal guilt envelopes me to this very day every time I think of it" (p. 370). For having deliberately shut his eyes to what had been going on around him, Albert Speer was prepared to admit as a free man that he considered himself personally responsible for Auschwitz. "Being in a position to know and nevertheless shunning knowledge," wrote the former Nazi leader, "creates direct responsibility for the consequences—from the very beginning. . . By entering Hitler's party I had already in essence assumed a responsibility that led directly to the brutalities of forced labor, to the destruction of war, and to the deaths of those millions of so-called undesireable stock . . . I will never be rid of that sin" (pp. 19-20).

In 1976, after Speer had paid his penalty and was released, I arranged to meet the former Reichminister. I would not have done so had I not been convinced from his public statements that Speer felt a sincere sense of remorse for what he had done. I wanted his opinion on the merits of the position taken by the German firms.

The meeting in a lounge near the Frankfurt airport was cordial. We shook hands and Speer expressed his satisfaction that he could exchange views with a former Nuremberg prosecutor who was a Jew. We talked about the slave labor program and the Nazi plan of extermination through work. The former minister of armaments was not ready to concede that extermination was the proximate goal of the forced labor program, noting how inefficient it would have been to train a man for several months and then work him to death. He was obviously not thinking of the unskilled toilers in the mines, the quarries, the construction work, the bridges, the tunnels, or Auschwitz. He reminded me that one of his close co-workers, Dr. Walter Schieber, in May 1944 had deplored the SS tactic of arresting trained armaments workers and transporting them to the concentration camps and that Schieber had argued for better treatment to encourage better work. Speer failed to mention that Schieber had been a general in the SS and that the humanitarian overtones of the letter, written when it was quite apparent that the war was lost, might have been prompted more by concern for efficiency or bureaucratic power than concern for the welfare of the forced laborers. Speer felt guilty not because he was responsible for the employment of the inmates but because he did not insist upon getting more of them out of the camps and into the armaments factories, where conditions were better and their chances for survival were greater.

I then asked the former armaments minister whether in his judgment his fellow prisoner Friedrich Flick had been right in refusing to pay anything to the former Jewish inmates who had worked in Flick factories. Speer replied, "No, Flick was wrong."[16]

The events I have described happened to have been committed by Germans against Jews. Although the annals of history contain no record of more systematic attempts at annihilation of any people, that does not mean that they could not be committed elsewhere, by others against other victims: one need only recall the treatment of the American Indians, or the exploitation of the black man, or the Gulag camps, or the mass murder of "enemies of the state" in Asia, Africa, and elsewhere. Contemporary society is replete with examples of torture, false imprisonment, and repression of large groups of innocent people whose only offense is that they do not share the color, religion, or political convictions of those in power. Humankind throughout history has been willing to shut its eyes to cruelty if it could be rationalized as being in the interest of the state or a popular cause.

The evils here recounted, and the failure of so many to recognize them, stemmed not so much from hatred as from an indifference that made it possible for otherwise decent people to accept or ignore what was happening. The last word, as in Genesis, is not hate but what we owe one another.

Then the Lord said to Cain, "Where is Abel your brother?"
He said, "I do not know; am I my brother's keeper?"
And the Lord said, "What have you done? The voice of your
    brother's blood is crying to me from the ground . . . "

**APPENDIXES**
**NOTES**
**INDEX**

SS-Wirtschafts- Verwaltungshauptamt     Oranienburg, 29. August 1942
Amtsgruppe D - Konzentrationslager
    D II/1 21 Ma./Hag.

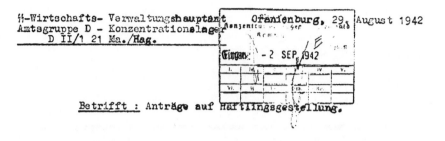

Betrifft : Anträge auf Häftlingsgestellung.


An die
Kommandanturen - Arbeitseinsatz -

K.L. Arb., Au., Bu., Da., Flo., Gr.Ro., Lu., Mau.,
Na., Neu., Nie., Rav., Sah., Stutth., Moringen.


1.) Ich mache erneut darauf aufmerksam, daß Anträge auf
Häftlingsgestellung <u>v o r</u> Abstellung des Kommandos
mir zur Genehmigung vorzulegen sind. Nur in Ausnahme-
fällen, bei denen es sich um dringenden Einsatz in
der Landwirtschaft handelt, kann von dieser Regel ab-
gewichen werden. Die Anträge sind dann nachzureichen.

Es ist selbstverständlich, daß sämtliche Anträge
von der Stelle,die das Häftlingskommando anfordert,
<u>selbst</u> unterschrieben sein müssen.

2.) In den täglichen Übersichten ist in Spalte 36
"Posten" auf der ersten Spalte die Gesamtzahl der
Wachmannschaften (Führer, Unterführer und Männer),
die für die Bewachung aller Häftlinge zur Verfügung
stehen, einzusetzen.

          Der Chef des Amtes D II



          SS - Obersturmbannführer


[From the files of the Bundesarchiv, Koblenz, Buchenwald Records,
NS-3391]

# Appendix 1

Translation of letter dated August 29, 1942, in which SS Lieutenant Colonel Maurer orders all concentration camp commanders to refer requests for inmates to him before assignment (opposite).

---

SS Economic and Administrative Main Office
Section D - Concentration Camps          Oranienburg, Aug. 29, 1942
D II/1 21 Ma./Hag.                        *Stamped by Concentration Camp*
                                          *Buchenwald Received 2 Sept. 1942.*

Subject: Requests for Assignment of Prisoners.
To the
Commanders-Work Assignments -
[Camp initials only in original] Auschwitz, Buchenwald, Dachau, Flossenbürg, Gross Rosen, Lublin, Mauthausen, Natzweiler, Neuengamme, Niederhagen, Ravensbrück, Sachsenhausen, Stutthof, Moringen.

1.) I again draw attention that requests for the assignment of inmates are to be placed before me for approval *b e f o r e* the transfer of the work gangs takes place. An exception to this rule can be made only in extraordinary cases, where it relates to an urgent assignment for farming. These applications are then to be submitted later.

It is obvious that all applications for prisoner work gangs must be *personally* signed by the office making the request.

2.) In column 36 of the daily status report, under the heading "Guards" the total number of security personnel (leaders, deputy leaders, and men) who are available to guard all of the prisoners, should be put in the first column.

The Chief of Section D II
[Signed Maurer]
SS-Lieutenant Colonel

# Appendix 2

Translation of document NI-1065: beginning and end of nine-page affidavit from SS Captain Karl Sommer, taken and translated by the Office of the United States Chief of Counsel for War Crimes, listing German companies that used inmates from different concentration camps and describing the procedure to be followed by companies when requesting inmate labor. (From Staatsarchiv, Nuremberg.)

## AFFIDAVIT

I. I, Karl SOMMER, born on 25 March 1915, SS-Hauptsturmführer of the Reserve of the Waffen-SS, SS-Obersturmführer of the General-SS, non-Party member, General-SS since 30 January 1934, Waffen-SS since 5 May 1942, employed in the SS Economic and Administrative Main Office (WVHA) (since 20 April, 1944 Departmental Head), declare herewith under oath that I am acquainted with the following facts from personal experience:

II. During the course of interrogation conducted by representatives of the Office of US Chief of Counsel, a number of documents were shown or read to me as well as other informational material in order to refresh my memory.

III. After the conclusion of these interrogations this affidavit, to which the statements I made regarding relevant matters have been reduced, was presented to me in the German language. According to my recollection, prisoners from concentration camps were employed at the following places of work:

A. *From the Concentration Camp of Buchenwald:*
   1. BMW Eisenach, approximately 1,000 prisoners (from the end of 1943 on)
   2. Siebel, Halle-Saale, approximately 800 prisoners (from 1944 on)

3. Dr. Heymann, Darmstadt, approximately 300 prisoners, responsible head, Dr. Heymann (from the middle of 1944 on)
4. Construction enterprise S 3 Ohrdruf. (Construction Department of the SS-WVHA, responsible head: Dr. Kammler) approximately 10,000 prisoners (from the end of 1944 on)
5. Brabag Boehlen, approximately 500 prisoners, responsible head: Dr. Wilde (from 1944 on)

[6 through 47 lists other companies using inmates from Buchenwald. Paragraphs B through M list twelve other concentration camps and many companies that employed inmates from each camp.]

IV. . . . The following gentlemen are known to me through negotiations concerning the allotment of concentration camp prisoners with Standartenfuehrer Maurer from Office Group (Amtsgruppe) D of the Economic Administration Main Office (WVHA):
1. Dr. Gommern of the firm OSMAG.
2. Kranefuss of Brabag
3. Rickney of Damag Armor Works.
4. Walther Schieber from the Gustloff Works.
5. Professor Heinkel and Director Hayn of the Heinkel Works.
6. Wide from Messerschmitt.
7. Nathusius jr. from Polte, Magdeburg.
8. Porsche and Thyrhold of the Volkswagen Works, Fallersleben.
9. Dr. Duerrfeld from I.G. Farben, Buna.
10. Dr. Heyne and Paul Pleiger of the Hermann Goering Works.
11. Lueschen of Siemens.

The I.G. Farben was given priority in Buna over all other armament plants for the allotment of concentration camp prisoners. Maurer had informed me of the order, to allot inmates to other plants only after the requirements of Buna had been met.

V. The allotment of concentration camp prisoners as workers was regularly directly requested by the firm from the Economic Administration Main Office (WVHA), Office Group (Amtsgruppe) D (Maurer, in individual cases Gluecks, and only in the case of personal connections Pohl). Occasionally the firms referred directly to the commanders of the individual concentration camps, in order to be given prisoners, contrary to the prescribed procedure. When the permission for the utilization of the concentration camp inmates had gone from the Office Group to the firms,the billeting and security conditions in the plants were either inspected by Maurer or a commander of a concentration camp. When the prerequisites for employment had been fulfilled, in particular with regard to security, a directive was issued to the concentration camp concerned to furnish a corresponding number of prisoners. The firms in question were ordered to select the most suitable workers in the concentration camps concerned or from several concentration camps, if necessary.

The representatives of the latter entered the interior of the camp for this purpose, and/or entered the camp accompanied by the camp-commander or his representative, and thereby they had an insight into the conditions which prevailed in the concentration camp in question.

Altogether about 5-600.000 concentration camps prisoners inmates were furnished by the Economic Administration Main Office (WVHA) for the commitment of labor (Arbeitseinsatz) (This at the end of 1944).

I have carefully read over the 9 pages of this affidavit and have countersigned it in my own handwriting; I have made the necessary corrections in my own handwriting and have countersigned them with my own initials and herewith declare under oath that, to the best of my knowledge and my conscience, and all the facts stated by me in this affidavit correspond to the whole truth.

s/ KARL SOMMER

Sworn to and signed before me
on this 4th day of October 1946
    s/ ALFRED H. BOOTH.

# Appendix 3

Translation of document NI-4434-A: affidavit of Auschwitz commandant Rudolf Höss, taken and translated by the Office of the United States Chief of Counsel for War Crimes. It confirms that one-fifth of the prisoners died each month because of the difficult working conditions, that concentration camp inmates were never offered to industry but had to be requested by industry after the applicant established that adequate security measures were provided, and that those unable to work were immediately exterminated *("sofort vernichtet")*. (From National Archives, Washington, D.C.)

AFFIDAVIT

Warsaw, 12 March 1947

Present: John E. FRIED, Consultant to the U.S. Secretary of War
Hertha C. KNUTH, Interpreter at the Office of Chief of
Counsel for War Crimes, Nuremberg, Germany
Rudolf HOESS

From May 1940, until 1 December 1943, I was commandant of the concentration camp at Auschwitz. Thereafter I was Chief of Office of the Department I of Wirtschafts Verwaltungs Hauptamt (W.V.H.A.-main office for economics and administration). Until 1 December 1943, one of my official functions was to inspect the use as labor (Arbeitseinsatz) of concentration camp prisoners from the Auschwitz camp and subsequently to inspect the use as labor of prisoners from all German concentration camps whenever Pohl, the chief of the Main Office (Hauptamt); especially ordered me to do so.

According to my knowledge, the large scale use of concentration camp prisoners in the German private industry began in 1940/41. This utilization increased constantly until the end of the war.

Towards the end of 1944, there were approximately 400,000 concentration camp prisoners used in the private armament industry and in establishments essential for armament purposes. How many prisoners were used prior or after that time I cannot say. According to my estimate, in enterprises with particularly severe working conditions—for instance, in mines—every month one fifth died or were, because of inability to work, sent back by the enterprises to the camps in order to be exterminated.

The concentration camps have at no time offered labor to the industry. On the contrary, prisoners were sent to enterprises only after the enterprises had made a request for concentration camp prisoners. In their letters of request the enterprises had to state in detail which measures had been taken by them, even before the arrival of the prisoners, to guard them, to quarter them, etc. I visited officially many such establishments to verify such statements and this was always before the inmates would be sent.

The enterprises did not have to submit reports on causes for death, etc. On the basis of reports which we received in the camps from the S.S. guard personnel and from the leaders of the labor details, on the decrease of the number of prisoners working in the respective enterprises, the number of deaths and of persons unable to work was communicated, and on that basis new prisoners were continuously sent out to the respective enterprises for replenishing.

During my official trips I was constantly told by executives of the enterprises that they want more prisoners.

In the beginning of the war the enterprises paid little for this labor, perhaps Mk. 1.-, Mk. 1.20. Later on, they paid up to Mk. 5.00 for skilled workers. Among the prisoners sent out to be used as labor, there were
1)   non-Jewish prisoners who were selected by reason of their professional training, and
2)   Jews who were selected merely because of their ability to work.
The age of the prisoners utilized for labor ranged from approximately 13 years upwards. Prisoners over 50 years were but rarely utilized for labor—when they were particularly strong or were trained along special lines—otherwise they were exterminated at once.

Prisoners utilized for labor who every evening returned from the plant to the concentration camp, had to work in the concentration camp on the same evening whenever collective or individual punishment to this effect had been imposed. Such additional collective or individual penal labor would be imposed because of minor offenses against the discipline, for instance, saluting not according to regulations. In such cases the prisoners had to work as long as daylight would permit, in the summer for two to three hours. In addition, the other customary punishments were imposed.

[signed] Rudolf Hoess

[signed] John H. E. Fried
[signed] Hertha C. Knuth


We, the undersigned, herewith declare that Rudolf Hoess signed his name on all three pages of this document by his own hand in our presence, after having carefully read, in our presence, every page including the corrections as they now appear.

John H. E. Fried,
Consultant to the U.S. Secretary of War

Warsaw, 12 March 1947

Hertha C. Knuth,
Interpreter, OCCWC

# Appendix 4

Translation of document NI-280: affidavit of Anton Kaindl, commandant of the concentration camp at Sachsenhausen, taken and translated by the Office of the United States Chief of Counsel for War Crimes. In it Kaindl swears that all factories which used concentration camp inmates had to request the assignment from the SS Economic and Administrative Main Office, Group D, which was under the direction of Oswald Pohl, Richard Glücks, Gerhard Maurer, and Karl Sommer. (From the National Archives, Washington, D.C.)

## AFFIDAVIT

I, Anton Kaindl, born on 14 July 1902, declare hereby in lieu of oath:

A. 1. I am a merchant by profession and was a professional soldier since the age of 18. My NSDAP membership number is 4390 500, my SS number is 241 248.

2. From 22 August 1942 until the collapse I was camp commandant at the Sachsenhausen concentration camp.

3. My superior authority was the Economic and Administrative Main Office of the SS; chief: SS-Obergruppenfuehrer Oswald Pohl and/or his division D, chief: SS-Gruppenfuehrer Richard Gluecks.

4. Glueck's deputy, Standartenfuehrer Gerhard Maurer and his deputy, Hauptsturmfuehrer Sommer were in charge of the employment of concentration camp labor. (Sommer, who in my opinion is best informed about the over-all aspect of the employment of concentration camp labor, was a young man between 25 and 30, whose leg had been injured in the war. As

far as I know, Sommer is in the Neumuenster internment camp.

5) At the Sachsenhausen concentration camp SS-Untersturmfuehrer Rehn was responsible for the employment of inmates.

6) Out of the approximately 25 000 inmates of the Sachsenhausen concentration camp, about 15 000 were employed either at outside places of work or were sent to work from the main camp.

7) All plants, employing concentration camp internees, applied to Division D for their assignment, and then I was charged by this agency which was my superior authority, to supply the manpower, as far as available, to the applying plants.

8) My own office as well as the office of my director of outside places of employment (Einsatzstellen) SS-Untersturmfuehrer Rehn, were located in the so-called ante-camp (Vorlager) which formed a part of the concentration camp. The persons who were responsible for the employment of internees at the individual plants—mostly labor employment directors (Arbeitseinsatzleiters) of the firms concerned—did all call on Rehn in order to discuss questions concerning employment. Rehn also had a list of available skilled labor and effected its distribution according to it. I, myself, carried on basic negotiations only.

9) Anyone visiting me or Rehn in the ante-camp, though he had no insight into the protective custody camp, did see the camp internees who worked in the ante-camp.

B. During my service in the Sachsenhausen concentration camp I met the following persons:

1) Director Hayn, Heinkel works, Oranienburg. He once visited also the actual Sachsenhausen camp.

2) Director Erich (?) Koch, Heinkel works, Oranienburg.

3) Director Dr. Friedrich Zuercher, Auer works, Oranienburg.

4) Director Robert Vorbau, Auer works, Oranienburg.

5) NSFK (NS Flying Corps) Gruppenfuehrer, SS-Standartenfuehrer (?) Albert Bormann (Martin Bormann's brother).

6) Gauleiter of Berlin, Schach. Bormann and Schach were present during a conducted visit of the Sachsenhausen camp by Reich Chancellery representatives.

7) SS-Obergruppenfuehrer Oswald Pohl.

I myself conducted Pohl through the actual protective custody camp on 29 September 1942.

Furthermore the following chiefs of outside places of work, belonging to other than privately owned:

8) SS-Obersturmbannfuehrer Mummenthey.
9) SS-Sturmbannfuehrer Schondorff.
10) SS-Obersturmfuehrer Ludewig.
11) SS-Untersturmfuehrer Buettner.
12) SS-Hauptsturmfuehrer Bestle.
13) SS-Untersturmfuehrer Meissner.
14) Police Captain Abraham.

C. In the appendix of this affidavit on lists 1, 2 and 3, I have indicated all plants I was able to remember where inmates of the Sachsenhausen concentration camp were employed.

In my capacity of commandant of the concentration camp, I was invited by the Auer-Works, Oranienburg, and by the Heinkel-Aircraft-Plants to visit the main plants, and did so wearing my SS uniform. I was at the Siemens Concern in Siemensstadt for a conference with the labor employment director.

I have made these statements voluntarily and without any compulsion.

I have carefully read and personally signed each of the 5 pages of this affidavit as well as each of the pages 1 and 2 of lists 1 and 2, and list 3, and declare that the statements which I made in this affidavit and in the appendix are correct to the best of my knowledge and ability.

[Signed] Anton Kaindl

Sworn to and signed before me on this 22 day of June 1946 in Nuernberg, Germany.

[Signed] Alfred H. Booth.

# Appendix 5

Audited statement prepared by Loeb and Troper, Certified Public Accountants, New York, showing payments made by Compensation Treuhand to slave labor claimants from different countries, from inception to December 31, 1973. (From archives of the Conference on Jewish Material Claims against Germany, filed at the Central Archives for the History of the Jewish People, The Hebrew University, Jerusalem.)

*(overleaf)*

| Country of residence | Total No. of claimants paid | Amount (DM) | I. G. Farben No. of claimants paid | Amount (DM) | Krupp No. of claimants paid | Amount (DM) |
|---|---|---|---|---|---|---|
| Argentina | 103 | 388,000 | 51 | 241,500 | 19 | 62,700 |
| Austria | 79 | 319,700 | 42 | 216,500 | 5 | 16,500 |
| Australia | 334 | 1,184,300 | 134 | 619,500 | 104 | 339,300 |
| Belgium | 235 | 1,032,700 | 166 | 825,500 | 24 | 79,200 |
| Bolivia | 12 | 51,700 | 8 | 38,500 | 4 | 13,200 |
| Brazil | 90 | 312,500 | 41 | 181,000 | 24 | 76,300 |
| Canada | 630 | 2,157,000 | 269 | 1,197,000 | 129 | 423,100 |
| Chile | 18 | 56,000 | 8 | 34,000 | 1 | 3,300 |
| Costa Rica | 3 | 12,000 | 2 | 10,000 | — | — |
| Columbia | 1 | 2,000 | — | — | — | — |
| Cuba | 1 | 3,300 | — | — | 1 | 3,300 |
| Czechoslovakia | 491 | 1,843,900 | 222 | 1,119,500 | 11 | 36,300 |
| Denmark | 7 | 19,700 | 1 | 2,500 | 3 | 9,900 |
| Dominican Republic | 3 | 7,300 | — | — | 1 | 3,300 |
| France | 899 | 3,805,900 | 783 | 3,472,000 | 47 | 148,600 |
| Greece | 77 | 420,600 | 51 | 340,000 | 22 | 72,600 |
| Great Britain | 104 | 355,500 | 44 | 192,000 | 16 | 52,800 |
| Guatemala | 2 | 8,300 | 1 | 5,000 | 1 | 3,300 |
| Hungary | 1,184 | 3,849,700 | 225 | 1,209,500 | 109 | 355,800 |
| Israel | 5,295 | 17,814,000 | 1,540 | 7,978,000 | 1,232 | 4,012,700 |
| Italy | 34 | 135,800 | 25 | 114,000 | 3 | 9,900 |
| Luxemburg | 5 | 23,300 | 4 | 20,000 | — | — |
| Mexico | 7 | 30,000 | 5 | 25,000 | — | — |
| Netherlands | 376 | 1,275,600 | 191 | 879,000 | 5 | 16,500 |
| New Zealand | 3 | 7,300 | — | — | 1 | 3,300 |
| Norway | 19 | 80,200 | 15 | 67,000 | 2 | 6,600 |
| Pakistan | 1 | 3,300 | — | — | 1 | 3,300 |
| Paraguay | 1 | 5,000 | 1 | 5,000 | — | — |
| Peru | 1 | 5,000 | 1 | 5,000 | — | — |
| Philippines | 1 | 2,500 | 1 | 2,500 | — | — |
| Poland | 75 | 305,800 | 59 | 259,500 | 14 | 41,000 |
| Rhodesia | 1 | 3,300 | — | | 1 | 3,300 |
| Rumania | 94 | 155,400 | 6 | 12,000 | 7 | 11,000 |
| South Africa | 20 | 59,700 | 7 | 29,000 | 2 | 6,600 |
| Sweden | 294 | 973,900 | 56 | 291,000 | 147 | 483,800 |
| Switzerland | 24 | 73,800 | 11 | 37,000 | 6 | 19,800 |
| Uruguay | 44 | 148,400 | 18 | 73,000 | 15 | 49,500 |
| U.S.A. | 3,709 | 12,555,800 | 1,521 | 6,622,500 | 981 | 3,186,400 |
| U.S.S.R. | 16 | 24,595 | 3 | 15,500 | — | — |
| Venezuela | 9 | 35,700 | 5 | 22,500 | 3 | 9,900 |
| West Germany | 526 | 2,205,800 | 320 | 1,598,500 | 138 | 451,500 |
| Yugoslavia | 50 | 180,800 | 18 | 81,500 | 11 | 36,300 |
| **Totals** | **14,878** | **51,935,095** | **5855** | **27,841,500** | **3090** | **10,050,900** |

| A.E.G. | | Siemens | | Rheinmetall | |
|---|---|---|---|---|---|
| No. of claimants paid | Amount (Dm) | No. of claimants paid | Amount (DM) | No. of claimants paid | Amount (DM) |
| 12 | 22,500 | 16 | 52,800 | 5 | 8,500 |
| 13 | 24,000 | 19 | 62,700 | — | — |
| 38 | 72,500 | 38 | 119,000 | 20 | 34,000 |
| 8 | 15,500 | 31 | 102,300 | 6 | 10,200 |
| — | — | — | — | — | — |
| 12 | 23,500 | 6 | 19,800 | 7 | 11,900 |
| 86 | 166,000 | 81 | 261,100 | 65 | 109,800 |
| 6 | 12,000 | 1 | 3,300 | 2 | 3,400 |
| 1 | 2,000 | — | — | — | — |
| 1 | 2,000 | — | — | — | — |
| — | — | — | — | — | — |
| 83 | 157,000 | 146 | 481,800 | 29 | 49,300 |
| 2 | 4,000 | 1 | 3,300 | — | — |
| 2 | 4,000 | — | — | — | — |
| 27 | 51,500 | 39 | 128,700 | 3 | 5,100 |
| 4 | 8,000 | — | — | — | — |
| 16 | 29,500 | 21 | 69,300 | 7 | 11,900 |
| — | — | — | — | — | — |
| 296 | 585,500 | 474 | 1,562,900 | 80 | 136,000 |
| 884 | 1;716,500 | 831 | 2,734,600 | 808 | 1,372,200 |
| 2 | 3,500 | 1 | 3,300 | 3 | 5,100 |
| — | — | 1 | 3,300 | — | — |
| — | — | 1 | 3,300 | 1 | 1,700 |
| 159 | 316,500 | 19 | 60,200 | 2 | 3,400 |
| 2 | 4,000 | — | — | — | — |
| — | — | 2 | 6,600 | — | — |
| — | — | — | — | — | — |
| — | — | — | — | — | — |
| — | — | — | — | — | — |
| 1 | 2,000 | 1 | 3,300 | — | — |
| — | — | — | — | — | — |
| 22 | 27,000 | 26 | 50,000 | 33 | 55,400 |
| 9 | 17,500 | 2 | 6,600 | — | — |
| 41 | 80,500 | 21 | 69,300 | 29 | 49 ,300 |
| 1 | 2,000 | 3 | 9,900 | 3 | 5,100 |
| 8 | 16,000 | 3 | 9,900 | — | — |
| 456 | 888,000 | 371 | 1,212,900 | 380 | 646,000 |
| — | — | — | — | 13 | 9,095 |
| — | — | 1 | 3,300 | — | — |
| 29 | 56,000 | 30 | 84,500 | 9 | 15,300 |
| 2 | 3,500 | 17 | 56,100 | 2 | 3,400 |
| **2223** | **4,312,500** | **2203** | **7,184,100** | **1507** | **2,546,095** |

# Notes

The records of the International Military Tribunal and the dozen subsequent war crimes trials at Nuremberg have appeared in the English language in three distinct publications, each one in a binding of a different color. In the notes that follow:

"Blue" refers to the forty-two-volume edition, *Trial of Major War Criminals before the International Military Tribunal* (Nuremberg, 1947). These are the official transcripts and the original text of the German documents admitted into evidence at the International Military Tribunal trial.

"Red" refers to the eight volumes, plus supplement, *Nazi Conspiracy and Aggression* (Washington, D. C. : United States Government Printing Office, 1946), which contain some of the documents and guides submitted to the International Military Tribunal by the United States and British prosecution staffs.

"Green" refers to the fifteen volumes, *Trials of War Criminals before the Nuernberg Military Tribunals under Control Council Law No. 10* (Washington, D. C.: United States Government Printing Office, 1949). These are extracts from the trial records of the twelve "Subsequent Proceedings" conducted by the United States.

The symbols and numbers referred to, such as NI, NO, PS, and so on are taken from Nuremberg trial documents. For convenience a further reference to the Nuremberg volumes is given if the document has been published. The originals, together with English translations or summaries, may be found in the Collection of World War II War Crimes Records, Record Group 238, at the National Archives in Washington, D. C. The *Bundesarchiv* in Coblenz and other document centers have copies of many of the Nuremberg records.

Much of the information contained in this book is derived from the claims submitted to Compensation Treuhand by former concentration camp inmates. The files of Compensation Treuhand are in the archives of Yad Vashem, the Martyrs' and Heroes' Remembrance Authority in Jerusalem.

Descriptions of meetings at which I was not present are derived from contemporaneous correspondence or reports. Such correspondence is indicated by reference to the name or initials of the writer and receiver. E. K. refers to Ernst Katzenstein, S. K. refers to Saul Kagan, and B. B. F. refers to Benjamin B. Ferencz. The correspondence files will also be sent to Yad Vashem.

## 1. The Final Solution—A Brief Reminder

1. Vol. 1 Blue, p. 251.
2. Adolf Hitler, *Mein Kampf* (Boston: Houghton Mifflin, Sentry Ed., 1943), pp. 296, 383.
3. Ibid., p. 623.
4. Ibid., pp. 640, 651.
5. *Documents on German Foreign Policy,* series D, 1937-1941 (Washington, D. C.), vol. IV, p. 170.
6. NO-5194.
7. PS-1816, vol. XIII Green, p. 119.
8. See Jakob Apenszlak, *The Black Book of Polish Jewry* (New York: American Federation of Polish Jews, 1943).
9. PS-1412, vol. XIII Green, p. 129, and PS-1816, p. 127.
10. NG-2586-A, vol. XIII Green, p. 129.
11. PS-2360, vol. XIII Green, p. 131; PS-3054, vol. V Red, p. 831.
12. See Telford Taylor, *Sword and Swastika* (New York: Simon and Shuster, 1952), p. 310.
13. PS-386, vol. III Red, p. 295; vol. XV Blue, p. 403; see also vol. I Red, p. 387; vol. I Blue, p. 188; PS-789, vol. XXVI Blue, p. 327.
14. Hitler, *Mein Kampf,* p. 652.
15. L-79, vol. I Red, p. 392; vol. II Green, p. 389; compare vol. XIV Blue, p. 179.
16. See Judgment of The IMT, vol. I Blue, pp. 198-204.
17. Vol. XII Blue, p. 4.
18. PS-2233, vol. IV Red, p. 883.
19. Vol. XII Blue, p. 13.
20. L-185, vol. VII Red, p. 997.
21. NO-019(a), vol. V Green, p. 294.
22. PS-3047, vol. V Red, p. 769; see also vol. II Blue, p. 448.
23. PS-3363, vol. VI Red, p. 97; vol. XIII Green, p. 133; EC-307-1, vol. IV Green, p. 119; trans. based on German text in *Faschismus-Getto-Massenmord* (Berlin: Rütten and Loening, 1961), p. 37.
24. PS-3363, vol. VI Red, p. 99.
25. See vol. IV Green, pp. 134, 415.
26. PS-2233, vol. XXIX Blue, p. 358.
27. Ibid., pp. 361, 363, 366, 367.
28. See International Tracing Service of the International Committee of the Red Cross, *Vorläufiges Verzeichnis der Konzentrations-lager und deren Aussenkommandos* (Arolsen: International Tracing Service, 1969).
29. *Kölnische Zeitung,* Sept. 5, 1941, citied in John Fried, *The Exploitation of Foreign Labor by Germany* (Montreal: International Labor Office, 1945), p. 251.
30. See Isaiah Trunk, *Lodzher Geto* (New York: Yivo-Yad Vashem, 1962), p. 50.
31. NG-2586-B, vol. XIII Green, p. 154; PS-2233, vol. XXIX Blue, p. 378; PS-1816, vol. XIII Green, p. 127.
32. NG-2586-B, vol. XIII Green, p. 154; see also NG-2586-J, p. 243.

33. See Gerald Reitlinger, *The Final Solution* (London: Valentine Mitchell, 1953), p. 46, where the Madagascar Plan is referred to as an "official pretense."

34. PS-2233, vol. XXIX Blue, p. 458.

35. Ibid., p. 405.

36. Ibid., p. 415.

37. 034, Supp. A Red, p. 1277; see also Jan Sehn, *Auschwitz-Birkenau Concentration Camp* (Warsaw: Wydawnictwo Prawnicze, 1961), p. 13.

38. Vol. XI Blue, p. 397.

39. NI-11784, vol. VIII Green, p. 336, and NI-11782, p. 351.

40. See vol. VIII Green, p. 1319.

41. Rudolf Höss, *Kommandant in Auschwitz* (Stuttgart: Deutsche Verlag, 1958), p. 174.

42. Ibid., p. 175.

43. Ibid., p. 176. Reitlinger thinks it was 1942; see Reitlinger, *Final Solution*, p. 104; see also Sehn, *Auschwitz*, p. 112.

44. Vol. XI Blue, p. 398.

45. NI-15148, vol. VIII Green, p. 376.

46. See German text in Leon Poliakov and Josef Wulf, *Das Dritte Reich und die Juden* (Berlin: Arani Verlag, 1955), p. 67.

47. NO-2890, vol. IV Green, p. 92; PS-2620, vol. IV Green, pp. 205, 415.

48. See vol. IV Green, pp. 276-307.

49. PS-2233, vol. XXIX Blue, p. 361.

50. Vol. IV Green, p. 415.

51. See NO-3841, affidavit of *Einsatzgruppen* defendant Erwin Schulz, Dec. 20, 1945.

52. David Irving, *Hitler's War* (New York: Viking Press, 1977).

53. File MA 316, *Institut für Zeitgeschichte,* Hitler's speech to generals and officers on May 26, 1944, at Platterhof, pp. 50-56. For other repudiations of the revisionist theory of Nazi history see Martin Broszat, "Hitler und die Genesis der Endlösung," *Vierteljahrshefte für Zeitgeschichte,* Oct. 1977, pp. 739-776; Eberhard Jäckel in *Frankfurter Allgemeine Zeitung,* Aug. 25, 1977, p. 17; Gitta Sereny and Lewis Chester in the *Sunday Times,* July 10, 1977, Alan Bullock in the *New York Times* Book Review, May 26, 1977; Hugh Trevor-Roper in the *Sunday Times* Weekly Review, June 12, 1977; Sebastian Hafner, *Anmerkungen zu Hitler* (Munich: Kindler, 1978).

54. See vol. IV Green, pp. 393, 406, 409.

55. Vol IV Green, pp. 414-589.

56. L-180, vol. XXXVII Blue, p. 689: "Die nicht mehr arbeitsfähigen Juden erfasst und demnächst in kleinen Aktionen exekutiert." Trans. in vol. VII Red, pp. 978-996.

57. PS-1138, vol. III Red, p. 800; see also PS-3428, vol. IV Green, p. 191.

58. PS-710, vol. IV Green, p. 132; German text in vol. XXVI Blue, p. 267.

59. Vol XI Blue, p. 416.

60. PS-212, vol III Red, p. 222. "Verstösse gegen deutsche Massnahmen, *insbesondere die Entziehung vom Arbeitszwang,* sind bei Juden grundsätzlich

mit der *Todesstrafe* zu ahnden." Trans. from German text in *Dokumente über Methoden der Judenverfolgung in Ausland* (Frankfurt: United Restitution Organization, 1959), p. 39; also in Staatsarchiv, Nuremberg.

61. See Uwe Dietrich Adam, *Judenpolitik im Dritten Reich* (Düsseldorf: Droste Verlag, 1972), p. 310.

62. NO-4540, unpublished *Einsatzgruppen* report no. 52.

63. L-180, vol. VII Red, p. 978; German text in vol. XXXVII Blue, pp. 670-711.

64. Vol. VII Red, p. 992.

65. NO-3140, vol. IV Green, p. 147; see also vol. IV Green, p. 430, and Anatoly Kuznetsov, *Babi Yar* (New York: Dial Press,1967).

66. Vol. IV Green, p. 415.

67. PS-3663, vol. VI Red, p. 402.

68. PS-3666, vol. VI Red, p. 402; German text in Poliakov and Wulf, *Dritte Reich*, p. 191.

69. Trial transcript, Case IX, Oct. 8, 1947, p. 526.

70. NO-365, vol. I Green, p. 870; Adalbert Rückerl, *NS- Vernichtungslager* (Munich: Deutsche Taschenbuch, 1977).

71. See PS-4328, vol. IV Green, p. 191.

72. PS-2233-D, vol. IV Red, p. 891; German text in Poliakov and Wulf, *Dritte Reich*, p. 181.

73. NI-11130, vol. VIII Green, p. 409.

74. NI-14556, vol. VIII Green, p. 405.

75. NI-14543, vol. VIII Green, p. 393.

76. NI-15253, vol. VIII Green, p. 410.

77. See vol. VIII Green, p. 1184, and Sehn, *Auschwitz,* p. 64.

78. See Sehn, *Auschwitz,* pp. 47, 49.

79. Vol. VIII Green, p. 1184.

80. See Reitlinger, *Final Solution,* p. 97.

81. NG-2586-G, vol. XIII Green, p. 210; German text in Robert Kempner, *Eichmann und Komplizen* (Zurich: Europa Verlag, 1961), p. 130.

82. Höss, *Kommandant,* p. 154; English Trans. cited in Sehn, *Auschwitz,* p. 114.

83. Vol. XI Blue, p. 416.

84. See vol. XIII Green, pp. 210-217; trans. from German text in Kempner, *Eichmann,* pp. 130-147.

85. NO-500, vol. V Green, p. 365.

86. PS-3311, vol. V Red, p. 1104.

87. ITS, *Verzeichnis der Konzentrationslager,* p. 482.

88. Ibid., pp. xxii, 482.

89. R-124, vol. XXXVIII Blue, p. 359; vol. XVI Blue, p. 472.

90. Josef Goebbels, *The Goebbels Diaries,* ed. L. Lochner (New York: Doubleday, 1948), p. 147.

91. PS-1472, vol. IV Red, p. 49.

92. NO-111, vol. V Green, p. 317; see also pp. 589, 593, 595, 602, 605.

93. R-129, vol. XXXVIII Blue, p. 362; vol. V Green, p. 299.

94. R-129, vol. XXXVIII Blue, p. 366.

95. Höss, *Kommandant,* p. 179.

96. NI-14514, vol. VIII Green, p. 462.

97. NI-838, vol. VIII Green, pp. 1322-1323.

98. NG-183, vol. XIII Green, p. 233; NG-802, German text in Kempner, *Eichmann*, p. 197.

99. ITS, *Verzeichnis der Konzentrationslager,* pp. 482-483.

100. PS-3311, vol. V Red, p. 1104; PS-1553, vol. I Green, p. 865.

101. Rückerl, *NS-Vernichtungslager,* p. 199.

102. Vol. XI Blue, p. 417.

103. See Gerstein's affidavit dated May 4, 1945, reported in *Vierteljahreshefte für Zeitgeschichte,* I, no. 2 (April, 1953): 185-196; also affidavit of April 26, 1945, in PS-1553, vol. I Green, p. 865. See also Poliakov and Wulf, *Dritte Reich,* p. 101; Gerstein's efforts to obtain the pope's intervention became the basis for the play *Der Stellvertreter* (The Deputy) by Rolf Hochhuth (Frankfurt: Rowahlt Verlag, 1963).

104. PS-2620, vol. IV Green, p. 205.

105. PS-2992, vol. V Red, p. 701; vol. IV Green, p. 437.

106. PS-2992, vol. V Red, p. 703.

107. Ibid., pp. 697-698; German text in vol. XXXI Blue, p. 441.

108. Unpublished decree dated Aug. 29, 1942, from *Amtsgruppe* D of WVHA, signed by Maurer; *Bundesarchiv,* Coblenz. See appendix 1.

109. Aug. 20, 1942, RGBL (Reich Laws), 1942, p. 535; cited in vol. III Green, p. 207; see also vol. III Green, p. 36.

110. PS-682, vol. III Red, p. 496. See also vol. V Blue, p. 442; vol. VI Blue, p. 379; vol. XVIII Blue, p. 486; vol. XIX Blue pp. 497, 555.

111. PS-654, vol. III Green, p. 504; vol. III Red, p. 468; vol. XXVI Blue, p. 201.

112. Vol. IV Green, pp. 134, 415.

113. PS-2273, vol. IV Red, p. 944; vol. IV Green, p. 197; vol. XXX Blue, p. 71.

114. Berlin Document Center, Doc. Series 4070-4075, B. B. F. general file, Oct. 30, 1959.

115. L-61, vol. II Green, p. 413.

116. NO-611, vol. V Green, p. 617.

117. R-124, vol. XXXVIII Blue, p. 359; vol. VIII Red, p. 186. See also Speer testimony, vol, XVI Blue, pp. 472, 517-518.

118. Walter Schieber's testimony, vol. IX Green, p. 836.

119. See vol. IX Green, p. 839.

120. Vol. VIII Green, pp. 1184, 1323.

121. See vol. VIII Green, p. 1186.

122. Vol. VIII Green, p. 624; NI-4829, vol. VIII Green, p. 576; NI-11696, vol. VIII Green, p. 607; see also NI-12388, p. 617.

123. See vol. VIII Green, p. 583.

124. NI-12388, vol. VIII Green, p. 618; see also NI-11692, p. 623.

125. PS-2171, vol. IV Red, p. 833; NO-1523, vol. V Green, p. 372.

126. Vol. XI Blue, p. 422. In 1977 the German government listed 1,634 concentration camps and subcamps; *Bundesgesetzblatt* (Federal Laws), Bonn, Sept, 24, 1977, pp. 1787-1852.

127. PS-016, vol. III Red, p. 57.

128. Vol. I Blue, p. 293.

129. D-736, vol. VII Red, p. 190.

130. NI-15256, vol. VIII Green, p. 510, see also R-91, vol. VIII Red, p. 60.

131. NI-12194, vol. VI Green, p. 261.

132. NI-903.

133. PS-1472; L-41, vol. VII Red, p. 784.

134. See Kempner, *Eichmann,* p. 118.

135. See Poliakov and Wulf, *Dritte Reich,* p. 198; cites *Documents from Central Jewish Historical Commission,* (Lodz: N. Blumenthal, 1946), p. 110.

136. See NI-9807, vol. VIII Green, p. 589.

137. PS-1061, vol.III Red, pp. 718, 728; German text in vol. XXVI Blue, pp. 628-694.

138. For an excellent summary of Jewish resistance, see Lucy S. Dawidowicz, *The War against the Jews* (New York: Holt, Rinehart and Winston, 1975), pp. 311-341.

139. NI-10040, VIII Green, p. 532.

140. NI-7569, Vol. VIII Green, p. 553.

141. NI-15253, vol. VIII Green, p. 540.

142. NO-1905, vol. VIII Green, p. 554.

143. NI-6851, vol. VIII Green, p. 567.

144. NI-903.

145. NO-597.

146. See Joseph Billig, *Les camps de concentration dans l'économie du reich hitlérien* (Paris: Presses Universitaires de France, 1973).

147. PS-1584, vol. IV Red, p. 117.

148. Albert Speer, *Inside the Third Reich: Memoirs* (New York: Macmillan, 1970), p. 370.

149. PS-3319, vol. VI Red, pp. 4-38.

150. R-124, vol. XXXVIII Blue, p. 361; vol. VIII Red, p. 146.

151. PS-109, Speer Defense Doc. Letter from Schieber to Speer, Personal and Confidential, May 7, 1944; see vol. XVI Blue, pp. 442, 579.

152. See Sehn, *Auschwitz,* p. 126.

153. Vol. XI Blue, p. 415.

154. L-161, vol. VII Red, p. 908; see also Sehn, *Auschwitz,* p.141.

155. See vol. II Green, p. 577; also Krupp Prosecution Brief, Count Three, pp. 182-183.

156. Vol. II Green, p. 558.

157. Vol. VIII Green, p. 315.

158. NI-4829, vol. VIII Green, p. 576.

159. Vol. XI Blue, p. 403.

160. PS-3868, vol. XI Blue, pp. 415-416; vol. VII Red, p. 787; see also Sehn, *Auschwitz,* p. 9.

161. See Kazimierz Smolén, *Auschwitz, 1940-1945* (Oswiecim: Panstwowe Museum, 1961), p. 76.

162. Gerald Reitlinger, *The SS* (New York: Viking, 1957) p. 266.

163. See vol. V Green, p. 445.

164. See Fried, *Exploitation,* p. 255.

165. See Smolén, *Auschwitz*.

166. See Höss, *Kommandant*,p. 8.

167. See Hannah Arendt, *Eichmann in Jerusalem* (New York: Viking Press, 1963), p. 228.

168. See Telford Taylor, *Final Report to the Secretary of the Army* (Washington, D. C.: United States Government Printing Office, 1949).

## 2. Auschwitz Survivors v. I.G. Farben

1. NI-10030, vol. VIII Green, p. 532. Vol. VII and vol. VIII Green contains a summary of the Farben case.

2. Vol. VIII Green, pp. 1183-1187.

3. See the judgment in the Farben case, vol. VIII Green, pp. 1081-1307.

4. Vol. VIII Green, pp. 1307-1325.

5. See vol. VII Green, p. 6 (photo).

6. See Allied High Commission Law No. 35, and *Report on Germany* (Office of the United States High Commissioner, Sept. 21, 1949–July 31, 1952), pp. 114-115.

7. Vol. I Blue, p. 365; vol. V Green, p. 1062.

8. Summaries of trial statements are based on the official Frankfurt court records.

9. Decision in *Wollheim v. I.G. Farben in Liquidation,* Frankfurt District Court, June 10, 1953, court file no. 2/3/0406/51.

10. JRSO was a New York corporation on whose board sat a dozen major Jewish charitable agencies. Similar organizations were later established for the other western zones and Berlin. See Charles Kapralik, *Reclaiming the Nazi Loot* (London: Sidney Press, 1962), and *The History of the Work of the Jewish Trust Corporation* (London: A. Wheaton and Co., 1971); see also Walter Schwarz, *Rückerstattung nach den Gesetzen der Allierte Mächte* (Munich: Beck Verlag, 1974).

11. *Documents Relating to the Agreement Signed on 10 Sept. 1952* (Israel Ministry of Foreign Affairs); G. Blessin and H. Wilden, *Bundesentschädigungsgesetze* (Munich: Beck Verlag, 1954).

12. The Claims Conference printed annual reports showing its organization and activities.

13. L-180, vol. XXXVII Blue, pp. 687, 702; trans. in vol. VII Red, pp. 985,992.

14. PS-2273; extract in vol. IV Green, p. 197.

15. See Norman Bentwich, *An Autobiography: My 77 Years* (Philadelphia: Jewish Publication Society, 1961). The URO secretary was Dr. Hans Reichman and his principal deputy was Dr. Fritz Goldschmidt.

16. Letter from Schoenfeldt to B.B F., April 7, 1954.

17. Report of B.B.F., June 24, 1954.

18. Letter from Schmidt to B.B.F., July 13, 1954.

19. Report by Ormond of court hearing, July 14, 1954.

20. Report of B.B.F., Nov. 15, 1954.

21. See Telford Taylor, *Final Report to the Secretary of the Army* (Washington, D.C. 1949), pp. 312, 333-334.

22. Dr. Alfred Werner wrote the main brief for the plaintiff.

23. Story by Albion Ross.

24. Order of Oct. 21, 1955, *Oberlandesgericht* Frankfurt, court file no. 5 U 122/53.

25. The influential Sen. Everett Dirkson of Illinois was in the forefront of the efforts to return the vested German assets. See *The Reporter,* June 14, 1956; *Chemical Week,* April 14, 1956; Joseph Borkin, *The Crime and Punishment of I.G. Farben* (New York: Free Press, 1978).

26. Report of B.B.F., Jan. 9, 1956.

27. Letter from S.K. to B.B.F., Jan. 16, 1956.

28. Reports of B.B.F., Feb. 17, Feb. 26, 1956.

29. See vol. VII Green, pp. 64-65, 256; vol. VIII Green, p. 1159. See also Josiah DuBois, *The Devil's Chemists* (Boston: Beacon Press, 1952).

30. Letter from May to S.K., Mar. 20, 1956.

31. Letter from May to S.K., May 14, 1956.

32. Report of Dr. Alfred Schüler, July 30, 1956, of Farben shareholder's meeting on July 27, 1956.

33. Report of B.B.F., Sept. 12, 1956. The contract went through many drafts and it was also necessary to enact special Allied and German laws to establish a new and definitive legal deadline for the submission of claims against Farben.

34. Letter from S.K. to E.K., Jan 24, 1957.

35. *Congressional Record,* appendix, Feb. 14, 1957, p. A1010.

36. *Congressional Record,* appendix, Feb. 19, 1957, p. A1201.

37. Report of Alfred Schüler, April 8, 1957; see *Deutsche Zeitung,* Mar. 27, 1957.

38. *Bundesgesetzblatt* (Federal Laws), part I, 1957, p. 569.

39. Farben let it be known that it would not favor any reference to Auschwitz. The offices of Compensation Treuhand GmbH were at Stauffenstrasse 29 in Frankfurt; Katzenstein was chairman of the board, which included S.K. and B.B.F. The general manager was required to issue progress reports at least twice a year.

40. See *Information Bulletin, Comité International d'Auschwitz,* May 17, June 18, 1957; report of E. G. Lowenthal, June 3, 1957; *New York Times,* Dec. 1, 1957.

41. Letter from E.K. to S.K., Dec. 2, 1957.

42. *Industriekurier,* Dec. 3, 1957; *Deutsche Zeitung,* Dec. 4, 1957, Mar. 3, 1958.

43. The screening committee in Israel was headed by Dr. Philip Korngrun, a former judge, who was assisted by Samuel Shlomai and Rafael Olevski, who had both worked for Farben at Auschwitz. The French committee was headed by Professor Robert Waitz, assisted by Avocat M. Ayache and Marcel Stourdze. In Hungary the chairman was Dr. Géza Seifert, assisted by Oskar Betlin. Dr. Matoušek, of the Anti-Fascist Committee, helped in Prague, Dr. Wilhelm Krell, head of the Jewish Congregation in Vienna, Mr. Jacob and Josef Spring in Australia, Mr. Pagee in London, Mr. Levold in Brazil, and Mr. Eitinger in Oslo. They all served without pay. In Frankfurt Dr. Franz Unikower, a former registrar at Buna, and Walter Lewinski were employed by Compensation Treuhand to help with the screening.

44. *Frankfurter Allgemeine Zeitung,* April 1, 1958.

45. Letter from Schmidt to B.B.F., April 10, 1958.

46. Report of Lowenthal, Dec. 3, 1957, attaching translation of letter written in Yiddish by Hershel M., Sept. 1957.

47. Heinz Galinski, head of the Jewish Congregation of Berlin, and Ernst Landau, a journalist from Munich, completed the panel.

48. Letter from E.K. to S.K., Mar. 29, 1960; letter from B.B.F. to E.K., July 29, 1960.

49. NI-14543, vol. VIII Green, p. 393.

50. Report of E.K., June 26, 1961.

51. Report of E.K., Oct. 25, 1961.

52. The lawsuit was commenced on July 31, 1958, and disclosed by Farben in a press conference on Aug. 12, 1958; see *Frankfurter Allgemeine Zeitung, Frankfurter Rundschau, and Neue Presse,* Aug. 14, 1958.

53. Decision of Frankfurt *Landgericht,* July 9, 1959, court file no. 2/30 190/58.

54. Brief to the *Oberlandesgericht,* Sept. 20, 1960; supplementary brief, Oct. 26, 1960.

55. Vol. VIII Green, pp. 1318-1319.

56. A photocopy of the original letter is reproduced in Leon Poliakov and Josef Wulf, *Das Dritte Reich und die Juden* (Berlin: Arani Verlag, 1955), p. 67.

57. NI-10040, vol. VIII Green, pp. 532,1319.

58. Letter from E.K. to S.K., Dec. 1, 1960.

59. *Oberlandesgericht* decision, Jan. 4, 1961. See articles by Ministerial Director Féaux de la Croix in *Neue Juristische Wochenzeitung,* Dec. 9, 1960, and Hans Gurski in *Betriebs-Beraters,* Jan. 1961; but see Martin Domke, "Individual Anspruch fur völkerrechtliche Deliktshaftung?" *Schweizerische Juristen-Zeitung,* Jan. 1, 1962.

60. Farben had also established a panel to which a rejected claimant might appeal. It was headed by a German judge, Dr. Dombrowski.

61. Letter from Gutter to E.K., Jan. 30, 1961.

62. Report by E.K., Oct. 25, 1961.

63. See the *Saturday Review,* Feb. 16, 1963.

64. See Kazimierz Smolén, *Auschwitz, 1940-1945* (Oswiecim: Panstwowe Museum, 1961); Jan Sehn, *Auschwitz-Birkenau Concentration Camp* (Warsaw: Wydawnictwo Prawnicze, 1961).

65. I received a copy of a similar report which had also been smuggled out by the underground and which showed camp strength as of Aug. 21, 1944; see B.B.F. report, Nov. 13, 1961.

66. Sehn referred me to NI-14997, a 500-page report dealing with the Buna plant at Monowitz.

67. Report of E.K., Oct. 24, 1962. Farben was represented by Dr. Otto Wirner, Hans Göring, Dr. Ferdinand Kremer, Benvenuto Samson, and Dr. Erich Petri.

68. Report of E.K., July 10, 1963; letter from Farben to Claims Conference, July 9, 1963.

69. Decision of *Bundesgerichtshof,* Feb. 26, 1963, court file no. VI ZR 94/61.

70. Report of Compensation Treuhand, Sept. 1965.

71. The committee headed by Professor Robert E. Waitz dealt with hardship applications from France, Belgium, Holland, Luxembourg, and Italy. Gunter Ruschin of Santiago dealt with applications from Chile, Argentina, and Brazil. Dr. Hans Tramer organized the screening of hardship claims in Israel. Hungarian claims were handled with the aid of the director of the Hungarian National Bank, Dr. Laslo Deszery. Czech claims were screened by Robert Dub of Prague, and German claims were screened by Max Willner and Siegmund Freund of Frankfurt. In New York Wollheim and Gutter, aided by a few former Buna inmates, screened claims originating in the United States and Canada.

72. Report of Seidenberg, Nov. 9, 1965.

73. Letter to Compensation Treuhand, Aug. 27, 1965.

74. Correspondence dated Oct. 13, Oct. 26, and Nov. 16, 1965.

75. Report of Seidenberg, Dec. 22, 1965.

76. Norbert Wollheim was chairman, Ernest W. Michel and Haskel Tydor were co-chairmen, and Simon Gutter was the secretary. About two dozen other Buna survivors were listed as members.

77. Gutter later reported that all of the money collected by the Scholarship Memorial Committee was turned over to the Bar Ilan University in Israel for scholarships to needy children of camp survivors.

78. Letter from Gerhard Riegner, Executive Director of the World Jewish Congress office in Geneva, to B.B.F., Jan. 25, 1973.

79. Letter from Rafael Olevski to B.B.F.July 9, 1967; letter from E.K. to B.B.F., June 30, 1967.

80. *New York Times*, April 22, 1968, story by Jonathan Randal. Ten years later it was reported that a Jewish Memorial Pavilion was opened in Auschwitz on April 17, 1978. See Jewish Telegraphic Agency dispatch, Feb. 5, 1978.

81. See *Frankfurter Allgemeine Zeitung,* Sept. 21, 1968.

82. Interest-free loans, in amounts of between IL 2,000 and IL 3,000, were made to former Auschwitz inmates. There was a supervisory board of thirty-five former Nazi victims. See letter from Association of Former Inmates of Auschwitz-Buna Concentration Camps to B.B.F., Aug. 6, 1968; Loeb and Troper audit report, Mar. 31, 1974.

83. Letter to Compensation Treuhand, Dec. 23, 1963, file no. CP/9424 SP.

## 3. Accounting with Krupp

1. NI-2965, vol. IX Green, pp. 738-739. Photograph of original German carbon copy in vol. IX Green, pp. 1319-1320. Vol. IX, *The Krupp Case,* is a summary of the Krupp trial.

2. D-204, vol. IX Green, p. 338; PS-3725, vol. VI Red, p. 464; NI-910, vol. IX Green, p. 339.

3. NIK-12074, vol. IX Green, p. 237.

4. NIK-12074, vol. IX Green, p. 234.

5. NIK-9294, vol. IX Green, p. 232.

6. See William Manchester, *The Arms of Krupp* (Boston: Little, Brown, 1964), p. 605.

7. Vol. I Blue, pp. 129, 143.

8. Vol. I Blue, pp. 137, 145.

9. Vol. I Blue, p. 146.

10. Vol. IX Green, pp. 1329, 1331.

11. Vol. IX Green, pp. 1411-1412.

12. Vol. IX Green, p.1449.

13. See vol. IV Green, p. 591n. General Clay did not review the ministries case, case 11, since it was only completed after he left Germany. High Commissioner McCloy reduced all the sentences which had been in excess of ten years. Vol. XIV Green, p. 1004.

14. Statement made by McCloy to B.B.F. on Aug. 11, 1977.

15. Office of the United States High Commissioner for Germany, Staff Announcement No. 117, July 18, 1950. The terms of the appointment of the Clemency Board were explicit: "The Board shall not review the decision of such Tribunals on questions of law or fact." Clearly it was not an appellate review, but this distinction went largely unnoticed in the minds of the public and was apparently also overlooked by the high commissioner himself.

16. *Landsberg: A Documentary Report* (Office of the United States High Commissioner for Germany, Frankfurt, Germany, Jan. 31, 1951); reprinted from the Feb. 1951 issue of the *Information Bulletin,* the official magazine of the United States High Commissioner for Germany. [HICOG.]

17. Vol. IV Green, case no. 9, *The Einsatzgruppen Case.*

18. *Landsberg Report,* p. 20.

19. McCloy's release of convicted war criminals gave rise to widespread criticism. Extracts from an explanatory letter that McCloy had written to Eleanor Roosevelt were published in the *Information Bulletin* in May 1951, and the *State Department Bulletin* of June 11, 1951, reprinted portions of McCloy's letter to Senator Jacob Javits in which McCloy referred to "a fundamental principle of American justice that persons accused shall have a right of appeal." Telford Taylor, knowing that the defendants had already been given a full right of appeal and recognizing that clemency proceedings which are ordered to hear only one side do not remotely resemble an appellate procedure, tried to have his corrections published in the *Information Bulletin,* but to no avail. Manchester, *Arms of Krupp,* pp. 669-677, refers to Taylor's criticism and implies that McCloy's action was based on political considerations, a conclusion which McCloy vehemently denies. Letter from McCloy to B.B.F., June 7, 1977. It may be noted that McCloy did order the carrying out of five death sentences despite protests by German groups of varying political persuasion and that in many cases his final decision was more severe than the action recommended by the Clemency Board. See unpublished report of Advisory Board on Clemency for War Criminals to the United States High Commissioner for Germany, Aug. 28, 1950, State Department Archives, Washington D.C.

20. "I am disposed to feel that confiscation in this single case constitutes discrimination against this defendant unjustified by any considerations attaching peculiarly to him." *Landsberg Report,* p. 10. In this respect the high commissioner followed the unanimous recommendation of the Clemency Board.

21. *Herald Tribune,* Feb. 5, 1951.

22. *Germany Reports* (published by the Press and Information Office of

the Federal Republic of Germany, 1955), p. 102.

23. John J. McCloy, *Report on Germany* (Office of the United States High Commissioner for Germany, Frankfurt, Germany, Sept. 21, 1949–July 31, 1952), sec. 4.

24. See Allied High Commission Law No. 27 (May 1950), and Regulation 6 thereunder.

25. The Convention on Relations between the Three Powers and the Federal Republic of Germany, signed at Bonn on May 26, 1952, specifically required that Allied High Commission Law No. 27, on the "Reorganization of the German Coal, Iron and Steel Industries," remain in effect until carried out.

26. See *Daily Mirror,* Nov. 11, 1952, quoted by Manchester, *Arms of Krupp,* p. 704.

27. See Manchester, *Arms of Krupp,* p. 715.

28. Ibid., pp. 716-722.

29. The complaint was submitted by the attorney E. Jaegermann and received file no. 6 0 24/54. By 1956 the case was being handled by the attorney Hans Meyers. They served as corresponding lawyers for Theodore Mattern, Esq. of New York.

30. Complaint amended on July 19, 1956. The Krupp company was represented by a firm of Essen attorneys through one of the partners, Dr. Kurt Schürmann.

31. S.K. file memo, June 25, 1958. McCloy considered restitution a signpost of Germany's moral rehabilitation and in all matters affecting compensation to the survivors of Nazi persecution he could be relied upon to lend his strong support. See John J. McCloy, *Report on Germany* (Office of the United States High Commissioner for Germany, Sept. 21, 1949–July 31, 1952), pp. 131-145.

32. Henry Sachs was the researcher and his services were made available by the Yiddish Scientific Institute. (YIVO).

33. Sworn statement of Theodore Lehman, 355 Riverside Drive, New York, June 30, 1958.

34. S.K. memo, July 3, 1958.

35. Letter from Blaustein to McCloy, Sept. 11, 1958.

36. B.B.F. memo based on a conversation with Blaustein, Oct. 12, 1958.

37. Letter from B.B.F. to E.K., Jan. 5, 1959.

38. See *New York Times,* Jan. 18, 1959, article by Sidney Gruson.

39. Letter from Beitz to E.K., Jan. 14, 1959.

40. *New York Times,* Jan. 18, 1959.

41. See *New York Post,* Feb. 5, 1959, article by Marquis Childs.

42. *Newsweek,* Jan. 19, 1959, p. 33; see also News Analysis by Harold Callender, *New York Times,* Feb. 1, 1959, reporting on a change in the Allied view regarding the break-up of the Krupp industrial empire. The *Times* reported that there was "an unwritten gentlemen's agreement with the sympathy of their government" not to bid for the Krupp holdings (Feb. 1, 1959, article by Arthur J. Olsen).

43. Telford Taylor, *Final Report to the Secretary of the Army* (Washington D.C.: United States Goverment Printing Office, 1949), p. 333.

44. Letter from E.K. to B.B.F., Feb. 25, 1959.

45. Letter from E.K. to B.B.F., Mar. 5, 1959, referring to a *London Daily Telegraph* article of Mar. 4, 1959.

46. Report of E.K., April 23, 1959, on meeting with Krupp representatives, on April 22, 1959.

47. *New York Times,* Mar. 15, 1959.

48. Letter from Beitz to E.K., June 10, 1959.

49. The *New York Times,* Nov. 28, 1959, reported that a Dutch buyer was trying to acquire Rheinhausen for $350 million but Krupp would not even consider the offer.

50. B.B.F. report dated June 23, 1959, on meeting with McCloy on June 22, 1959.

51. B.B.F. memo to McCloy, June 23, 1959.

52. Blaustein letter to McCloy, July 2, 1959.

53. *Der Spiegel,* May 27, 1959, pp. 42-43.

54. Through Ambassador Bruce's office, E.K. arranged for McCloy to first meet Goldmann, who was then in Bonn; letter from E.K. to S.K., July 15, 1959.

55. B.B.F. memo, Aug. 14, 1959.

56. Letter from Blaustein to Beitz, Aug. 25, 1959.

57. Letter from B.B.F. to Warburg, Aug. 31, 1959. Warburg was also given copies of documents incriminating Alfried Krupp, including a statement, NIK-11234, by one of Krupp's directors warning that they might all be held criminally liable for their use of concentration camp inmates.

58. The German government assumed responsibility for enforcement of AHC Law No. 27 of May 20, 1950, subject to the supervision of the Mixed Commission. See *Paris Protocol on the Termination of the Occupation Regime,* Oct. 23, 1954, chap. I, art. 9. The United States member of the Mixed Commission was Spencer Phenix.

59. Letter from B.B.F. to S.K., Oct. 7, 1959.

60. The German lawyer in Essen was Dr. Hans Meyers, and the German brief was prepared by Dr. Max Stein of Israel. B.B.F. memo, Oct. 13, 1959.

61. B.B.F. memo, Oct. 22, 1959.

62. Letter from S.K. to Blaustein, Oct. 27, 1959.

63. Letter from E.K. to S.K., Oct. 23, 1959.

64. Letter from S.K. to B.B.F., Oct. 31, 1959.

65. *New York Daily News,* Nov. 27, 1959, article by Russ Braley.

66. See *New York Times,* Nov. 27, 1959.

67. Report of S.K. to E.K., Nov. 27, 1959. Beitz had been accompanied by Albrecht von Kessel. Blaustein was accompanied by S.K. Drafts of an agreement had been prepared by B.B.F., S.K., and Dr. Nehemiah Robinson, an outstanding restitution expert employed by the World Jewish Congress.

68. Katzenstein was accompanied by Dr. Max Stein. The Krupp lawyers were Dr. Hermann Maschke, Frau Dr. Knoll, and Dr. Schürmann; E.K. report, Dec. 2, 1959.

69. E.K. memo, Dec. 4, 1959; letter from E.K. to S.K., Dec. 4, 1959; telegram from Beitz to Blaustein, Dec. 23, 1959.

70. *New York Times,* Dec. 24, 1959, story by Theodore Shabad.

71. See Jewish Telegraphic Agency bulletin, Dec. 28, 1959, and Feb. 3, 1960.

72. Mackay Radio cable 113/110, Dec. 23, 1959.

73. See *Die antisemitischen und Nazistischen Vorfälle in der Zeit vom 25 Dez. bis zum 28 Jan. 1960* (Bonn:Bundesregierung, 1960); Jewish Agency for Israel, *Digest on Germany and Austria,* no. 86 (Feb. 1960).

74. See *Manchester Guardian,* Mar. 16, 1960; letter from Langbein to Krupp, Mar. 2, 1960.

75. See *Information Bulletin, Comité International d'Auschwitz,* Mar. 25, 1960.

76. Letter from E.K. to S.K., Mar. 16, 1960.

77. Letter to E.K., signed Hans Schwartz, Secretary, Mar. 15, 1960.

78. Letter from Krupp signed by Knoll and Maschke, Feb. 25, 1960. The letter was drawn to our attention by Caroline Ferriday of New York, an ardent champion of compensation for those Polish women of Ravensbrück who had been subjected to Nazi medical experiments. In transmitting the letter she wrote: "Fomenting a bit of anti-semitism would be just their cup of tea." Letter to B.B.F., April 10, 1960.

79. See the *Jewish Chronicle,* Feb. 17, 1961.

80. Annual report of Krupp's War Material Dept. for 1941-1942, NIK-11504, vol, IX Green, pp. 684-685.

81. NI-2868, vol. IX Green, pp. 708-711.

82. NIK-11569.

83. NIK-1722.

84. NIK-6565, vol IX Green, p. 719.

85. NI-3754, vol. IX Green, p. 722.

86. NI-3754, memo of engineer Weinhold dated Mar. 26, 1943, unpublished.

87. NIK-4723, vol. IX Green, p. 725.

88. NIK-4719.

89. NIK-8805.

90. NI-2965, vol. IX Green, pp. 738-739, 1319-1320.

91. NIK-4720.

92. NIK-15452.

93. Vol. IX Green, p. 1423.

94. NIK-11584, vol. IX Green, pp. 683-687.

95. NIK-15512.

96. Vol. IX Green, p. 1419.

97. Ibid.

98. Vol. IX Green, p. 1418.

99. NIK-12342, vol. IX Green, p. 1421.

100. NIK-9209.

101. See NIK-9039; NIK-7454, vol. IX Green, p. 753; NIK-10368.

102. NIK-8487; see Krupp Prosecution Brief, Count Three, p. 205.

103. NIK-11699; vol. IX Green, p. 1423.

104. Affidavit of Trudi G., dated Sept. 15, 1959.

105. Vol. IX Green, p. 1412.

106. Vol. IX Green, p. 1425.

107. See D-274, vol. IX Green, pp. 812-813.

108. D-238, vol. IX Green, pp. 1137-1139.

109. Vol. IX Green, pp. 1425-1426.

110. NIK-11676, vol. IX Green, pp. 1158-1159.

111. See Vol. IX Green, p. 1428.

112. D-277, affidavit of Rosa Katz, unpublished.

113. Krupp transcript, Commission I, pp. 8936-8937, May 21, 1948.

114. Ibid; See D-274, vol. IX Green, pp. 812-815; NIK-5919.

115. Vol. IX Green, pp. 1428-1429.

116. Letter from Beitz to E.K., May 9, 1963.

117. Letter from Goldmann to Bietz, June 12, 1963.

118. Letter from Beitz to Goldmann, June 26, 1963.

119. Letter from Rabbi Prinz to Secretary of State Rusk, Oct. 28, 1963.

120. Letter from E.K. to S.K., Nov. 8, 1963.

121. Letter from E.K. to S.K., Dec. 2, 1963.

122. Letter from Beitz to Goldmann, Dec. 20, 1963.

123. Letter from Goldmann to Beitz, Jan. 11, 1964.

124. Letter from Beitz to Goldmann, Jan. 15, 1964.

125. Letter from Goldmann to Beitz, Jan. 24, 1964.

126. Vol. IX Green, p. 1429.

127. PS-3319, vol. VI Red, p. 34.

128. Vol. IV Green, p. 557.

129. NG-4817, letter from Rademacher, May 12, 1942, reproduced in URO's report, *Dokumente über Methoden der Judenverfolgung im Ausland,* (Frankfurt: United Restitution Organization, 1959), p. 63.

130. Detailed descriptions were provided by survivors of the Trichati camp. See file notes for Feb. 22, 1960, and May 25, 1961.

131. Memorandum from the Association for the Protection of Rights of Forced Laborers from Trichati, Aug. 15, 1962.

132. Details are contained in Matatias Carp, *Cartea Neagra: Suferintele Evreilor Din Romania, 1940-1944* (The Black Book of the Suffering of the Jews of Romania) (Bucharest, 1946-1948), vol. III, Transnistrien.

133. File memos dated Sept. 23, 1960, Sept. 29, 1960, Mar. 15, 1961, and Oct. 16, 1962.

134. Letter of Abraham W., Newark, New Jersey, to Krupp, Nov. 4, 1964.

135. Letter from Krupp company to Abraham W., Nov. 27, 1964.

### 4. The Electrical Companies See the Light

1. Ella Lingens-Reisner, *Prisoners of Fear* (London: Gollancz, 1948), p. 36.

2. Letter from AEG to Zentralrat der Juden in Deutschland, Nov 1, 1957.

3. Letter from van Dam to AEG, Dec. 9, 1957.

4. Letter from AEG to van Dam, Dec. 19, 1957.

5. Letter from van Dam to AEG, Dec. 21, 1957.

6. Letter from AEG to van Dam, Dec. 24, 1957.

7. Affidavit of Rivka W. of New York, Oct. 14, 1958.

8. Decision of Berlin District Court, Mar. 25, 1958, in the case of *Ellfers and 115 others v. Telefunken and Hagenuk.* (Hagenuk was another German firm which later employed many of the same persons.) Werner reported to his clients, May 10, 1958.

9. Letter from Telefunken to Schildbach, June 26, 1958.

10. Complaint filed in the Berlin District Court, June 30, 1958, court file no. 14 0 152/58. Another former Reichenbach Jewish worker wrote on Feb. 23, 1960: "They treated us worse than dogs . . . it was hell . . . it was just a miracle that I survived."

11. Berlin *Kammergericht* decision in case of *Ellfers v. Telefunken,* Feb. 23, 1959, court file nos. 4 U 1057/58, 6 0 329/57.

12. Vol. V Green, p. 593.

13. Ibid., pp. 601-604.

14. Ibid., p. 595.

15. Ibid., p. 596.

16. Vol. V Green, p. 1033. Sommer was sentenced to death, but General Clay commuted the sentence to imprisonment for life (vol. V Green, p. 1255). The sentence was further reduced from life to twenty years by the United States High Commissioner John J. McCloy. See *Landsberg: A Documentary Report* (Office of the United States High Commissioner, Jan. 31, 1951), p. 6.

17. NI-280 (unpublished document submitted in the Farben case and used in the prosecution of Gerhard Maurer in Poland. Appendix 4.

18. See vol. IX Green, p. 1425.

19. NI-4434 (unpublished affidavit of Höss, Warsaw, Mar. 12, 1947, before John Fried, Consultant to the United States Secretary of War); Appendix 3. See also NI-039 (unpublished interrogation of Höss by Alfred Booth, Nuremberg, May 17, 1946).

20. The original German document, bearing Maurer's signature, as chief of Dept. D II, was sent out of Oranienburg to all the commanders of sixteen concentration camps identified only by initials. As far as is known, the document has not been published. See appendix 1.

21. NI-638, vol. V Green, pp. 588-590.

22. NI-1065; see appendix 2. Referred to in vol. V Green, pp. 1033, 1201. (Original at the National Archives in Washington; photocopy at the State Archives in Nuremberg.)

23. E.K. was accompanied by Max Stein, who was on the staff of Compensation Treuhand.

24. See *Deutsche Zeitung,* July 27, 1963; *Frankfurter Allgemeine Zeitung,* July 27, 1963.

25. Letter from E.K. to S.K., Mar. 25, 1960. A subsequent meeting failed to alter AEG's position. See letter from E.K. to S.K., April 26, 1960.

26. Goldmann had apparently relied on the advice of a man who purported to be an important AEG stockholder, William Robinson, who had arranged the meeting and who informed Goldmann that AEG would not pay more than DM 6 million. See letter from E.K. to S.K., May 16, 1960.

27. E.K. report to S.K., July 12, 1960.

28. E.K. report to S.K., July 28, 1960.

29. Letter from E.K. to S.K., July 28, 1960.

30. Letter from E.K. to S.K., Aug. 15, 1960.

31. Letter from E.K. to AEG, Aug. 23, 1960; reply from AEG's legal department to the Claims Conference, Aug. 24, 1960; E.K.'s confirming letter to AEG, Aug. 24, 1960.

32. Letter from E.K. to S.K., Aug. 24, 1960.

33. See letter from B.B.F. to E.K., June 10, 1963.

34. Letter from E.K. to B.B.F., June 20, 1963; letter from E.K. to B.B.F., July 19, 1963.

35. Dachau prisoners who went out on regular "AEG *Kommandos*" (work gangs) had to be turned down because they did not work inside an AEG factory.

36. See Loeb and Troper audit report, Aug. 15, 1974. Appendix 5.

37. In 1958 Siemens had sales of over DM 3 billion and employed 188,000 people. Reported in Siemens *Geschäftsbericht* (annual report) for 1958/59.

38. See letter from Nehemiah Robinson of World Jewish Congress to B.B.F., June 13, 1957.

39. See Max Stein, "Report on the Employment of Slave Work by the Siemens Concern during World War II" (Frankfurt: unpublished, Feb. 24, 1961). The declaration by Hermann v. Siemens signed on Jan. 10, 1946, is referred to on pp. 6-7.

40. George Siemens, *History of the House of Siemens,* 3 vols. (privately published by Siemens, vol. II, p. 269. The beatings given to Jews as they mounted deportation trucks is described in a letter from an SS captain dated Mar. 4, 1943, and reproduced in Robert M. W. Kempner, *Eichmann und Komplizen* (Zurich: Europa Verlag, 1961), pp. 118-119.

41. See Stein, "Report on Employment of Slave Work," which cites NI-034, NI-036, NI-382, and NI-1065. See also Bruno Baum, *Wiederstand in Auschwitz* (Berlin: Kongressverlag, 1957); letter from Stein to S.K., Dec. 16, 1960, attached information received from the State Museum in Auschwitz, dated Nov. 18, 1960. The information was confirmed in a special report prepared by Siemens on Oct. 31, 1945, "Einsatz ausländischer Ziviliarbeiter, Kriegsgefangener, Juden und KZ-Häftlinge im Hause Siemens," p. 38, referred to in *Buchenwald-Mahnung und Verpflichtung* (Berlin: Kongressverlag, 1960), p. 239.

42. PS-1584, vol. IV Red, p. 120.

43. NI-395, National Archives, Record Group 242; Karl Sommer's affidavit (extract in appendix 2), NI-1065 (unpublished), confirmed that between five and six hundred inmates were taken from Flossenberg to two different Siemens factories.

44. NI-1065, NI-280 (extract in appendix 4).

45. NI-1791 (unpublished).

46. Much of the information was obtained initially from inmates who had worked in the different locations. The facts were confirmed by documents discovered later. On June 9, 1964, the concentration camp commanders received secret code reference numbers from WVHA Dept. D II to be used on all correspondence with hundreds of listed firms regarding the use of camp inmates. NO-597 (unpublished), National Archives, Washington, D.C., "Records of World War II War Crimes (Nuremberg)," Record Group 238.

47. Letter from Siemens-Archiv, Munich, to Max Stein, Dec. 20, 1960.

48. Letter from Siemens and Halske in Erlangen to Ester Freundlich in Israel, Mar. 15, 1960; letter from Siemens-Schuckertwerke to Frederich Pins, Vienna, Jan. 22, 1958. See the *Jewish Chronicle*, London, May 27, 1960; letter from Siemens & Halske to Karl Leonhard, Sept. 15, 1960.

49. Letter from E.K. to Adolf Lohse, May 29, 1961; letter from E.K. to S.K., July 3, 1961.

50. Letter from E.K. to S.K., July 24, 1961. By that time the Claims Conference had assembled the names of about two thousand claimants and dozens of documents concerning the employment of inmates by Siemens.

51. See *German-American Trade News,* Jan. 1962.

52. Report from E.K. to S.K., Oct. 30, 1961, of meeting in Munich on Oct. 27, 1961.

53. Letter from E.K. to B.B.F., July 30, 1961. It was learned later that the report was also in the Archives of the Socialist Unity Party in East Berlin; see letter from Deutsche Institut für Zeitgeschichte to Stein, June 14, 1961.

54. Stein met Warburg in Hamburg on Nov. 28, 1961; see letter from Stein to E.K., Nov. 30, 1961; letter from Stein to S.K., Nov. 30, 1961.

55. See report by Stein, Nov. 30, 1961, p. 4.

56. The reduced figure had been suggested by S.K., on the transatlantic phone with Warburg the day before.

57. Report from E.K. to S.K., Dec. 20, 1961, of meeting on Dec. 18, 1961.

58. Letter from E.K. to S.K., Mar. 15, 1962.

59. Report from E.K. to S.K., May 10, 1962, of meeting on May 8, 1962.

60. The agreement was dated May 24, 1962.

61. SSW drew Sachsenhausen inmates for its plant at Berlin's Siemenstadt, Flossenberg inmates for its plants in Nuremberg, Auschwitz inmates for its plant at Bobrek, and Mauthausen inmates for its work in Ebensee. SBU drew Gross Rosen inmates for its plants at Ober Altstadt and Christianstadt, and Mauthausen inmates to work at Ebensee. It used slave laborers at Cracow/Plaszow and at Bor in Yugoslavia. A Siemens subsidiary, Cable and Wire Works used inmates from Buchenwald; and another subsidiary, Vienna Cable and Metal Works, used inmates from Mauthausen. The details about the various Siemens camps were assembled in "guides" prepared by Max Stein, Simon Gutter, and Hans Seidenberg, based on information derived from personal interviews, affidavits, and questionnaires submitted by claimants, as well as documentary evidence.

62. Report by Hans Seidenberg on Bobrek, Feb. 28, 1964.

63. See Siemens special report, Oct. 31, 1945, p. 31 (note 41, above).

64. See reports dated Jan. 19, 1965, June 17, 1965, July 8, 1965, June 26, 1967.

65. A detailed description was obtained from Ebensee's chief registrar, Albert Schockenweiler of Luxembourg; see Compensation Treuhand report, Aug. 11, 1966.

66. See PS-1584, vol. XXVII Blue, pp. 358, 361; Siemens special report, Oct. 31, 1945, p. 32 (note 41, above).

67. Siemens special report, Oct. 31, 1945, p. 36.

68. International Tracing Service, Preliminary List of Concentration Camps (1969), p. 192.

69. Compensation Treuhand report, Feb. 4, 1965.

70. Circular letter of the SS, Dec. 14, 1942, cited in T. Berenstein, A. Eisenbach, B. Mark, and A. Rutkowski, eds., *Faschismus-Getto-Massenmord* (Berlin: Rütten and Loening, 1961), p. 448. These are documents collected by the Jewish Historical Institute of Warsaw.

71. Compensation Treuhand report, Oct. 22, 1965.

72. Speech by Frank in Cracow, Aug. 2, 1943, cited in Leon Poliakov and Josef Wulf, *Das Dritte Reich und die Juden* (Berlin: Arani Verlag, 1955), p. 185.

73. Speeches by Frank in Warsaw, Jan. 25, 1943, and in Cracow, May 31, 1943, Mar. 4, 1944; cited in Poliakov and Wulf, *Dritte Reich,* p. 185. Details about the work at Cracow/Plaszow are contained in Compensation Treuhand reports, Sept. 21, Sept. 28, 1964; March 5, July 8, Sept. 28, 1965; Jan. 25, Feb. 15, 1966.

74. Memo D III 218 g from Fränk of Organization Todt, Feb. 20, 1943, in German Foreign Office files; Document NG-5629, Feb. 23, 1943, from the files of the Institut für Zeitgeschichte, Munich; telegram, February 25, 1943, Foreign Office file Z.D III 218 g,—all reproduced in *Judenverfolgung in Ungarn,* ed. Kurt May (Frankfurt: United Restitution Organization, 1959), pp. 133-135. See also Lucy S. Dawidowicz, *The War against the Jews* (New York: Holt, Rinehart and Winston, 1975), pp. 381-383.

75. Document 736 D from the State Archives in Nuremberg, file minutes of meeting between Hitler and Horthy, April 17, 1943, Fuh. 25/43 gRs., full text in *Judenverfolgung in Ungarn,* pp. 142-145.

76. Letter from Organization of Nazi Victims in Hungary to Compensation Treuhand, May 17, 1963.

77. Letter from Istvan K., Budapest, to Compensation Treuhand, April 17, 1963.

78. Compensation Treuhand reports, Feb. 4, Feb. 9, Aug. 19, 1966; Mar. 31, 1969.

79. See letter from Seidenberg to URO Israel, Jan. 19, 1966.

80. Audit report of Deutsche-Treuhand-Gesellschaft, Munich, Oct. 31, 1966, p. 14.

81. Final Loeb and Troper audit report, Aug. 15, 1974 (appendix 5).

## 5. The Cannons of Rheinmetall

1. Court file no. VI ZR 186/61.

2. Based on reports received by Compensation Treuhand from German banks, Jan. 19, Sept. 1, 1961.

3. Complaints filed Dec. 30, 1957, Civil Chamber of the District Court in Berlin.

4. Schildbach received assistance from Dr. Kurt Wehle of the URO office in New York. The arguments of the defendant were recapitulated in a decision of the Berlin District Court, Feb. 27, 1959, court file no. 3 0 12/58. See letter from Wehle to B.B.F., June 5, 1958.

5. Order of the Berlin District Court, July 8, 1958.

6. See letter from Wehle to Schildbach, Nov. 13, 1958, referring to Rheinmetall brief of Sept. 22, 1958.

7. Petition by Schildbach filed in Berlin District Court, Nov. 15, 1958; letter from Schildbach to E.K., Nov. 18, 1958.

8. Annual Report of Rheinmetall Berlin A.G., 1959, p. 5.

9. Decision, Berlin District Court, Feb. 27, 1959.

10. Berlin Appellate Court decision in *Ellfers and 115 others v. Telefunken and Hagenuk,* Feb. 23, 1959, court file no. 4 U 1057/58, 6 0 329/57.

11. Letter from Rheinmetall to E.K., June 26, 1961; letter from E.K. to Rheinmetall, June 28, 1961.

12. Letter from Rheinmetall to E.K., Aug. 3, 1961. Rheinmetall had won in the appellate court which followed its own decision in the Ellfers case (decision July 12, 1961, court file no. 10/4 U 873/59, 3 0 12/58). The Claims Conference instructed Schildbach to file an appeal, which was handled by Professor Bernhard Wieczorek with the assistance of E.K.

13. Letter from Rheinmetall to Eric Warburg, Feb. 2, 1962.

14. Decision of the supreme court in the case of *Staucher v. I.G. Farben,* Feb. 23, 1963, court file no. VI ZR 94/61.

15. Decision of the supreme court Mar. 17, 1964, court file no. VI ZR 186/61.

16. Decision of the Stuttgart District Court in the case of *Bartl v. Heinkel,* Mar. 11, 1964, court file no. 1 U 16/63.

17. Rachel and Helen signed the submission of the case to the German Constitutional Court on May 4, 1964.

18. Information based on fact sheet attached to text of speech delivered by Springfield Mayor Charles V. Ryan, Jr., at a governors' conference, Dec. 9, 1964.

19. *New York Times,* Nov. 15, 1964. *Wall Street Journal,* Nov. 16, 1964.

20. See articles in *Springfield Union,* Dec. 1, 1964, and *Springfield Daily News,* Nov. 30, 1964.

21. *Springfield Union,* Dec. 1, 1964.

22. Letter from Mayor Ryan and Congressman Edward P. Boland of Springfield to Secretary of Defense Robert S. McNamara, Dec. 2, 1964.

23. Letter from the secretary of the army to Mayor Ryan, Jan. 6, 1965.

24. See the *Springfield Daily News,* Nov. 30, 1964.

25. B.B.F. file memo of meeting, Jan. 21, 1965. Mayor Ryan was accompanied by Dr. Lowell E. Bellin.

26. See NI-382, NO-1065 (appendix 2), NI-4181, International Tracing Service List of Concentration Camps.

27. Nazi Party no. 4 913 523; Caesar entered the party on May 1, 1937. Source: Berlin Document Center, Nazi Party files.

28. Nazi Party no. 3 672 731. Source: Berlin Document Center, Nazi Party files.

29. Nazi Party no. 6 934 374; he entered the party on Nov. 1, 1935. Source: Berlin Document Center, Nazi Party files. See also vol. XIV Green, p. 1142.

30. Guth's Nazi Party no. was 3 267 530 and he entered the party on May 1, 1933; von Salmuth had Nazi Party number 7 821 021 and he joined the party on Jan. 1, 1940. Source: Berlin Document Center, Nazi Party files.

31. See vol. XIV Green, p. 1142.

32. B.B.F. report to E.K., Feb. 25, 1965, of a meeting with Cyrus Vance on Feb. 24, 1965.

33. Letter from Julius Klein to Assistant Secretary William R. Tyler, April 5, 1965.

34. See Harry Schneiderman and Itzhak J. Carmin, eds., *Who's Who in World Jewry* (New York: Monde Publishers, 1955); *New York Times,* April 30, 1966; "Interpretative Report" by Syndicated Washington columnist Richard Wilson, Gannett newspapers, July 9, 1966.

35. Letter from B.B.F. to Julius Klein, April 8, 1965.

36. See letter from B.B.F. to E.K., April 8, 1965.

37. B.B.F. file memo, April 27, 1965.

38. Letter from B.B.F. to S.K., May 5, 1965.

39. Letter from E.K. to S.K., May 7, 1965.

40. Letter from Rheinmetall to E.K., July 21, 1965 (trans. from German). At about that time William Korey of B'nai B'rith was preparing a survey, *Slave Labor Survivors: German Industry's Moral Responsibility* (Washington, D.C.: B'nai B'rith, 1965).

41. The meeting with Ambassador Heinrich Knappstein took place in the embassy of the Federal Republic of Germany on Nov. 18, 1965, and was attended by Philip Klutznick, William Wexler, President of B'nai B'rith, Rabbi Jay Kaufman, Executive Vice-President, and B.B.F.; see B.B.F., *aide memoire* sent to Amb. Knappstein, Nov. 22, 1965.

42. Minutes of meeting, United States Army Weapons Command, Rock Island, Ill., Oct. 21, 1965; letter from Mayor Ryan to B.B.F., Jan. 7, 1966. See letter from B.B.F. to Rabbi Jay Kaufman, Dec. 23, 1965; Department of the Army Scientific and Technical Intelligence Bulletin TU-381-6-3, Sept. 1965, pp. 22-24.

43. *New York Times,* Feb. 6, 1966, story by Jack Raymond; *Springfield Republican,* Feb. 6, 1966; *Christian Science Monitor,* Feb. 7, 1966, story by Kenneth D. Nordin; Associated Press dispatch in the *Washington Post,* Feb. 7, 1966.

44. See memo from Bernard Simon to William Wexler, Feb. 7, 1966; letter from Bernard Simon to B.B.F., Feb. 9, 1966.

45. *H.R. 12744,* 89th Congress 2d Session, Feb. 9, 1966.

46. *H.R. 12909,* 89th Congress 2d Session, Feb. 17, 1966.

47. Letter from Rheinmetall AG Washington Information Office, 1038 Pennsylvania Bldg., Washington, D.C. An article by syndicated columnist Drew Pearson, written in conjunction with Jack Anderson in Feb. 1966, described Kenneth Buchanan as the man who "ran Klein's Washington office." See "Washington Merry-Go-Round: Dodd's German Trip," Feb. 1966. A special report from Washington to the *Daily News* began with the statement, "A former national commander of the Jewish American War Veterans is the chief congressional lobbyist here for the Rheinmetall company of West Germany" (Feb. 1966).

48. Letter from Congressmen Emanuel Celler and Jonathan B. Bingham to Secretary of Defense McNamara, Feb. 9, 1966.

49. Press release from Jewish War Veterans of the United States of America, 1712 New Hampshire Ave., Washington, D.C., Feb. 16, 1966.

50. Letter from John T. McNaughton to William Wexler, Feb. 15, 1966.

51. Letter from Julius Klein to Congressman Farbstein, Feb. 16, 1966.

52. See *Bild Zeitung,* Feb. 15, 1966, article from Bonn by Friedrich Ludwig Muller (trans. from German).

53. Letter from B.B.F. to E.K., Feb. 17, 1966.

54. See letter from B.B.F. to E.K., Feb. 18, 1966.

55. B.B.F. file memo, Feb. 21, 1966.

56. Letter from Assistant Secretary of State John M. Leddy to William Wexler, Feb. 18, 1966.

57. Letter from Charles V. Ryan, Jr., Mayor of Springfield, Massachusetts, to President Lyndon B. Johnson, Feb. 23, 1966.

58. B.B.F. file memo, Feb. 28, 1966.

59. See letter from E.K. to B.B.F., Mar. 2, 1966; articles in the *Washington Post* by Drew Pearson on Jan. 26, Jan. 29, Jan. 31, 1966; *New York Times,* Feb. 6, 1966; *Aufbau,* Feb. 11, 1966; and the *Chicago Tribune,* Feb. 13, 1966.

60. E.K. cabled B.B.F., "Rheinmetall absolutely refuses," Mar. 2, 1966.

61. Letters from William Wexler to Secretary of State Rusk, Mar. 3, 1966, and to Secretary of Defense McNamara, Mar. 4, 1966. See the*Denver Post,* Mar. 4, 1966, article by Charles Roos, and the *Jewish Week,* Washington, D.C., Mar. 3, 1966.

62. *Der Spiegel,* Mar. 7, 1966, pp. 52-53 (trans. from German).

63. Letters from B.B.F. to Congressman Bingham and Congressman Celler, Mar. 9, 1966.

64. Letter from State Department Assistant Secretary for Congressional Relations Douglas MacArthur II to Senator Javits, Mar. 7, 1966; see also *New York Times,* Mar. 11, 1966, article by Philip Shabecoff.

65. Letters from Rabbi Seymour J. Cohen, Synagogue Council of America, to President Johnson, Secretary of State Rusk, Secretary of Defense McNamara, Congressman L. Mendel Rivers, Congressman Richard B. Russell, Senator Jacob J. Javits, and Senator Robert F. Kennedy, Mar. 11, 1966.

66. See letter from Senator Javits to Jewish Nazi Victims Organization of America, Mar. 18, 1966.

67. See *Springfield (Mass.) Union,* Mar. 14, 1966.

68. See letter from E.K. to B.B.F., Mar. 23, 1966.

69. Letter from B.B.F. to Rabbi Kaufman, Mar. 30, 1966.

70. See memo from Rabbi Kaufman to Klutznick, April 8, 1966; letter from B.B.F. to E.K., Mar. 31, 1966. Another meeting with Ambassador Knappstein took place on April 1, 1966, which was attended by B.B.F.; see B.B.F. letter to E.K., April 4, 1966; B.B.F. letter to Ambassador Knappstein, April 4, 1966.

71. B.B.F. file memo, May 5, 1966.

72. Report from E.K. to S.K., May 10, 1966, of meetings on May 9 and May 10, 1966.

73. Ibid.

74. *Die Welt,* May 16, 1966 (trans. from German).

75. *Frankfurter Rundschau,* May 16, 1966 (trans. from German).

76. Letter from E.K. to S.K., May 16, 1966.

77. B'nai B'rith press release, May 17, 1966.

78. *New York Times,* May 18, 1966; *New York Times International Edition,* May 20, 1956.

79. *National Zeitung und Soldatenzeitung,* June 3, 1966 (trans. from German).

80. *Wehrdienst,* June 1966, as reported in letter from E.K. to B.B.F., June 20, 1966 (trans. from German).

81. Unpublished report from files of the International Tracing Service; see report from Seidenberg to Compensation Treuhand, July 14, 1966.

82. See reports from Seidenberg to Compensation Treuhand, July 14, 1966, Mar. 22, 1967; see NI-1065 (unpublished; extract in appendix 2).

83. Mannheim Criminal Court, file no. L is 381/64; see report from Seidenberg to Compensation Treuhand, July 14, 1966.

84. Detailed information contained in reports from Seidenberg to B.B.F., June 7, 1967, July 3, 1967.

85. See letter from B.B.F. to Seidenberg, July 18, 1967.

86. See report of Compensation Treuhand, Oct. 27, 1967.

87. Loeb and Troper final audit report, Aug. 15, 1974 (appendix 5).

88. *Aufbau,* Aug. 26, 1966 (trans. from German).

89. Letter from Rheinmetall to Comité International des Camps, Mar. 6, 1969 (trans. from German).

90. *New York Times,* Aug. 13, 1966, article by Hanson W. Baldwin.

91. *New York Post,* Dec. 18, 1967, article by Charles Nicodemus.

92. B.B.F. memo of phone conversation with Col. Patrick Lynch, Nov. 16, 1976; see also letter from Lynch, Oct. 14, 1976.

93. *New York Times,* Feb. 1, 1978, article by Bernard Weinraub.


## 6. The Shark Who Got Away

1. Vol. VI Green, p. 1187; vol. VI Green, *The Flick Case,* is a summary of the Flick trial.

2. *Frankfurter Allgemeine Zeitung,* Aug. 5, 1972.

3. See vol. VI Green, pp. 36-47.

4. NI-12187, vol. VI Green, pp. 263-264.

5. NI-3506, vol. VI Green, p. 252.

6. NI-5397, vol. VI Green, p. 207.

7. NI-3510, vol. VI Green, p. 297.

8. NI-5253, vol. VI Green, pp. 694-700.

9. Vol. VI Green, p. 9.

10. Vol. VI Green, pp. 1044-1090, 1157.

11. Vol. VI Green, pp. 1172-1185.

12. Vol. VI Green, pp. 1223-1233; also see *Flick v. Johnson,* 174 Fed. Rep. 2nd 983 (1949), 338 U.S. Rep. 879, 940.

13. NI-5587 (unpublished); see also *Handbuch der Aktiengesellschaften* [*Handbook of Corporations*] *(1941), p. 5093.*

14. For detailed analysis of the structure of various Flick companies, see NI-1526, NI-5587, NI-5685, NI-6780, NI-7711, NI-7771, NI-9192, NI-9446, NI-10030, NI-15062, NI-15063 (all unpublished); B.B.F. memo, Jan. 8, 1965.

15. See report by Simon Gutter to Compensation Treuhand, April 23, 1962.

16. Ibid.; see also memo from Bruno Fischer, Feb. 6, 1964.

17. See annual report of Feldmühle A.G., the personal holding company of Friedrich Flick, 1964-1965.

18. Fabian von Schlabrendorff, *Offiziere gegen Hitler* (Zurich: Europa, 1946); English ed., *They Almost Killed Hitler* (New York, 1947).

19. Report by E.K. to S.K., June 21, 1963, of meeting on June 20, 1963.

20. A lawsuit against the company by a former forced laborer was vigorously opposed by Dynamit Nobel. The case was brought by Chana R., represented by a Munich attorney, Dr. Otto Betz, and filed in the district court at Bonn, court file no. 30384/61. See letter from E.K. to B.B.F., June 27, 1963.

21. Report by E.K. to S.K., June 21, 1963.

22. See letters from B.B.F. to E.K., July 17, 1963, and from E.K. to B.B.F., July 18, 1963.

23. See *Time* magazine, July 26, 1963. On his sixtieth birthday Flick had also donated 400,000 marks to be placed at the disposal of Reich Marshal Hermann Göring (vol. VI Green, p. 424).

24. NI-5587; see report of E.K. to B.B.F., Feb. 12, 1964, of meeting on Feb. 10, 1964; B.B.F. letter to E.K., Dec. 30, 1963; memo from Henry Sachs to B.B.F., Dec. 30, 1963.

25. Vol. VI Green, p. 9; see Telford Taylor, *Final Report to the Secretary of the Army* (Washington, D.C.: United States Government Printing Office, 1949), p. 332.

26. Letter from E.K. to B.B.F., Feb. 12, 1964.

27. Letter from E.K. to B.B.F., April 17, 1964; see also letter from Wolfgang Pohle to von Schlabrendorff, April 11, 1964. Letter from E.K. to von Schlabrendorff, April 20, 1964, attaching a signed copy of the contract and a declaration by Eric Warburg attesting to the reliability of the Claims Conference.

28. Letter from von Schlabrendorff to E.K., May 6, 1964.

29. Letter from E.K. to S.K., May 22, 1964.

30. Ibid.

31. Report from E.K. to S.K., Aug. 19, 1964, of meeting with von Schlabrendorff, Aug. 18, 1964.

32. Letter from B.B.F. to E.K., Aug. 24, 1964; see also letter from B.B.F. to E.K., May 27, 1966.

33. See B.B.F. memo, Mar. 1, 1965, and report from E.K. to B.B.F., Mar. 18, 1965, on meeting with von Schlabrendorff on Mar. 13, 1965.

34. See letter from E.K. to S.K., June 28, 1965. Kronstein was a German refugee who had converted to Catholicism and who had acquired United States citizenship. He lectured at the University of Frankfurt and at Georgetown University in Washington, D.C.

35. See E.K. letter to S.K., Feb. 4, 1966. At just that time there was much publicity in the United States against the purchase of guns from Rheinmetall.

36. See letters from E.K. to S.K., May 24 and June 29, 1966.

37. Letter from E.K. to B.B.F., Sept. 30, 1966 (trans. from German).

38. Report from E.K. to S.K., Feb. 7, 1967, of a meeting with von Schlabrendorff on Feb. 3, 1967.

39. See *Die Welt,* Sept. 21, 1966.

40. See letter from E.K. to S.K., Feb. 17, 1967.

41. See letter from E.K. to S.K., Feb. 7, 1967.

42. Letter from B.B.F. to E.K., Feb. 13, 1967.

43. Letter from S.K. to E.K., April 13, 1967.

44. See letters from E.K. to S.K., July 31 and Aug. 25, 1967.

45. Letter from Goldmann to Abs, Jan. 12, 1968. Abs was the director of the Deutsche Bank, which held 25 percent of the shares of Daimler-Benz, the manufacturer of Mercedes cars, which was controlled by Flick; see *Forbes Magazine,* Feb. 1, 1969.

46. Letter from Abs to Goldmann, Feb. 5, 1968.

47. Letter from B.B.F. to S.K., Feb. 27, 1968, and letter from E.K. to B.B.F., Mar. 29, 1968.

48. See letter from McCloy to von Schlabrendorff, Jan. 13, 1969; letter from von Schlabrendorff to McCloy, Jan. 24, 1969; letter from Kronstein to McCloy, Jan. 29, 1969. Kronstein had carried on various discussions with von Schlabrendorff, Abs, Warburg, Wolfgang Pohle, and Dieter Bührle of Switzerland, the minority shareholder of Dynamit Nobel, and he also claimed credit for having intervened in Washington to prevent the withdrawal of certain orders from the munitions company: see letter from E.K. to S.K., June 5, 1968. The Israel newspaper *Haaretz* (April 17, 1969) reported that the Bührle concern was heavily engaged in building rockets in Egypt.

49. See letter from Blaustein to S.K., May 13, 1969.

50. See letter from Blaustein to S.K., May 20, 1969. Blaustein also sought assistance from Rolf Pauls, the ambassador of the Federal Republic of Germany in Washington.

51. See letter from Blaustein to E.K., June 26, 1969.

52. McCloy had received a comprehensive memorandum which reviewed the long history of the negotiations with Flick and some of the documentary evidence from the Nuremberg trials; B.B.F. memo, "Compensation to Former Slave Laborers of Dynamit-Nobel," July 8, 1969; see letter from B.B.F. to S.K., Sept. 17, 1969.

53. Letter from von Schlabrendorff to E.K., Dec. 8, 1969.

54. See *Welt am Sonntag,* Mar. 29, 1970.

55. See letter from E.K. to von Brauchitsch, Mar. 16, 1970, and reply from von Brauchitsch to E.K., May 11, 1970.

56. See letter from Pauls to Blaustein, July 30, 1970; letter from Pauls to S.K., Feb. 11, 1971; letter from Pauls to S.K., June 2, 1971; letter from E.K. to Pohle, June 25, 1971; letter from E.K. to Flick, Oct. 29, 1971, enclosing a sixteen-page list of needy Jewish claimants who had worked for Dynamit Nobel; letter from Kaletsch to E.K., Nov. 16, 1971.

57. See letter from E.K. to Pauls, Dec. 2, 1971; letter from B.B.F. to E.K., Jan. 3, 1972.

58. The report was prepared by Harris Schoenberg of B'nai B'rith, Jan. 1972.

59. *New York Times,* July 22, 1970.

60. George Ogger, *Friedrich Flick der Grosse* (Munich: Scherz Verlag, 1971), pp. 15-16.

61. See letter from E.K. to B.B.F., Nov 20, 1972.

62. Letter from E.K. to B.B.F., July 24, 1972; letter from B.B.F. to Kurt

May, with copy to E.K., Aug. 1, 1972.

63. Flick's playboy son, Friedrich Karl, reportedly "pocketed $1 billion when in 1976 he sold to a German bank 29% of the stock of Daimler-Benz," *Time* magazine, June 5, 1978.

## 7. A Medley of Disappointments

1. Stuttgart court file no. 10 U 8/1965, p. 30.

2. The story of Adolf Diamant first appeared in the German press without disclosing his identity; see *Frankfurter Rundschau,* June 22, 1965.

3. Letter from Büssing to Leo Konstam, Mar. 15, 1957; identical certificate given to Abraham Hochmann, Aug. 27, 1957.

4. See *Frankfurter Rundschau,* June 22, 1965.

5. Letter from Adolf Diamant to the *Aufbau,* Aug. 10, 1965.

6. Letter from E.K. to Dr. Paul Meister and Dr. Wolfgang Boening, Frankfurt, June 23, 1965.

7. Decision of the Braunschweig District Court, *Diamant v. Büssing,* June 20, 1965, court file no. 13 C 566/64; reported in *Aufbau,* Aug. 27, 1965.

8. PS-1584, vol. IV Red, pp. 117-124.

9. See letter from E.K. to S.K., May 9, 1962, based on a report from the Bavarian Ministry of Finance.

10. Letter from E.K. to S.K., July 11, 1962; letter from E.K. to S.K., Sept. 12, 1962.

11. Letter from E.K. to S.K., Oct. 16, 1962.

12. Letter from Rudorf to E.K., Jan. 4, 1963; letter from E.K. to S.K., Dec. 14, 1962; a letter from Rudorf to E.K. on Jan. 4, 1963, argued that the company could pay "no more" (sic) since it had suffered too many losses itself.

13. Letter from E.K. to B.B.F., Jan. 25, 1963.

14. *New York Times,* April 3, 1963, and April 5, 1963, articles by Gerd Wilcke. Messerschmidt died in Sept. 1978 and according to a United Press International dispatch he had been building airplanes in cooperation with Spain since 1952; [New York] *City News,* Sept. 17, 1978.

15. Letter from Rudorf, Feb. 28, 1964. The letter was the culmination of several discussions between E.K. and B.B.F. with representatives of the Messerschmidt company. Willy Messerschmidt later became the co-founder and chairman of Messerschmidt-Bölkow-Blohm GmbH, which in 1978 was reported to be the largest air- and spacecraft company in Germany. See *Frankfurter Allgemeine Zeitung,* June 24, 1978.

16. See PS-1584, vol. XXVII Blue, p. 361.

17. Facts taken from the decision of the Stuttgart Appellate Court, *Bartl v. Heinkel,* Mar. 11, 1964, court file nos. 1 U 16/1963, 12 O 334/59.

18. Decision of the Augsburg District Court, *Bartl v. Heinkel,* July 31, 1962, court file no. 12 O 334/59.

19. Decision of the Stuttgart Appellate Court, *Bartl v. Heinkel,* May 19, 1965, p. 30; court file nos. 10 U-8/1965, 12 S 334/59. This was the court's second decision, the case having been remanded for technical reasons.

20. *Der Spiegel,* May 13, 1964.

21. See *Süddeutsche Zeitung,* June 20, 1967.

22. Decision of the German Supreme Court, *Bartl v. Heinkel,* June 22, 1967, court file no. VII ZR 181/65. See Benjamin B. Ferencz, "German Supreme Court Bars Claims of Forced Laborers," *American Journal of Comparative Law,* 15 (1966-1967): 561-566.

23. See NI-382; NI-1065 (appendix 2).

24. See vol. VIII Green, p. 659.

25. See report by Max Stein, June 14, 1961, based on National Archives files, contained in Buchenwald boxes 113, 122, 131, 151; see B.B.F. letter to Stein, Feb. 7, 1961.

26. Testimony of Oskar L., Nov. 23, 1959; see letter from Schildbach to E.K., Mar. 14, 1960.

27. See Stein report, June 14, 1961, p. 9. Kurt Wehle, a Czech lawyer employed by the URO office in New York and a former forced laborer for BRABAG, assembled the names of many claimants and set forth many of the facts of persecution; see letter from Wehle to Schildbach, Oct. 9, 1958.

28. See Stein report, June 14, 1961, p. 4.

29. Letter from Schildbach to S.K., Dec. 30, 1957.

30. Letter from Schildbach to E.K., referring to article in the *Hannoversche Presse*, Dec. 28, 1957.

31. Court file no. 4 O 320/57, filed in the district court in Berlin on Dec. 30, 1957.

32. See Schildbach memo to the Berlin District Court, June 16, 1958.

33. Testimony of Abraham L., Nov. 23, 1959; see letter from Schildbach to E.K., Mar. 14, 1960.

34. See minutes of annual meeting of BRABAG in Cologne on Aug. 7, 1961.

35. See letter from E.K. to attorney Peter Schulien, April 16, 1968, who intervened, on court order, when Schildbach resigned.

36. PS-2273, vol. IV Red, pp. 944-945; L-180, vol. VII Red, pp. 978-996.

37. Affidavits of witnesses Greta B., Margot W., and Lucy S., all of New York, May 18, 1959. Dr. Rudolf Löhnis of the URO office in Frankfurt was instructed to submit test cases against Holzmann.

38. See report by Simon Gutter, Mar. 16, 1962, based on testimony of survivors, describing the employment of Dachau inmates by Holzmann at Kaufering and Landsberg, and the employment of Gross Rosen inmates at Waldenburg, as well as other camps.

39. Information based on financial report furnished by a German bank, Mar. 16, 1962.

40. Letter from E.K. to S.K., May 6, 1960. Information assembled by the Claims Conference indicated that Holzmann had employed at least two thousand Jews in at least eight different locations; letter from B.B.F. to E.K., April 29, 1960.

41. See letter from E.K. to S.K., June 26, 1962; letter from E.K. to B.B.F., Sept. 10, 1962; letter from E.K. to S.K., Oct. 7, 1964; *Frankfurter Allgemeine Zeitung,* July 4, 1962.

42. See *K. et al. v. Holzmann,* Frankfurt District Court, hearing on Oct. 5, 1964, court file no. 2/13 O 215/58; E.K. letter to S.K., Oct. 7, 1964.

43. Decision of Frankfurt District Court *K. et al. v. Holzmann,* Oct. 8,

1968; see letters from E.K. to S.K., April 18, 1968, and Oct. 21, 1968.

44. Letter from Dr. Heinz Roth, attorney for Moll, to Dr. Hans Wolf, attorney for former slave laborers, Dec. 18, 1957. Wolf had been on the URO staff in Munich and he acted in close cooperation with the URO office in New York. Nahum Gershwin of URO, New York, had been sent to work for Moll while he was an inmate at Dachau and he assembled information from many claimants. See report of Simon Gutter, Mar. 15, 1962.

45. Decision of the Commercial Court in Vienna (*Handelsgericht*), in case of *Jacob S. v. Rella and Porr,* June 21, 1972, court file no. 29 Cg 54/71, p. 23.

46. Meeting between B.B.F. and Veith, Oct. 2, 1957; letter from Veith to B.B.F., Nov. 11, 1957.

47. Letters from Froehlich to B.B.F., Nov. 13, 1957, and May 21, 1958.

48. Letter from B.B.F. to Froehlich, Oct. 22, 1958.

49. See letter from E.K. to Goldmann, April 5, 1962.

50. See letter from Goldmann to Beitz, Jan. 24, 1963. At just about that time, efforts were being made to persuade Krupp to increase the settlement sum; when those efforts failed, further contact was broken off.

51. Article in *La Merchav,* Aug. 2, 1970, as reported by Seidenberg in letter to E.K. on Aug. 6, 1970; see also letter from Friedmann to B.B.F., Sept. 17, 1970, attaching article from the *Jerusalem Post,* Sept. 13, 1970.

52. Letter from B.B.F. to The World Jewish Federation of Victims of the Nazi Regime, Oct. 3, 1970.

53. See *Frankfurter Allgemeine Zeitung,* Jan. 21, 1971; *Baseler National Zeitung,* Jan. 22, 1971.

54. See the *Jerusalem Post,* Mar. 11, 1970; Jewish Telegraphic Agency dispatch from Tel Aviv, Mar. 11, 1970.


## 8. The Last Word

1. Rolf Hochhuth, *Der Stellvertreter* (Hamburg: Rowohlt, 1963), p. 74.

2. See PS-1739, vol. XXVII Blue, p. 573; Edward L. Homze, *Foreign Labor in Nazi Germany* (New Jersey: Princeton University Press, 1967), pp. 83, 148, 153, 267; John Fried, *The Exploitation of Foreign Labor by Germany* (Montreal: International Labor Organization, 1945).

3. See Ino Arndt-Wolfgang Scheffler, "Organisierter Massenmord an Juden," *Das Parlament,* May 8, 1976.

4. See vol. IV Green, *The Einsatzgruppen Case.*

5. NI-1065 (appendix 2); see vol. V. Green, p. 1201. During the Hitler period about 1,650,000 persons in the prime of their lives were "selected" to work within the formal concentration camp system. By the time the war ended, less than half a million were still alive. See Joseph Billig, *Les camps de concentration dans l'économie du reich hitlérien* (Paris: Presses Universitaires de France, 1973), p. 99.

6. See Fried, *Exploitation of Foreign Labor,* p. 253.

7. NI-4434 (appendix 3).

8. NI-5598, vol. VI Green, p 754; vol. V Green, p. 595; vol. IX Green, pp. 838-839, 1412; NI-039; NI-382; NI-387; NI-388; NI-390; and appendixes 1, 2, 3, and 4.

9. NI-382.

10. See Fried, *Exploitation of Foreign Labor,* p. 255.

11. See Saul Friedländer, *Kurt Gerstein: The Ambiguity of Good* (New York: Knopf, 1969).

12. PS-2992, vol. V Red, pp. 697-698; vol XXXI Blue, pp. 441-450.

13. See Kurt Grossman, *Die Unbessungenen Helden* (Berlin: Arani Verlag, 1957).

14. Taken from an interview with Kranzbühler in the Marcel Ophul's film, *Memories of Justice* (Paramount Pictures, 1976).

15. Albert Speer, *Inside the Third Reich* (New York: Macmillan, 1970). German edition:*Erinnerungen* (Berlin: Ullstein, 1969).

16. Confirmed by Speer in note to B.B.F. July 23, 1978.

# Index

Warburg, Eric: intervention with
Farben, 48; assistance in Krupp
claims, 81, 83, 84; meetings with
Lohse, 120–121; intermediary with
Rheinmetall, 132; attempt to
persuade Flick, 159; meeting with
Nobel representative, 160; on DAG's
intentions, 163; meeting with Von
Schlabrendorff, 165
Wegener, Rudolf, 101–102
Weinhold (Krupp engineer), 89–91
Werner, Alfred, 107
Werner Works, 118
Wexler, William, 138, 140, 142–143
Wilhelmi, Hans, 145, 148
Wollheim, Norbert: deportation from
Berlin, 26–27; witness at Nuremberg
trial, 35; seeks help from Jewish
organizations, 40–41; screening of
claims, 52; search for Buna
survivors, 62; attitude toward Claims
Conference, 63; proposal for
memorial, 64, 65
*Wollheim v. I. G. Farben in*

*Liquidation,* 35–37, 42–45
Women: Dutch and Polish forced
laborers, 28; Hungarian forced
laborers, 29, 99; use by Krupp, 91,
93, 94–95, 95–96; use by AEG, 107;
use by Telefunken, 108–109;
compensation to survivors of
electrical firms, 116; use by Siemens,
117–119, 122, 124, 125; at
Auschwitz, 123, 124; claimants
against Rheinmetall, 130; at
Buchenwald, 149–150; at Hundsfeld
slave labor camp, 151; use by Nobel
munitions factories, 158–159; use by
construction companies, 179
World Jewish Congress, 38
World Jewish Federation of Victims of
the Nazi Regime, 182

Yad Vashem, 66
"Youth protection camp," 124–125

Zelenko, Herbert, 49

BENJAMIN B. FERENCZ was the prosecutor at the Nuremberg trial of the SS *Einsatzgruppen*. Now past 81, Ferencz remains active as a teacher, lecturer, and author of books on international law and articles dealing with the creation of an international criminal court.